Religious Education
TOPICS
for the Primary School

▶ **John Rankin** ▾ **Alan Brown** ▴ **Mary Hayward** ◀

Longman ▦

LONGMAN GROUP UK LIMITED,
Longman House, Burnt Mill, Harlow,
Essex CM20 2JE, England
and Associated Companies throughout the world.

© Longman Group UK Limited 1989

First published 1989
Second impression 1990

Set in 10/13 Helvetica Light, Linotron 202
Produced by Longman (FE) Ltd
Printed in Hong Kong

ISBN 0 582 00334 2

John Rankin

formerly Head of Religious Studies at the West Sussex
Institute of Higher Education

Alan Brown

RE (Schools Officer), Church of England Board of Education;
Director, The National Society's RE Centre, London

Mary Hayward

Deputy Director of the York Religious Education Centre,
College of Ripon and York St. John

Responsibility for each section is as follows.

Section 1 (for 5–7 year olds): Alan Brown

Section 2 (for 7–9 year olds): John Rankin

Section 3 (for 9–11 year olds): Mary Hayward

General editor: **John Rankin**

We wish to acknowledge the help of the following in preparing the units, although the authors take full responsibility for the final text.

David Barton	Soho Parish School, London
Peter Doble	Director, York RE Centre
John Enticknap	formerly a Primary School Headmaster
Judith Evans	West Sussex Institute of Higher Education
Fay Hodgson	Hob Moor Junior School, York
Ruth Mantin	West Sussex Institute of Higher Education
David Metcalfe	Kingsway Junior School, York
Josephine Moxon	Sproatley C of E Endowed Primary School, Humberside
Erica Musty	Co-ordinator for RE and Special Educational Needs, West London Institute of Higher Education
Elizabeth Owens	Kentish Town C of E Primary School, London
Jenny Sanders	Laceby Acres First and Middle School, Grimsby
Sandra Starkey	Fairfield Middle School, Grimsby
Mary Williams	Primary RE Adviser, Diocese of Southwark
Andrew Woodhouse	Bedale C of E Primary School, North Yorkshire

Thanks are due to Sheila Jack, Jean Metcalfe, Judy Thursby, Gillian Vigne and Judy Perkins for their patience and understanding in typing the several versions of the manuscript and helping with the resources.

Contents

About this book

▶ ## SECTION 1: for 5–7 year olds

▶ ## SECTION 2: for 7–9 year olds

SECTION 3: for 9–11 year olds ◀

About this book

Religious Education in the primary years makes great demands on teachers, especially in the area of World Religions. This book is designed to provide material to help with this part of the task.

It is deliberately limited to *religious* topics and is not intended to cover everything which is called religious education in current syllabuses. There are many indications in the text about how these religious topics can fit in with wider themes in the primary curriculum.

For easy reference the book is divided into groups of topics suitable for three separate age ranges, 5–7, 7–9 and 9–11. However, teachers should feel free to draw on information throughout the book as it seems useful to them.

Note that the convention CE and BCE is adopted throughout the book. CE stands for the 'Common Era' and BCE for 'Before the Common Era'. These expressions are acceptable to adherents of *all* religions. For the spelling of religious terms we have generally followed that recommended in *Religious Studies—a Glossary of Terms*, 1986, produced by the Secondary Examinations Council in collaboration with the Religious Education Council. Exceptions have of course been made in material directly quoted from other publications.

The Topics

In 1985 the Chichester Project decided to set up a Primary programme to help teachers with the teaching of RE in the classroom. We decided from the outset that we would include topics drawn from Christianity, Islam, Judaism, Buddhism, Sikhism and Hinduism. We also decided that there were sufficient resources available already to help teachers explore what is sometimes referred to as the 'implicit' area of religious education. Such topics are often headed with titles such as 'Hands', 'Homes', 'Who am I?', and so on. These topics are both useful and important and their absence from this book must not be taken to imply that they should be dispensed with. Our efforts are directed very specifically at recognisable 'religious' topics, in order to encourage teachers to develop confidence in this area.

Some of the topics will be familiar in schools and these appear in each of the age range lists; for example, Christmas, Easter and Jesus. In each age range we have tried to provide a different approach and in all cases we have laid emphasis on the *religious* content.

There is a preponderance of 'Christian' topics as this corresponds realistically to the needs of the majority of primary schools in the United Kingdom. However, the treatment demonstrates how such topics can be studied within a World Religions syllabus.

The topics have considerable range but this is by no means exhaustive or exclusive. It is hoped that they will provide models through which the teacher can enlarge the scope to meet particular circumstances.

The Approach

We have tried to avoid telling teachers *everything* they should do! Each topic begins with a simple statement of 'Aims'. Then comes some 'Information' for the teacher which can of course always be supplemented from other sources. The book nevertheless provides the basic outline. Then a variety of 'Approaches' are suggested. These are no more than hints as to where to begin and are certainly not intended to displace the teachers' own ideas. The same is true of the 'Activities' suggested. We hope that the combination of 'Approaches' and 'Activities' will allow teachers to construct their own units according to their own needs. Any of these topics can be extended into 1, 2, 3 or 4 week long projects and we have not prescribed how much of the curriculum they should fill.

The style changes progressively. At the infant level we propose no more than a 'flavour' of some elements, whereas at the upper junior level there is material for quite careful and reflective study. The 'Information' section goes beyond the level possible for the age range, but we believe that an awareness in the teacher of deeper implications helps in the selection of appropriate teaching modes.

We hope that the book will be a genuinely useful contribution to teachers' resources and that it reflects the needs of today.

About the Chichester Project

This book is a result of a long consultation with primary teachers under the auspices of the Chichester Project. The Project acknowledges the financial support received from the United Society for Christian Literature and the National Society in carrying this out. These bodies are in no way responsible for the text as it appears.

The Chichester Project is an independent Trust set up in 1977. The impetus came from the *Shap Working Party on World Religions in Education.** It was felt that there was a need to carry out research into the teaching of Christianity as a world religion. This initial research led to the publication of ten books for pupils in the secondary school. These have been influential in helping foster a new approach to the teaching of Christianity. In 1987 there appeared also *Teaching Christianity: A World Religions Approach*, a symposium written by authors and teachers associated with the Chichester Project. It reflects the approach developed by the Project over a period of ten years. The Project is now actively engaged in producing video cassettes to accompany the secondary books. Further research both in primary school RE and in GCSE criteria is also proceeding.

John C Rankin
Director, Chichester Project

* The Shap Handbook on *World Religions in Education 1987* is a useful source for all teachers. It can be obtained from the Commission for Racial Equality (Elliot House, 10–12 Allington Street, London SW1E 5EH) at £4.50.

1 Christmas: The Theme of Birthdays

Aims	The aims of this unit are to help pupils to understand that Christmas is a birthday celebration and to relate these experiences to the feelings of joy that **Christians** have about the birth of Jesus.

Information

Christmas was not celebrated by Christians until three hundred years after the life of Jesus. Jesus' actual birthday is unknown and it was only when Constantine became the Roman emperor early in the fourth century CE that the festival began to be celebrated. Constantine had become a Christian while fighting to become emperor, and when in charge he encouraged the Church to take over the festival of 'Sol Invictus' (the Unconquerable Sun) on 25 December. The idea of an 'official birthday' is familiar in Britain—the monarch has an official as well as a personal birthday. (All horses have their birthday on 1 January!)

The Virgin and Child by Botticelli

Modern celebrations of Christmas have become much affected by traditions building up over the years. St Francis of Assisi in the thirteenth century CE is believed to have begun the use of the crib scene; Christmas trees came from Germany in the nineteenth century and with holly and mistletoe are taken over from pagan traditions. Santa Claus (or Father Christmas) takes his name from St Nicholas, a saint from Myra, in present-day Turkey, who cared for children and gave them presents (if good!). His Dutch name 'Sinter Klaas' has been more famililiar as Santa Claus. St Nicholas is remembered on 6 December.

However, Christmas has not been universally celebrated. A number of the Protestant churches did not celebrate the festival and some still don't, though common practice today is for most to join in. Generally it is considered to be the second great festival in the Christian year after Easter. The cycle begins with Advent, a period of preparation; then the festival lasts from Christmas Day to Epiphany (manifestation) which is twelve days after Christmas.

Approaches

1   Since Christmas can be approached in so many ways, it is important to bear in mind that the focus of the approach in this unit is 'birthdays'. It may be possible to identify a family with a new baby whose mother or father will be able to visit the class with the baby to answer questions and generally talk about looking after a new-born baby. Some pupils may be able to bring in photographs of themselves as tiny babies.

2   Part of the story of the birth of Jesus involves a journey and the pupils may be able to talk about where they were born, or where their parents or relatives were born; perhaps 'birth' traditions are carried out in some homes.

3   Most children are named at birth, though the name may not be decided until the child is registered. Jewish babies are given an 'ordinary' name and a Hebrew name. Boys are given their names at the ceremony of circumcision eight days after birth—Jesus (meaning 'Saviour') would have received his name at this time. A girl is given her names and a blessing on the first Sabbath after her birth. Find out what the pupils' names mean. Did a ceremony surround their naming?

Read one of the stories of Jesus' birth either from Luke's gospel or Matthew's gospel (Luke 2:1–21; Matthew 2:1–12). The two accounts are different and it would be as well to check on the two accounts, to decide which would be more appropriate, before retelling the story.

Activities

1   Pupils will often be interested in birth, birth announcements—the time of birth, weight and sex of baby, and so on—and a collection of birth cards and birth announcements from the local papers can be displayed.

2   The children can make crib figures from clay, or use bottles as a base and decorate them with material; using stick puppets the pupils can act out the story of Jesus' birth. A collection of Christmas cards will help tell the story of Christmas.

3   Many pupils already make their own Christmas cards, so an **Advent crown** of four candles in a ring of holly might be a good idea in the four weeks before Christmas, with an additional candle being lit in the week before Christmas. To make an Advent crown pupils will need:

> 5 small candles (8–10 cm tall) 4 red and 1 white
> A square piece of wood (*c.*25 cm square)
> Silver foil
> Plasticine
> Holly and other evergreen (preferably a non-spiky sort)

This Advent crown has four red candles; a white one may be added in the centre. Light one candle each week during Advent and the centre (white) one on the last day of term.

Cover the wood with foil and draw a circle in the centre. Arrange the four red candles around the circle and keep them in position with softened wax. The white candle goes in the centre of the circle. Roll the plasticine into strips and place around edge of circle to join candles. Arrange evergreen to cover the plasticine. One candle can be lit each week during Advent and the white candle on the last day of the term.

4   Birthday celebrations are often associated with special food like birthday cake. Christmas conjures up images of turkey, mince pies and Christmas pudding (in Britain anyway). But in other countries different foods are part of the Christmas story. In Holland, St Nicholas' Day is celebrated with parties and St Nicholas 'letters' can be fun to make in the classroom as well as being tasty to eat—for the story in rhyme see *The Oxford Merry Christmas Book* by R Winstanley (OUP 1987), p 44.

St Nicholas 'letters'
400 g frozen shortcrust pastry
200 g marzipan
milk

Defrost pastry, roll out and cut into strips of about 4 cm by 10 cm. Roll out marzipan into a long sausage about the width of a pastry. Cut marzipan into strips slightly smaller than the pastry. Dab milk around the edges of the pastry and press the edges firmly together to seal the marzipan inside. Strips can be joined or bent to make a letter but always ensure the pastry is sealed. Place on a greased baking sheet and bake for 10–15 mins at Gas Mark 7 (210°C, 425°F).

A Christmas Crossword   Fit the words into the squares

ANGELS
BETHLEHEM
CANDLE
CAROLS
CHRISTMAS
CRIB

DONKEY
INNKEEPER
JESUS
JOSEPH
LIGHTS
MARY
MERRY

NATIVITY
PEACE
SHEEP
SHEPHERDS
STABLE
STAR
WISEMEN

Resources

Books

H Aoki and I Gentscheu, *The Christmas Story by Father Christmas*, Neugebauer Press 1982

L Berg, *Christmas: Celebrations* series, Ginn 1985

P Blakeley, *Christmas Cat*, A & C Black 1986

Bright Ideas for Christmas Art & Craft, Ward Lock 1985

Christmas: Make It Yourself series, Franklin Watts 1983

Christmas Tinderbox Book, A & C Black 1986

C Dickens, *The Life of our Lord*, Macdonald 1987

I Fedrigotti, *The World of Christmas*, Macdonald 1986

C Gregorowski, *Why a Donkey Was Chosen*, Benn 1980

Images of Christmas, Shepheard-Walwyn 1984

A Lindgren, *Christmas in the Stable*, Hodder 1980

S Miyoshi, *The Christmas Lamb*, Methuen 1980

The Oxford Merry Christmas Book, OUP 1987

J Pienkowski, *Christmas*, Heinemann 1984

J Ridgway, *Festive Occasions*, OUP 1986

A Scholey, *Lucy and Tom's Christmas*, Lion 1982

R Thomson, *My Class at Christmas*, Franklin Watts 1986

AVA

Advent candle, obtainable from many religious bookshops

Baboushka filmstrip, BBC Radiovision

Christian Festivals poster pack, E745, Pictorial Charts Educational Trust

Christmas cassette, NCEC

Christmas Pack posters, Macmillan

Christmas poster set, CEM

The Christmas Story filmstrip and notes, Philip Green Education

Christmas Story frieze, Lion

First Christmas cut-outs, Macdonald

2 Easter: New Life

Aims

The aims of this unit are to develop an awareness of Easter as a spring festival and to help pupils to become familiar with the Easter story and its importance for **Christians**.

Information

Easter is the most important festival in the Christian year. The story of Jesus' entry into Jerusalem, crucifixion and resurrection is the cornerstone of the Christian faith and is universally celebrated throughout the Christian world. Like Christmas, it has a period of preparation, and the Easter cycle of festivals lasts nearly three months. The date of Easter is determined by the phases of the moon. It is a movable festival which may occur very late in March or early in April. Easter Day is, however, always on a Sunday. (NB: the dates when Easter is celebrated can vary in the Western and Orthodox churches.) For Christians, Easter is the triumph of life over death, light over darkness; it is the resurrection that Christians believe brings the promise of eternal life.

In many churches, events leading up to the death of Jesus are read each day during Holy Week with the whole account of the Passion being read on Good Friday usually from Matthew's gospel (Matthew 26 and 27). The gospels record Jesus' trial and condemnation as well as his last meal (the Last Supper) with his disciples. The Jewish Sabbath begins just before dusk on Friday and Christians today remember Jesus' time on the cross with three-hour services (from 12 noon to 3 pm) as that is the length of time the gospels record Jesus as hanging on the cross. He was then laid in the tomb before the Sabbath began.

Approaches

The pain of the crucifixion of Jesus has been a common theme in Christian art during the centuries. This sculpture by Enzo Plazzotta captures the agony remembered by Christians during Holy Week.

1 Whatever personal views a teacher may have about the Easter festival, there seems to be no reason why pupils should not hear the whole story or, at least, episodes from it chosen by the teacher. Questions may arise during the telling, but the Easter story is fundamental for Christians. Pupils will be unable to understand why Christians celebrate at Eastertime unless they are aware of the events of Holy Week and the first Easter. There is no need to explain every detail; it is a story full of mystery, the truth of which is dependent upon faith. Teachers should not feel obliged to explain away each detail and in fact by doing so are misrepresenting the Christian approach. For most Christians the resurrection is a mystery not to be explained. It is an act of God which brings the offer of salvation and there are many questions surrounding the resurrection that cannot be answered factually. In a sense the resurrection is an experience that cannot be put into words.

2 Easter will be studied usually in the spring term and the theme of 'new life' observed in the natural world could lead to a discussion of festivals of spring, eg Passover (see section 2, page 76) and Easter in particular.

3 In preparation for Easter, pupils could be told the story of Jesus in the wilderness and they should be encouraged to talk about what it would have been like— what sort of emotions and feelings might they experience? Would it be frightening, dangerous? Would it be a happy experience? As a way of sharing in this experience, Christians today may eat more simple food during Lent, or give up something so that they will be reminded of Jesus' hardship.

Activities

1 Pupils could make **hot cross buns**—traditionally made and eaten on Good Friday. You will need:

300 g plain flour	100 g currants
1 level tsp salt	50 g mixed peel
$\frac{1}{2}$ tsp mixed spice	Yeast liquid
$\frac{1}{2}$ tsp cinnamon	1 level tblsp dried yeast
$\frac{1}{2}$ tsp sugar	1 level tsp sugar
50 g melted butter	550 ml warm milk and water, less 3 tblsps
1 beaten egg	100 g plain flour

Blend yeast, warm milk, water, sugar and flour and leave for 20–30 minutes in a warm place until 'frothy'. Sift rest of flour, salt, spices, sugar and add fruit. Stir egg and melted butter into yeast liquid and add flour and fruit. Mix well and knead dough for 10 minutes. Divide dough into 12 pieces and space out on floured baking sheet. Leave in warm place until doubled in size. Make a cross on bun with knife and bake in hot oven for 15–20 minutes (Gas Mark 7, 210°C, 425°F). To glaze, bring 3 tablespoonfuls of milk and water to boil, add 35 grams of sugar and stir. Boil for 2 minutes. Brush on to buns.

2 To celebrate Easter Day itself pupils could design Easter cards linking the resurrection of Jesus with the emerging new life in nature and longer days. In the classroom, bulbs or baby animals will reinforce the theme of 'new life'. What colours are common at Eastertime—in the shops, in the countryside? (In many churches the Easter colour is white or gold.) In many areas there are particular local Easter customs—like a walk or egg-rolling. Pupils could decorate eggs (hard-boiled) or make Easter biscuits.

These activities, together with the story of Easter, should help the pupils to acquire a concrete feeling of this festival. Stories, music and poems too can all illuminate the affective atmosphere in the classroom.

In some parts of the Christian world painted eggs symbolise the new life and joy of the resurrection of Jesus. These are Hungarian.

Resources

Books
M Batchelor, *The Lion Easter Book*, Lion 1987
B Birch, *Assemblies Round the Year*, Ward-Lock 1985
B Cass-Biggs, *A Musical Calendar of Festivals*, Ward-Lock 1983 (collection of musical celebrations for many festivals)
J Chapman, *Pancakes and Painted Eggs*, Hodder & Stoughton 1981
R Chapple, *The Man from Galilee*, Wheaton/Pergamon 1982 (the Easter story in words and music)
L Cox, *Countdown to Easter*, Macmillan 1984
The Easter Book, Macdonald 1986
M Eastmand, *The Easter Book*, dist. Wm Collins 1987
J Fox, *Festivals* series; *Easter*, Wayland 1984
P Frank, *The First Easter: Lion Story Bible* series, Lion 1986
Harlequin 44 Songs Round the Year, A & C Black 1981
A Farncombe, *The Easter Book*, NCEC 1984
R Purton, *First Assemblies*, Basil Blackwell 1981 (contains a first person account of two children's experiences of Palm Sunday)

AVA
Christian Festivals poster pack, E745, Pictorial Charts Educational Trust (4 charts including teachers' notes)
Easter Primary Pack, CEM

Music
Beethoven, Symphony No 6—'Pastoral'
Dvorak, Symphony No 5—'New World'
Mendelssohn, 'Spring Song'
Rimsky Korsakov, 'Easter Festival Overture'
Vivaldi, 'The Four Seasons'—Spring

Hymns, eg 'Lord of the Dance', 'Morning has broken, like the first morning'

3 Divali

The aims of this unit are to help pupils to become aware of the richness and vitality of celebrating festivals and to become familiar with one of the stories from the **Hindu** tradition.

Information

Hinduism has many festivals and one of the best known and most celebrated is Divali. It may sometimes be referred to as Diwali or Deepavali. In the West it is often referred to as the festival of light because light plays such an important part. The main theme of the festival is the *triumph of good over evil*, light over darkness. By using this symbolism people are reminded of the good and bad sides of their personality and encouraged to make a fresh start.

Hinduism is a vast religion, indeed India is a vast country. There are many different beliefs and practices, many gods, many stories. Most Hindus recognise one 'ultimate being', Brahman, but this being is far removed from the everyday lives of people; it is an abstract concept. Worship and a personal relationship are associated with a personal god and in Hinduism there are very many gods. The most commonly revered are Shiva and Vishnu. The latter is worshipped in the form of Rama and Krishna, among others. Through stories about its gods, Hinduism expresses something of the nature of 'ultimate being'.

For many Hindus these stories are handed on through the oral tradition and expressed through drama and dance. They, and the rituals which surround them, are real living activities in the Hindu tradition and will therefore lend themselves very easily to a variety of classroom activities. Divali in particular is a time for hope and optimism, the emphasis is placed on light, music, food, and generosity, with the Divali lamp (or *diva*) as the central symbol.

The Hindu calendar follows a lunar cycle, so Divali does not happen on the same date each year. Different communities in England may celebrate Divali on different weekends, but the festival usually occurs in the October/November period.

There are wide variations in India regarding the celebration of Divali. In some areas, particularly the north, the god Rama is remembered in story and music; in the south it is often the god Krishna. In this section we will concentrate on Rama, but you will find more about Krishna under section 3, page 126.

This *diva* lamp can be made from clay with cotton-wool wicks dipped in cooking oil. Roll the clay into a ball. Press thumb into the centre and pinch one end, then press gently on a hard surface to flatten the base. Once it has hardened, paint the lamp. Roll the cotton wool until it is 2–3 cm long. Pour oil into lamp and float the wick. Let the oil soak into the wick and light (**under supervision**).

Approaches

In some schools there may be pupils who celebrate Divali and whose mother or father would be willing to come to the school to talk about their family celebration.

One of the most important aspects of Divali is the story; what follows is a résumé of *one* of the stories associated with the festival. It is beautifully told in *Stories from the Hindu World* by Jamila Gavin (Macdonald 1986).

There was once, in India, a king who had three wives. Each wife had sons, but no daughters. One of the sons was called Rama, who grew up to be tall and strong. Some miles away lived a princess called Sita. She was honest and truthful and many young men wanted to marry her. She owned an enormous bow and had vowed that she would marry the prince who could string it.

The Ramayana being performed in Bali. Hanuman the monkey god comes to the rescue of Sita.

Many princes came to try to string the bow but it was so heavy and powerful that some could not even lift it. At last Rama came to seek the hand of Sita, and he picked the bow up as if it were a feather and drew it back. So powerful was he that the bow snapped. Sita became his bride.

Rama's father was old and as he neared death Rama knew that his stepmother wished to have him banished from the kingdom so that her own son could be king. She claimed that the old king (her husband) had promised her that her son Bharat would be king and that Rama should be banished from the kingdom for fourteen years.

So Rama and Sita went to live in the safety of the forest and while Rama hunted he left Sita in a magic circle to protect her from danger. In his absence a demon king, Ravana, came and tricked Sita into stepping out of the circle. As soon as she had done so he carried her off to Lanka, his kingdom.

Rama was heartbroken, and he searched for Sita everywhere. One day as he searched he met Hanuman, the monkey god, who helped him find and rescue his beloved Sita. Rama killed the demon with an arrow and he and Sita returned. Everyone was so happy that they lit lamps and decorated their houses with them and Rama and Sita became king and queen.

Activities

Rangoli patterns

1 This story is also told more lavishly in *The Slaying of the Dragon* by Rosalind Kerven (André Deutsch 1987). The story could be retold through painting and collage, though a teacher might like to develop Divali through a topic on light by looking first at light and shadow, and things which give light—electric lights, fires, candles, for example. Candles could be decorated as part of the celebration of Rama and Sita's homecoming.

2 Rangoli patterns are traditional decorations for Divali. They can be made from coloured lentils or rice, or flour mixed with sand (or coloured chalks can be used instead), on sheets of paper or card. Rangoli patterns are often found at Divali on the floors of houses in India and in some parts of India there are traditions of decorating the hands. Garlands made from tissue paper, and Divali cards, are fun to make.

3 Divali can be a colourful end to the Hindu year. The classroom can be decorated with cards and patterns, and pupils might be encouraged to make cakes or sweets and come to school in their 'best' clothes (Hindu children are often given new clothes at Divali). Incense sticks might be lit and sitar music played while the story is being retold or acted.

Resources

Books
O Bennett, *Festivals: Exploring Religion* series, Bell & Hyman 1984
O Bennett, *Festival!—Diwali*, Macmillan Education 1986 (plus Teacher's Notes and Worksheets)
H Banks, *Bright Ideas—Assemblies*, Scholastic 1987
B Candappa, *Diwali: Celebrations* series, Ginn 1985
C Deshpanda, *Diwali: Celebrations* series, A & C Black 1985
V Kanitkar, *Hindu Stories*, Wayland 1986
M Lynch, *Diwali*, West London Institute (loose leaf) 1981
H Marsh, *Divali: Living Festivals* series, RMEP 1982
Minority Group, *Diwali Pack*, Coventry Education Authority 1983

S Mitter, *Hindu Festivals: Festivals* series, Wayland 1985
J Solomon, *Gifts and Almonds*, Hamish Hamilton 1980
B Thompson, *The Story of Prince Rama*, Kestrel 1980
R Thompson, *My Class at Divali*, Franklin Watts 1986
G Ram, *Rama and Sita*, Blackie 1988

AVA
Garlands, Bhavneeta Shop, 7 Upper Tooting Road, London SW17
Hindu Festivals, E748, Pictorial Charts Educational Trust (4 large colour charts and teachers' notes)
Hinduism posters, CEM
Indian Dance—Divali, R745 Pictorial Charts Educational Trust

4 Harvest

The aim of this unit is to help the pupil to recognise the importance of harvest in religious celebrations.

Information

Children building a *sukkah* at their school; they are covering the ceiling with leaves and hanging up fruit.

Harvest is one of the most familiar festivals in school life, yet pupils are often far removed from the original concerns of harvest. A failed harvest once meant death, poverty and starvation but today in the West the presence of supermarkets and freezers detracts from the importance of a good harvest for survival. However, the publicity given to famine and failed harvests in Africa may help pupils to become more sensitive to this aspect; it may also help them to understand that giving and sharing of food (the fruits of the harvest) is an important part of most harvest-time festivals.

Harvest is not only a Christian festival though many churches celebrate harvest festival today. In different climates harvest will come at different times of the year so it is important to remember the varieties of celebration worldwide. In Britain perhaps the best known 'harvest festival' outside the Christian tradition is the Jewish festival of Sukkot. This occurs two weeks after the start of the Jewish New Year in late September/mid-October and is often called the Feast of Tabernacles. It is a festival to remind the Jews of their wanderings in the wilderness and many Jews will build a tabernacle (*sukkah*) in the garden or even in a room in the house. It is a temporary 'living place' and may be made out of leaves, branches and so on. Jews are required to 'live' in the *sukkah* for seven days. It is traditional during the harvest festival to offer hospitality to all, Jews and non-Jews.

There are several rules about building a *sukkah*: (1) it should be temporary; (2) it should be built specially for the festival; (3) the ceiling is the last thing to go on, though the sky should be visible; (4) the ceiling should be made from 'plant' material but any material can be used for the walls (the ceiling is often made from fruit tree branches); (5) it should be big enough for a table and a person to be fitted in.

During the festival, four plants—citron, palm, myrtle and willow—are waved three times up and down in every direction, to symbolise blessings over all. The festival recalls the temporary homes the Israelites lived in during their wandering in the wilderness after escaping from Egypt. This prayer sums up the seven-day festival of Sukkot; it is recited on the first day.

> May it be Your will, O my God and God of my fathers, that You cause Your divine presence to live among us, and may You spread a covering of peace over us.
>
> (Prayer Book)

In Christian churches people often decorate the church with fruit and produce. A sheaf of corn may be brought in to the church together with gifts. Hymns are sung, and prayers are offered, of thanksgiving to God that the earth has provided enough food for the coming winter season. The bringing of the produce to church is a dedication of the fruits of the earth to God. There is also an awareness that some people may not have sufficient and the fruits of the harvest are shared with them.

Approaches　　The general approach of the teacher could be that of 'Thanksgiving', for all harvest festivals have that element in them. All the religious activities surrounding harvest festivals point towards thankfulness that God has created such a fruitful earth. The theme can of course be developed within the context of a larger programme of observation of the natural world in autumn.

Activities　　1　It might be possible to build a *sukkah* in the classroom as one way of symbolising a harvest thanksgiving to be celebrated alongside the usual school approach to harvest.

2　The school's harvest festival, if it has one, could emphasise the bringing of useful and acceptable gifts—and members of the local community could be invited to share in the celebration.

3　Pupils could use the fruits of harvest time to create collages or pictures—fruit- or vegetable-printing, pictures made of rice, seeds or lentils. They could learn a verse of one of the well known harvest hymns, or share a simple meal together. There is the opportunity to develop vocabulary by asking what the pupils felt as they gave a gift, ate their meal.

4　There is much that can take place in the classroom through activities such as painting, movement, music, but it would be unfortunate if the pupils were not aware of the religious dimension of harvest thanksgiving through thanksgiving and sharing. There may be local customs connected with harvest which could integrate with a topic on local studies to help the pupils to a deeper understanding of the meaning of harvest celebration.

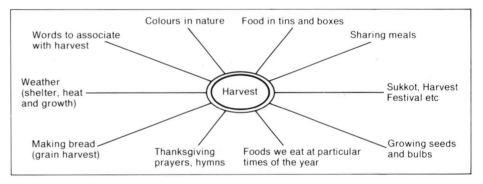

Resources

Books

B Birch, *Festivals: My First Library* series, Macdonald Educational 1984

A Brown, *Festivals in World Religions*, Longman 1986 (resource book for the teacher)

Harvest: Exploring a Theme series, CEM 1986

J McFarland, *Festivals*, Macdonald Educational 1984

P Morrell, *Festivals and Customs*, Piccolo Pan 1977

J Priestley and H Smith, *Harvest and Thanksgiving: Living Festivals* series, RMEP 1985

C Storr, *Feasts and Festivals*, Patrick Hardy Books 1983

D Vause, *The Infant Assembly Book*, Macdonald 1985

R Whitlock, *Harvest and Thanksgiving*, Wayland 1984

AVA

Autumn slides, Philip Green Education (this set of slides may be shown to accompany Vivaldi's Autumn—see below)

Harvest poster, CEM

Songs

Harlequin 44 Songs Round the World, A & C Black 1981

Music

Grieg, 'In Autumn'

Vivaldi, 'The Four Seasons'—Autumn

5 Jesus

The aims of this unit are to introduce pupils to the story of Jesus through incidents in his life and to help them understand that Jesus was a great teacher and healer.

Information

It has become a cliché to say that nothing is known of Jesus' life except what is recorded in the gospels and that the gospels were written for adults, not children. However, since Jesus is so important for Christians it seems reasonable that events in his life and the stories which he is recorded as having told should be made accessible to children. Most of the gospel narratives are concerned with the final events of Jesus' life and accounts of his resurrection appearances. Children will need to become familiar with stories about Jesus if they are to understand the significance of events such as Christmas and Easter.

The Christian tradition has always sought to reflect on the various activities and stories of Jesus in order to discover deeper layers of meaning. It therefore seems appropriate that children should be given the opportunity to listen to the stories and to comment on them at their own level of perception and understanding. Age does not necessarily bring deeper insight! It is through discussing the stories, and through a recognition that there are some puzzling questions that pupils will realise that there are different ways of interpreting the story of Jesus' life.

Foxes Have Holes by Stanley Spencer. This painting of Jesus captures the reflective nature of his mission – a very twentieth-century-style representation.

Jesus lived (probably) between about 6 BCE and 31 CE. He was born in Bethlehem and lived the early part of his life in Nazareth. His father, Joseph, was a carpenter and though nothing is known of those formative years it is likely Jesus was brought up to follow the same trade, which was (and is) a skilled trade and would have been much respected. The teaching ministry of Jesus with which the gospels are mainly concerned is believed to have lasted about three years culminating in his crucifixion in Jerusalem. After his burial on the Friday of Holy Week, his disciples returned to the tomb on Sunday to find it empty, and the gospels record a number of Jesus' appearances to his followers in the succeeding weeks. It is the faith in Jesus' resurrection that forms the cornerstone of the Christian religion.

Approaches
Followers

Jesus had been teaching and some parents brought their children to him for him to bless them and pray over them. The disciples scolded them for it, but Jesus said to them, 'Let the children come to me; do not try to stop them; for the Kingdom of Heaven belongs to children like this.' So he laid his hands on the children and went on his way.

(Matthew 19:13–15; cf Mark 10:13–16)

Jesus is represented as drawing people to him—here he wants to ensure that the children are not prevented from coming to him. In Matthew 4:18–22 and Luke 5:2–11 we read that he called his disciples and they followed him without question.

Miracles

There are a number of stories in the gospels where Jesus heals young people: eg Healing of the Centurion's Son—Matthew 8:5–13; Healing of the Daughter of the President of the Synagogue—Matthew 9:18–26 (and see also Luke 8:49–56); Healing of the Daughter of the Canaanite Woman—Matthew 15:21–28; Healing of the Epileptic Boy—Matthew 17:14–18 (Luke 9:37–43).

These stories could be used as the central theme of a topic on, for instance, 'people whom we trust' or 'people who care for us'. If pupils raise the issue of whether these things really happened, then the teacher can respond by noting that today some people are healed in similar ways and some Christian churches hold healing services. However, the key element is *approachability*; that is, there are those who can help, who are welcoming—parents, friends, people in whom children are encouraged to have confidence.

Parables

Jesus used parables to teach. Some are long, like mini-stories, others are 'one-liners'. The essence of parables is that they transmit a message, though the message may be one thing to one person and another to a second person.

The parable of the Lost Son is an example.

The Lost Son

Once there was a man who had two sons. The younger one asked his father for all the money that was due to him for his work. The father gave him his money and a few days later the young son left home to live in a far distant country. He soon spent all his money on having a good time and when a famine came to the country he could not support himself. He had to get a job working on a farm looking after the pigs. He was so hungry that he would have gladly eaten the food given to the pigs and he decided to go home and ask his father to employ him as a servant.

As he drew near, his father heard of his coming and called for the best clothes to be made ready for his returning son. He ordered a great feast to be held in his son's honour, for the son he thought had gone forever had returned.

However, the elder son was working in the fields and when he heard about the festivities he asked what had happened. When he learned that his younger brother had returned home he was angry. He said to his father 'I've worked for you all these years and you've never done anything like this for me. But now *he* turns up having spent all his money and you welcome him with open arms.' His father replied, 'How could we do anything else? Your brother was lost, he'd gone away, now he is found and come home.'

(Luke 15:11–32)

This is a free translation of the gospel story and teachers may prefer to use a version of the Bible with which they are familiar. The story integrates well with a topic on forgiveness; it is an opening gambit for a discussion about jealousy and envy, about sharing and perhaps about family relationships. The rationale for using this parable is that it *is* a good story and can be used simply as a story or as a support to topic work. Other parables that may be helpful are the Good Samaritan (Luke 10:30–35), the Sower (Mark 4:3–9). They also lend themselves to drama, movement and dance, and the creative arts. Do the pupils have their *own* stories to share?

The Lord's Prayer

The most familiar and most used part of Jesus' teaching is probably the Lord's Prayer:

Our Father in heaven,
Hallowed be your name,
Your Kingdom come,
Your will be done,
On earth as in heaven.
Give us today our daily bread.
Forgive us the wrong we have done
As we have forgiven those who have wronged us.
And do not bring us to the test
But save us from the evil one.

(Matthew 6:9–13, NEB; cf Luke 11:2–4)

It is probably not helpful to encourage any analysis of the Lord's Prayer with very young pupils. The prayer was given by Jesus to his disciples when they asked him how they should pray, so it has become *the* model Christian prayer.

It is brief and there is no reason why pupils should not learn it as a very important Christian prayer, used privately as well as in many public services.

Activities

1   One type of activity would be for the children to sort through different pictures of Jesus. This depends upon the teacher collecting postcard-size pictures, but if it is possible to obtain a reasonable collection groups of children can sort through the cards in order to choose, for example, one they like, or one that illustrates a story they might recognise.

2   Tell a story of Jesus, or one which he told, and, without discussion, ask the children to model in clay (or in clay tiles) or paint an illustration for the story. It may be necessary to repeat the story. The aim of this activity is to encourage the children to express *their* response to the story in a creative way rather than just repeat directions from the teacher.

3 Some of the older pupils could in a group make a collage, using colour magazines, of the event or story told. An ambitious project could take a story, or part of a story, and use a life-size model by drawing around the pupils, then 'filling in' faces, clothes, hands and the setting of the story.

4 Some of the stories can be imaginatively explored with infants by using puppets made in the classroom. These can be 'potato puppets' or 'paper-cup puppets' or whatever degree of sophistication is possible. However, puppets made, given a personality, dressed, can provide an important learning activity and develop a number of useful skills. The final 'show' can be presented to the class or school at an assembly.

Resources

Resources for young children on 'Jesus' are nearly always from a 'faith' position. Teachers may find it more useful to tell the stories themselves or to use traditional pictures available on slides or on posters.

Books
Baby Jesus, Ladybird (Easy-Reading) 1961
M Doney, *Jesus*, Lion 1988
P Frank, *Secrets Jesus Told: Lion Story Bible* series, Lion 1987
Good News From Jesus!, Palm Tree Press 1983
F Henderson, *Learning about the Bible*, Lion 1984
F Henderson, *Learning about Jesus*, Lion 1983
D Hurst, *Leaders of Religion: Jesus*, Oliver & Boyd 1986
Jesus, Friend of Children, Lion 1980
N Martin, *The Life of Jesus*, Wayland 1986
C Storr, *The Birth of Jesus*, Franklin Watts 1982

AVA
The Life of Jesus posters, Bible Pictures, Macmillan
Tell Me the Stories of Jesus cassette, National Christian Education Council

6 Gautama

The aims of this unit are to help children to recognise Gautama as an important figure for some people, and also to develop an awareness of the foundations of the **Buddhist** religion.

Information

Gautama is the source of the teaching embodied in the religion called Buddhism. He was born about 2,500 years ago at the foot of the Himalayan mountains in India. As the son of a royal family he had many privileges of wealth and rank although it was foretold he would be a Buddha—an 'enlightened one'. Years past and he married and had a son but he was beginning to reflect more on the meaning and purpose of life. Why do people suffer? Is there a way to end the pain of life? One night he left his wife and child in order to seek for an answer; he gave away his fine clothes and became a poor wandering holy man. He was about 29 years old.

After much searching and listening to many teachers, he sat in the shade of a tree, determined to remain until he discovered what he was looking for—even if death came first. (The tree was later to be known as the *Bodhi* tree, that is 'the tree of enlightenment'.) He sat and meditated, looking inwards into his mind. He experienced various temptations but these passed and he found peace—called *nirvana* (this is a state within each person where nothing can be disturbed). Once he had found this peace or *nirvana* he became the Buddha (the Awakened or Enlightened One). He was now about 35. For the next forty-five years he taught throughout India. Some people left their families and followed him, forming the *sangha* (a fellowship of monks and nuns). He had many adventures. He revisited his family and his wife became a nun and his son a monk. When he was about 80 years old he ate some poisoned food, and died.

For Buddhists the truths Buddha taught would still exist even if Gautama had never lived. They are eternal and therefore Buddhism does not rely on the historical person of Gautama in the same way that, for example, Christians require the historical person of Jesus. So Buddhism has grown up around the teachings of the Buddha and although it began in India it had almost completely disappeared there by the thirteenth century CE. However, it spread to Sri Lanka, Thailand and on to other countries such as Tibet, China, Korea and Japan.

This Wesak card is typical of the cards sent to each other by Sri Lankan Buddhists. The Buddha meditates under the *Bodhi* tree and in another image is the monk with the alms bowl.

Approaches

At this stage stories surrounding the life of the Buddha will be enough for pupils; it is not appropriate to deal with his teaching.

The Swan

Gautama (or Prince Siddhartha) was a kind and thoughtful boy; he seemed to be brilliant at everything he did. One day a wounded swan fell at his feet. Gautama gently pulled an arrow out of the bird's wing and began to soothe the injured bird.

Suddenly his cousin, Devadetta, came up to him. He was holding a bow and arrow. 'It's mine,' he shouted, 'I shot the swan. It's mine! Give it to me at once!'

Gautama refused and the two boys argued for a long time. Finally they agreed to take the swan to a wise man who would give them some advice. The wise man listened to what had happened. He sat quietly for a long time thinking over the arguments of the two boys. At last he said, 'It is better to give life than to take it.'

So Gautama took the swan and cared for it. When it was completely better he let it fly away.

This story could be used as part of a topic on animals and how we care for them. It will also help the pupils to think about the suffering they can cause. In Britain a swan is a protected bird and may not be killed. It is a graphic story and can be illustrated with collage, painting or another medium.

The Elephant
One day a rich man asked for many blind men and women to be gathered together. When they were met, he placed an elephant in the middle of them. Then he asked each blind person to describe to him what they felt and what they thought they were touching.

One, who had felt the head, said that it was a pot. Another, who had felt the ears, said it was a basket for collecting corn. The tusk was described as the blade of a plough; the foot was a pillar.

Each person was so sure about what they were touching that they began to argue over which of them was correct. The rich man told them they had only touched a part of the whole and had not understood they were touching a large elephant.

This story is often used to illustrate that in the world we are like the blind man and understand only part of truth.

Activities

1   Touch and taste activities can be fun. Before telling the story above, explore, touch, taste and hearing senses with the pupils. They might be blindfold and asked to describe specific items that they touch. Can they recognise the object they feel? Can they taste food they can't see, and recognise it by taste alone? Can they recognise a sound, or a person's voice when they cannot see the person? Stories like this complement work on the body: how each of us reacts through our senses; see unit on 'Our Body' in *Religious Education and the Pupil with Learning Difficulties* by A Brown (Cambridge University Press 1987).

2   Very young children can be taught to meditate. By lighting a candle at the front of the room and asking the pupils to concentrate on it for a short time it is possible to experience the effect of attentive silence for a minute or so.

Resources

Books
C Barker, *Ananda in Sri Lanka: A Story of Buddhism*, Hamish Hamilton 1985 (the story of a child at school in Sri Lanka)
B Evans, *Gautama, the Indian Prince*, Galliard 1979
J Landow and J Brooke, *Prince Siddhartha*, Wisden 1984
P Morgan, *Buddhist Stories*, Westminster College Oxford 1984

J Snelling, *Buddhist Stories*, Wayland 1986
J Snelling, *The Life of the Buddha*, Wayland 1987 (a simply told story)
AVA
Buddhist Festivals posters, Pictorial Charts Educational Trust

7 Special Books

Aims

The aims of this unit are to encourage awareness of the value of books and to help pupils appreciate how special some books are in some religious traditions.

Information

Some religions place great emphasis on a book, others do not; but even among the 'book' religions there is no uniformity. It is not appropriate, or accurate, to regard the Qur'an (the Holy Book of Islam) as having the same significance for Muslims as, for example, the Bible for Christians.

Generally speaking, of the six religions usually taught in schools, Christianity, Islam, Judaism and Sikhism have a particular point of reference in a book. Buddhism and Hinduism, while having a vast literature, tend not to place the emphasis on the written word in quite the same way, although both do contain important literary works and use them devotionally. Here we will be largely concerned with those four religions which focus on a book.

Christianity

The Bible consists of the Old Testament and the New Testament. The Old Testament records the relationship of God with his chosen people, Israel. The New Testament records the effect of the life of Jesus Christ; it consists of four gospels, the Acts of the Apostles and a series of letters to young churches. As it contains almost all the known information about Jesus' life and teaching, it is indeed a special book for Christians. They believe that the New Testament is the completion of the Old Testament, for Jesus fulfilled and completed the promises of God made to Israel. The original language of the Old Testament is Hebrew and of the New Testament is Greek.

The Bible is used in personal worship—some Christians read a portion every day, attend Bible study groups and so on—and it has a central place in public worship. In some churches it is carried into the church at the beginning of a service. In many churches when the gospel is read the congregation will stand. Most Christians will own a copy of the Bible and there are still families which have a Family Bible. There are many different translations of the Bible.

Islam

The word *Qur'an* comes from an Arabic word meaning 'recite'. Muslims believe this book, the Qur'an, is the unaltered word of God revealed through the Prophet Muhammad by the Archangel Gabriel. Muhammad memorised the words and recited them so they could be written down. There are 114 *surahs* (or chapters) in the Qur'an. Muhammad was not educated and Muslims emphasise that he could not therefore have invented the Qur'an; for Muslims it is *the* Word of God and is not a book about Muhammad. As the Qur'an is the speech of God it is always recited in Arabic (the language in which it was revealed). Any translation is not regarded as the Qur'an. Any decorations in the Qur'an are abstract.

The Qur'an plays an important role in every aspect of Muslim life. It is used in all ceremonies and most Muslim children will begin to learn portions from it at an early age. It is treated with great respect: there are strict regulations governing the handling and text reading of the Qur'an: for instance (1) it is often kept wrapped in a clean piece of material, (2) it is placed on a shelf higher than any other book, (3) one should avoid turning one's back on it, (4) to read from the Qur'an a person must be clean, (5) it is usually read from a stand to keep it off the floor.

This Muslim girl reads carefully from her holy Qur'an. Notice her head is covered and the Qur'an placed on its own stand.

Judaism   The Jewish Bible is written in Hebrew; it is divided into Torah ('teaching' or Law), Prophets and Writings. The Torah, the first five books of the Bible, are traditionally believed to have been given by God to Moses on Mount Sinai. The Bible is the same as the Christian Old Testament but it is unhelpful and misleading to make this direct comparison as the two books (the same words) are used and interpreted in such different ways. The Torah is read in the synagogue on a regular cycle to ensure all of it is read. It will be read during Sabbath worship, in Hebrew, with people being called to read from the congregation. If they are unable to read Hebrew fluently the rabbi (or another person) will read on their behalf. The Torah is hand-written on a scroll which is kept in the 'ark', a cupboard in the synagogue which the congregation faces. Before and after its reading it is processed around the synagogue.

Religious Jews will have their own copy of the Bible to read and to study. A rabbi is a teacher and will normally use the week's reading from the Torah as a basis for the sermon. The Torah is extremely important to Jews as it was given by God to Moses and, while the Orthodox and Liberal and Reform Jews may interpret it differently, its significance cannot be doubted.

Sikhism   The Sikh book is called the Guru Granth Sahib, or sometimes the Adi (first) Granth. (Guru = teacher; Granth = collection or anthology; Sahib = title of reverence.) It is regarded as a living guru and became the focus for Sikh *gurdwara* (temple) worship and life after the last human guru (Guru Gobind Singh) died. He had said the Sikhs should treat the book in future as their guru. It is written in Punjabi in the Sikh script, Gurmukhi, and is a collection of hymns and poems written by Sikh gurus and some non-Sikhs.

In the gurdwara it is placed on cushions on a raised platform with a canopy over it. At night it is generally removed and kept in a safe place covered with a cloth.

The Granthi turns the page of the Sikh holy book, the Guru Granth Sahib. The Guru Granth Sahib is rarely found in private homes and has a special place of honour in the Sikh gurdwara (temple).

An Ethiopian Falasha boy in Israel enacts the Sabbath eve service.

A *chauri* (fan) is usually waved over it as a sign of respect. All entering the gurdwara bow to the book; no one sits with their back to it or points their feet towards it. At home few families will have a Guru Granth Sahib, as a special room has to be set aside for it where it can be treated with reverence: shoes must be removed and the head covered in its presence. Sikhs will use their own prayer books with selections from the Guru Granth Sahib at home.

Approaches

One approach could be that of a special book. Some of the children may have favourite books, which could lead to thoughts about special religious books. However, with this age range it might be helpful simply to begin by exploring the idea of 'what is special' and develop ideas of caring for and looking after those things which have value. From there you could move on to the idea of a special book.

Clearly all the information above will not be imparted to the pupils, but the chart below might suggest a variety of activities.

Activities

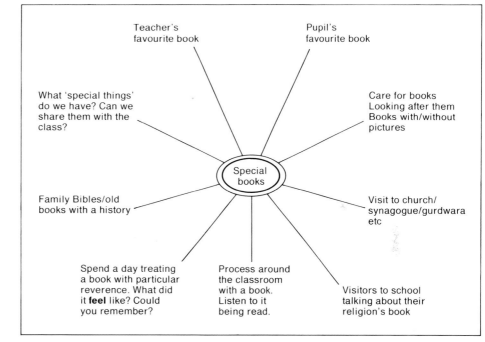

Resources

Books

M Batchelor, *The Children's Bible*, Lion 1987
The Bible in the Primary Classroom: 'What is the Bible?', CEM 1982
The Bible in the Primary Classroom: 'Classroom Practice', CEM 1983
Islam Primary RE Materials, Westhill College, Selly Oak, Birmingham B29 6LL (folder on the Qur'an)
J Mayled, *Holy Books*, Wayland 1986

AVA

Holy Books 1 and *2* posters, E726, E727, Pictorial Charts Educational Trust

8 Stories from Different Religious Traditions

Aims

The aims of this unit are to help children to become aware of a variety of stories from different religious traditions and to begin to perceive that stories often contain important meanings.

Information

Stories are one of the ways in which religions pass on their accumulated wisdom from generation to generation. By using stories teachers are able to capture the imagination of their pupils, to reflect and interpret, and to discover a meaning and a purpose that goes beyond the intellectual into the emotional and affective. Teachers who feel uncertain or ill-equipped to introduce young pupils to world religions will find a helpful way through story.

It is worth reading a number of stories before selecting a range to tell in class; in some stories, for example, it is not historical reality which is important. The stories are concerned simply with sharpening human religious experience. Children can often grasp the point of such stories very quickly for the animation of plants and animals presents no problem to them. Often too there are strong contrasts of good and evil that are uncomplicated in their meaning, and their very directness allows children to respond. Sometimes the stories have clear direct moral teaching.

There is a wide choice of stories and, generally, they fall into the following groups.

1 **Creation myths**. These can foster children's sense of awe and wonder at the natural world.

2 **Lives of important people** in the world's great religions: eg Jesus, the Buddha, Muhammad. In this context teachers might see the importance of presenting a complete 'life' of Jesus. To this group should be added the lives of people of faith: Guru Nanak, King David, St Francis, Gandhi.

3 **Parables and moral stories** emerge from the Jewish, Christian and Buddhist traditions and are immediately accessible because they are stories designed to be memorable and thought-provoking.

4 By contrast there are the **epic stories**, which at first, in both length and style, seem far removed from the infant class. Yet these are important stories, in their religious significance, their inner meaning and in their powerful sense of adventure and excitement. The Exodus, the story of Rama and Sita, and the tales of Monkey from the Chinese tradition (particularly the Peaches of Immortality) are among the world's greatest stories, and for that reason alone deserve a place in the curriculum.

5 Finally there are individual stories in all traditions that have a special quality because their **central figure is a child**, and they directly reflect a child's experiences. The story of David and Goliath (1 Samuel 17) is more than just a tale of a brave boy.

It is about a child who stayed faithful to his own skills and to the resources of childhood, refusing adult weapons. Children rarely fail to see this meaning, and such a story should be part of every child's interpretive equipment. To this group could be added the Call of Samuel (1 Samuel 3:1–18), the story of Ya Teo (see Owen Cole, *Religion in the Multi-Faith School*), Wu and the Yellow Dragon (see Mollie Clark, *Second Folk Tales Series*), the story of Gopala (*Buddhist Stories*), the Boy with the Loaves and Fishes (Matthew 14:13–21), and a number of others.

Approaches

A story from the Hindu tradition

The following are examples of enthralling stories from which activities can begin.

This story tells how Lord Shiva leaps forward to save the world from disaster. It also tells of the goddess Ganga—in whose waters people bathe, pray, heal themselves and cast their ashes after death.

The goddess Ganga

'How the River Ganga Came to Earth' (an epic story)
The goddess Ganga, a mighty river, lived in the heavenly regions of the Himalayas. She was the most sacred of rivers. Those who bathed in her waters were cleansed of their sins and gained everlasting life. Yet if it hadn't been for King Sagara the Ganga might never have come to earth.

King Sagara had two wives but no children. He prayed so devotedly that at last he was rewarded. One wife had one son, and the other had thousands.

To show his gratitude to the gods, the king wanted to make a most important sacrifice—a horse. He took the finest he could find, but it belonged to Lord Indra. Before it was slaughtered, Indra stole it away.

Sagara searched the world for this horse. His sons searched too, and finally began to dig towards the centre of the earth to see if it was there. The Earth goddess, wife of Lord Vishnu, cried in pain as the sons dug deeper. So Vishnu sent a terrible fire which burned Sagara's sons to death.

The king was grief-stricken. He hadn't meant to offend anyone. He begged the gods to return his sons.

'Your sons will come back to life and go to heaven,' he was told, 'when the River Ganga flows to earth.'

So once more Sagara began to pray. At last, Lord Brahma allowed Ganga to flow to earth.

The river gathered into a mighty torrent, her massive weight ready to hurl down on the earth below. Suddenly, Lord Shiva realised that the whole world would be engulfed if the river wasn't broken up first. As the great mass began to fall, he stood underneath. Ganga fell on to the god's head and was trapped in his tangled hair. She was unable to escape, until Shiva divided her up into seven streams.

With a roar like thunder the seven rivers of Ganga came streaming down through the sky. Fish and turtles came tumbling down, and spray which scattered like white birds. Gods, angels and heavenly warriors watched in amazement. Their jewels reflected in the drops of water and sparkled like suns.

Ganga fell to earth, and the seven rivers broke up into brooks and streams, waterfalls and pools. They rushed merrily through rocks and gulleys, and dashed down on to the hot, thirsty, Indian plain.

The water trickled through the earth until it reached the ashes of Sagara's sons. As water and ashes mingled, they came to life, and their souls rose rejoicing to heaven. Now the Ganga flows on earth, and everyone who bathes in her waters will have everlasting life.

(from *Stories from the Hindu World* by J Gavin, Macdonald 1986)

A story from the Buddhist tradition

'The Tricks of the Trade' (a moral story)

There was once a wise old stag who lived deep in the heart of the forest. He knew all the skills and tricks that a deer should know, and he taught them to his nephew, the young stag.

'A good education is a truly marvellous thing,' the old stag told his nephew time and time again. 'If you have it, you're set up for life. Without it, you could well find yourself in serious difficulties sooner or later.'

'Now, it so happened that not long afterwards the young stag went on a trip to a distant part of the forest. There he had the bad luck to be caught in a hunter's trap.

When his mother heard of this, she was very upset. She rushed at once to her brother, the wise old stag.

'Don't worry, sister,' the old stag reassured her. 'I've trained your son well. He'll be all right. You can go home—and calm down!'

Meanwhile, the young stag had not panicked. He had lain down at full length with his legs stretched out stiffly and, by holding air in his lungs, he had made himself swell up like a balloon. Finally, he was completely still, breathing only very gently through one nostril. In fact, he looked so lifeless that flies began to buzz around him and vultures circled in the sky overhead.

The hunter had grown very hungry after working all day in the forest. He was therefore delighted when he saw the young stag caught in his trap.

'There'll be a fine supper for me tonight!' he exclaimed, rubbing his hands together. He slapped the young stag's belly. 'Ah! There's plenty of good, tender meat here.'

Thinking that the young stag was dead, the hunter opened the trap and dragged him clear. After that, he went off, whistling, in search of firewood.

As soon as the hunter had gone, the young stag leapt to his feet. He shook himself twice, stretched his neck and sped off to freedom like a cloud flying before a driving wind.

'You see what a good education can do!' the wise old stag said when he saw his nephew coming home, none the worse for wear. 'It can get you out of the worst difficulties.'

'Yes indeed, uncle,' the young stag agreed heartily. 'I really am most grateful to you for the good training that you gave me.'

(from *Buddhist Stories* by John Snelling, Wayland 1986)

A story from the Muslim tradition

Muhammad and the Cave (life of an important person)

The Prophet Muhammad and his followers were in danger from those tribes who did not believe as they did. Muhammad told his followers to leave Mecca and to go to Medina where they would be safe. While his followers crept away secretly, Muhammad stayed in Mecca. At last only Muhammad, his friend Abu Bakr and their families were left.

One night word was brought to Muhammad that his life was in danger. Leaving their families behind, the Prophet and Abu Bakr slipped through a window and fled from the town. They made their way up a nearby mountain and hid in a cave near the top.

As soon as the two were in the cave, a spider came down and wove its webs over the opening. Soon after that, men came from Mecca hunting for the Prophet. They searched the mountain and found the cave. When they saw the curtains of spider's web covering the entrance, they said, 'Muhammad cannot be here. Those spider's webs have covered the entrance since the time of his birth!' At the same time they startled two wild pigeons which Allah had sent to perch outside the cave. This made the hunters even more certain that Muhammad was not there.

The men returned to Mecca, and the Prophet blessed the pigeons, saying that no follower of Islam should ever harm them.

(from *Stories from the Faiths* by A Sinclair and J Essame, Nisbet 1983)

Activities

The stories lend themselves to (1) dramatic representation,* perhaps embroidered to bring out the dramatic aspect of the story, or (2) straightforward discussion of the story: Who did the children like/dislike? What did they remember most? and so on. (3) The drawing or painting of the story is another creative outlet, where pupils could use torn paper, seeds and suchlike to make a frieze.

* NB. Muhammad must not be portrayed in any dramatic presentation.

Resources

Books

C Baker, *Ananda in Sri Lanka*, Hamish Hamilton 1985
M Clark, *The Second Folk Tales Series*, Hart Davis 1983
W O Cole, *Religion in the Multi-Faith School*, Hulton 1983 (story collection at end)
W Dargue, *Assembly Stories from Around the World*, Oxford 1983
Tao Tao Liu Sanders, *Dragons, Gods and Spirits from Chinese Mythology*, Lowe 1980 (in same series: *Greek Myths, Viking Mythology*)
Muslim Nursery Rhymes, The Islamic Foundation (223 London Road, Leicester) 1982
Buddhist Stories
Chinese Stories
Creation Stories
Guru Nanak and the Sikh Gurus   } *Religious Stories* series, Wayland 1986
Hindu Stories
Lives of the Saints
Old Testament Stories
Stories from the Christian World
Stories from the Hindu World   } Macdonald 1987
Stories from the Jewish World
Stories from the Muslim World
For other books, see under Divali, page 15; Gautama, page 23

9 Food and Festivals

Aims

The aims of this unit are to encourage an awareness of the importance of the sharing of meals and food in religion and to help children recognise that eating together builds up community life.

Information

There are special times in religion when meals carry great symbolism. The account of how to celebrate the Passover (section 2, pages 76–79) may help some teachers and pupils explore the significance of that meal for Jews. It does lend itself to the classroom and young pupils can explore the symbols regardless of age and religious background. Some religions, like Judaism and Islam, are very specific about what sort of food is acceptable and what is not, or what meat can be eaten and how it should be killed. Many Hindus and Buddhists are vegetarian— so are some Jews and Christians, though for different reasons.

Most religions have a special meal, though it may have become so stylised that the 'meal' aspect is not easily recognised. The Eucharist can be a memorial of the Last Supper Jesus had with his disciples but it has become so ritualised that it rarely seems to be a meal. As Jewish festivals are celebrated in the home, the idea of a family meal with friends—eating food for the particular occasion—is very strong.

For Sikhs the receiving of *karah parshad* (a ritually prepared mixture of clarified butter, sugar and semolina flour, cf section 3, page 165) during the service is a

The candles are lit at the beginning of the Passover meal. On the *seder* plate are symbols connected with the Passover and the *matzah* (unleavened) bread lies near the candles.

32

strong symbol of the wish of all Sikhs (and visitors) to express their 'togetherness' in sharing food. In Britain some *langars* (kitchens) attached to gurdwaras offer a meal 24 hours a day and the social gathering around the *langar* is very important to the Sikh religion.

Approaches

The most helpful approach can be simply that of sharing together. In this case it is a special meal and often the meal is related to a story. For young children, if they can begin to capture the atmosphere it will be a tremendous help towards an understanding of 'foods and festivals' as they grow up.

Activities

1 Some suggestions may be found on page 10 and 13 of this section, section 2 (pages 78, 79, 99, 100), and section 3 (pages 114 and 131), but for young pupils a useful approach is to 'collect' their special meals—a birthday, Christmas, class party, an occasion when family/friends come together (wedding, for example). Do they eat special food? Are special foods—eg wedding cake, turkey/chicken, Christmas pudding, latkes, hot cross buns, particularly sticky sweets or cakes—associated with the special meal?

2 The class could contribute to a table of special food, or food they like. The theme of a topic could be 'Bread' and the class become involved in the process of making bread, a staple diet in the West. Pupils could break the bread to share with someone—a private 'meal' together. This could link in with a Harvest theme.

3 As shops everywhere are increasingly making foodstuffs from other countries more available, the pupils could test and taste food often associated with other cultures. There are a number of cook books with easily prepared recipes which could be used in the classroom; some need a minimum of cooking in an oven. The preparation of the food and the eating of it together can help the pupils become aware of the sense of community and togetherness that can emerge. There are many stories attached to food in different religious traditions and a meal with a story linked to it may be particularly helpful.

4 Read the 'Story of Esther' in *Stories from the Jewish Tradition* by S Sheridan (Macdonald 1987). It tells the story behind the Jewish festival of Purim (February/March).

Eating and drinking are characteristic of Purim. Gifts are exchanged between families via the children, pastries are made (often three-cornered pastries filled with a paste of poppy seeds and honey). When the name 'Haman' is heard in the story the pupils can try to drown its sound by using rattles, cap-pistols, alarm clocks, booing or hissing. (Haman, a descendant of Amelek, was brutal to the Israelites.) Pupils can dress up in fancy dress. Purim, says one Jewish writer, 'is a day when only vital work should be done.'

It would be a noisy, exciting but special meal in the classroom.

Resources

Books
Food: Exploring a Theme, CEM 1985
C Lawton, *Matza and Bitter Herbs*, Hamish Hamilton 1984 (the story of Passover)
J Mayled, *Feasting and Fasting*, Wayland 1986
J Ridgway, *Festive Occasions*, OUP 1986 (recipes for every occasion)
Joan Solomon, *Sweet Tooth Sunil*, Hamish Hamilton 1984
C Storr, *Feasts and Festivals*, Patrick Hardy Books 1983 (calendar of British festivals and special days)

10 The Local Church

Aims

> The aims of this unit are to familiarise children with a religious building and to give them a conscious experience of being in a church.

Information

There are some basic principles to be followed. (1) Children should visit different churches and discover each has its own story to tell. By going to different churches children will pick up denominational distinctiveness as well as those things which unite Christians. (2) Co-operate with the priest/minister. (3) Make the visit part of a programme of work. (4) Going round in several small groups may be better than in a group of 30+. (5) The time spent in the church should be short and to the point.

Approaches

The following diagram may be helpful for teachers wanting to develop a programme of work around the local church. It is very comprehensive and the teacher of 5–7s will want to select out particular aspects which are appropriate to the age and experience of the pupils.

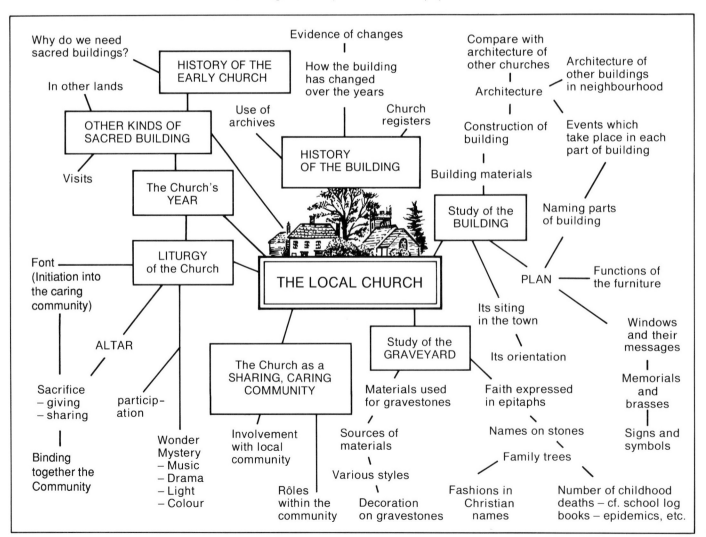

Why do we need sacred buildings?

Evidence of changes

Compare with architecture of other churches

Architecture of other buildings in neighbourhood

HISTORY OF THE EARLY CHURCH

How the building has changed over the years

Architecture

In other lands

Use of archives

Church registers

Construction of building

Events which take place in each part of building

OTHER KINDS OF SACRED BUILDING

HISTORY OF THE BUILDING

Building materials

Visits

The Church's YEAR

Study of the BUILDING

Naming parts of building

Font (Initiation into the caring community)

LITURGY of the Church

THE LOCAL CHURCH

PLAN

Functions of the furniture

ALTAR

Its siting in the town

Windows and their messages

Study of the GRAVEYARD

Its orientation

Sacrifice – giving – sharing

participation

The Church as a SHARING, CARING COMMUNITY

Materials used for gravestones

Faith expressed in epitaphs

Memorials and brasses

Binding together the Community

Wonder Mystery – Music – Drama – Light – Colour

Involvement with local community

Sources of materials

Names on stones

Signs and symbols

Family trees

Rôles within the community

Various styles

Decoration on gravestones

Fashions in Christian names

Number of childhood deaths – cf. school log books – epidemics, etc.

Activities

The traditional eagle lectern has been replaced in many churches by a modern style lectern.

What should we look for?

1 The outside of the church—Where is it in relation to the school? Is it near a main road? In the centre of a village? . . .

2 Inside the church—sit quietly for a short time to absorb the atmosphere. Look at any pillars, arches, windows and so on.

3 Inside the church will be various items: font, lectern, pulpit, altar or table, chairs or pews, and perhaps an organ. The examination of each can be followed up with activities in the classroom.

These could include baptism: collect photographs, a baptismal candle and a christening robe. The font has a part to play in baptism in some churches and is often placed near the church door to symbolise new members being received into the church. The story of Jesus' baptism by John could be read (Mark 1:9–11).

4 The senses could provide an excellent approach to a building. Some preliminary work on the senses could be followed by a visit to the church to experience through touch, smell, sight, hearing and possibly taste. **Touch** could be explored through rubbings, feeling textures of stone, wood, brass and so on. **Sight** could involve the identifying of parts of the building: font, pulpit etc. For **hearing**, can the organ be played, or the bell rung? If the pupils sang they might experience the echo. And, of course, do not forget silence. For **smell**, there might be polish, flowers, incense (perhaps), musty smells. **Taste** could be explored if the church celebrates the Eucharist; explain about bread and wine.

5 People who use the church
Talk about names of people involved with a church building: bishop, minister, priest, vicar, curate, deaconess, organist, church warden, verger. Learn something about their work. Ask the priest/minister to explain a typical week of his work. Let the children make 'The Vicar's/Minister's Diary'. Paint portraits of the church officials. Display them at the church. Why do people go to church? (To learn about God, to pray, to worship with others who belong to the Christian family of the church . . .) Allow the children to experience, as a small group, singing, praying, drama in the church; hold a class assembly with parents.

At the end of the Eucharist in some churches the priest says 'Go out to love and serve the Lord'. Look at the noticeboards. What organisations are part of the church and how is it serving the community both locally and worldwide?

6 Many churches have stories attached to their stained-glass windows—about saints, the Bible, local Christians, for example. After some preliminary class work, visit the church to discuss the stories. Children can make their own stained-glass windows or a collage of a story contained within a window.

Resources

Books
M Aird, *The Brown come to St Marks*, Church Information Office 1981 (written from within the Christian tradition)
K Baker, *Your Church*, Mowbray 1982
O Bennett, *Colin's Baptism*, Hamish Hamilton 1986
R Bowood, *Churches and Cathedrals*, Ladybird 1964
C Fairclough, *A Day with a Vicar*, Wayland 1981
E le Grice, *Peter's Two families*, Church Information Office 1985 (written from within the Christian tradition)
P J Hunt, *What to Look for Outside a Church*, Ladybird 1972

P J Hunt, *What to Look for Inside a Church*, Ladybird 1972
N Martin, *Christianity*, Wayland 1985
M Prowting and W Tooley, *Peter and Paula at a Communion Service*, CEM 1985
The Seasons in Stained Glass, Lion 1981
H T Sutton, *The Heritage Book of Cathedrals*, Longman 1985
C Swatridge, *Look Inside a Church*, Macmillan Education 1979

AVA
Jigsaw of a church, obtainable from many religious bookshops

11 Journeys

The aims of this unit are to develop the pupils' awareness of what it means to go on a journey and to explore different sorts of journey.

Information

Some religions place great emphasis on pilgrimage—Islam does so particularly—while for others it may be important but not unduly so. Many Jews try to visit Israel (as do many Christians) but there are often shorter journeys too. In Britain some Christians will visit Iona, Walsingham or Lindisfarne; or they may go further afield to Taizé or Lourdes. Some Hindus in India try to visit Benares (now called Varanasi), some Sikhs journey to Amritsar. For Muslims one of the main ambitions is to make the pilgrimage to Mecca* (called *hajj*) and about two million visit Mecca during Dhul Hijjah each year.

There are journeys within religions: Muhammad travels from Mecca to Medina, Abraham goes from Ur to Canaan, Jesus travels around Israel, Gautama travels throughout India as does Guru Nanak. (See this section, page 22; section 2, page 64, section 3, pages 148, 156.)

Approaches

The pupils' first-hand experience of journeys seems to be the most effective way of preparing children to develop an understanding of 'religious journeys'. One could begin with journeys the pupils make: to school, to a friend, to a relative. How long are these journeys? Are they walking distance? Do you travel in a train/bus/car? Sometimes journeys involve staying away from home—what do

The Ka'ba is one of the centres of all Muslim pilgrimage. It is situated in the city of Mecca in Saudi Arabia. When Muslims pray they always turn in the direction of Mecca.

* Note that Makkah is the preferred spelling, although Mecca has become more familiar in English.

you take with you? What would you think is important to take? These, and other questions the teacher can develop are largely *descriptive*.

The affective element also needs to be considered. Do you like travelling? Are you car-sick/sea-sick? What did you feel like when you first went on a boat or flew in a plane? Is it worth making journeys? Was it a long journey? Very hot? What is the alternative and would you prefer it?

Activities

1   Pupils can paint/draw and write about their journeys. There is also the dramatic aspect of an imaginary classroom journey—sitting in the coach, packing bags and so on. Perhaps the topic could follow up (or prepare for) a class outing.

2   There are other sorts of journey—blood going around the body; growing older; journeys of letters and parcels; rivers; moving house; changing schools or moving to a different class—all of which fit into different topic work.

3   Then there are similar descriptive and affective activities about special places. Where do you *like* to go? Why? What associations does it have? Is it a friend, a relative? Some happy times? Would you like to return? Are there places you don't like visiting and why? Are there journeys you are allowed to do alone? If not, who goes with you? Below is a child's account of a visit to Lourdes.

A visit to Lourdes

When my mother said we were going to Lourdes I wondered where it was. My father didn't want to come so my mother and my sister and I and lots of other people went to Lourdes. It is in France. The Virgin Mary, the mother of Jesus, was seen by St Bernadette and ever since it has been a place where people are healed. This happened about 100 years ago. Now lots of people go to be healed or to pray. I didn't see anybody healed but we all had a lovely time. My mother says we should go every year. My dad says he will come sometime.

It was a long way. I was very tired. It was noisy and my mum, who is a nurse, had a lot to do. We went for over a week and I was very tired when I got home. I enjoyed it. I hope we all go again next time.

There are some other stories to be told and some books are listed on pages 23 and 31. There is the story of Mary, Joseph and Jesus going into Egypt (Matthew 2), the story of Joseph (Genesis 39–50), Rama and Sita (pages 14–15), Pilgrimage (section 3, pages 157–158); and also pages 22–23 and 30–31 in this section.

Resources

Books
P Blakeley, *The Little Shepherd Boy*, A & C Black 1977
R Couldridge, *Christian's Journey*, Lutterworth 1979
D Craig, *Moses and the Flight from Egypt*, Macdonald 1984
P Frank, *The Story of the Good Samaritan: Lion Story Bible* series, Lion 1985
C Gregorowski, *Why a Donkey Was Chosen*, E Benn 1979

Journeys: Exploring a Theme, CEM 1985
S Lane and M Kemp, *Journey to Bethlehem*, CUP 1982 (a play)
S Lawhead, *Howard had a Submarine*, Lion 1987
J Mayled, *Pilgrimage*, Wayland 1986
J Perkins, *Haffertee Goes Exploring*, Lion 1977
J Robertson, *Paul the Traveller*, Ladybird 1980
A Scholey, *Baboushka*, Lion 1982 (also a BBC filmstrip)

12 Dress

The aims of this unit are to help pupils identify dress worn by some religious people and to make them aware of the distinctive forms of dress worn by religious communities.

Information

Christianity

In Britain many people are accustomed to the distinctive clothes worn by the clergy—the clerical or 'dog' collar being an obvious example. However, priests and ministers have special clothes they wear for a service; if you live near a church you will sometimes see the priest or minister walk around in a cassock, a long gown. The Salvation Army have a uniform because they consider themselves an army—there are modern and older versions of the uniform. Then there are monks and nuns: some wear ordinary clothes but most have a 'habit' which identifies them as belonging to a certain order. The nuns usually wear a veil over their hair and they, and monks, often have a cord around the waist of their habit, with three knots in to symbolise poverty, chastity and obedience.

Judaism

Many Jewish men wear a *cappel* or *kippah*—a skullcap—on their head, particularly during prayer. They also wear a *tallit* or shawl with a knotted tassel at each corner; it is worn around the shoulders during worship, though some Jews wear a similar garment under their shirt all day. During morning prayer *tefillin* are worn. These small leather boxes containing extracts from the Bible are strapped by leather thongs to the forehead and inside of the weaker arm so the writings are next to the brain and the heart.

Sikhism

Sikh men and women who belong to the *Khalsa* ('the Pure Ones') carry five symbols of the Sikh faith.

Kesh   – long uncut hair, often in young children tied into a top knot but older boys and men wear a turban

Kangha – a comb not usually seen as it is under the turban. (A turban is about 5 metres long.)

Kirpan   – a sword; often a miniature *kirpan* is worn in Britain

Kach   – short trousers usually worn as an undergarment

Kara   – steel bracelet

Islam

Generally Muslim women should cover the whole body except face and hands. The clothes should be loose to hide the outline of the body and thick enough not to show the skin colour or be attractive to men. The rules for men are basically the same, though men are not allowed to wear silk or gold. (Also men and women should not wear dress which is not distinctively male and female respectively.)

Approaches

One way can be to explore what the pupils *see* people wearing. Do they know what different sorts of dress mean; for instance, can they recognise, firemen, police, nurses? Do they know *why* people wear different sorts of clothing? Sometimes it is for *protection* (against weather, other people, natural objects and so on); sometimes it is for *identification*; sometimes it is for *personal reasons*.

Activities

1 The pupils could make a collage of 'special dresses'—cut out pictures of people wearing special dresses for particular occasions (for example, weddings, christenings)—or for 'people who help us' who are identified with particular clothes.

2 Ask a clergyman, for instance, to visit to show what he wears during a service; or perhaps a Sikh to show the turban and the five Ks; or perhaps an older sister/brother is a server in a church or a member of a particular religious community.

3 The chart suggests other types of approaches with ideas for discussion and creative activities.

These Japanese Buddhist monks have shaven heads and wear long robes. Each monk is given a robe on joining the sangha (the community of monks).

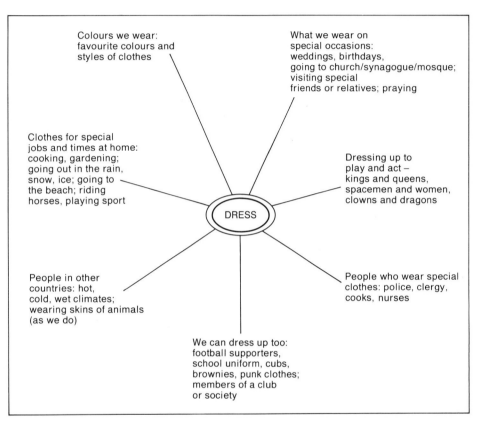

Colours we wear: favourite colours and styles of clothes

What we wear on special occasions: weddings, birthdays, going to church/synagogue/mosque; visiting special friends or relatives; praying

Clothes for special jobs and times at home: cooking, gardening; going out in the rain, snow, ice; going to the beach; riding horses, playing sport

Dressing up to play and act – kings and queens, spacemen and women, clowns and dragons

DRESS

People in other countries: hot, cold, wet climates; wearing skins of animals (as we do)

People who wear special clothes: police, clergy, cooks, nurses

We can dress up too: football supporters, school uniform, cubs, brownies, punk clothes; members of a club or society

Resources

Books
J R Bailey, *Worship, Ceremonial and Rites of Passage*, Schofield & Sims 1986 (the next may be helpful for teachers and the pictures will be useful for pupils)
J Mayled, *Religious Dress*, Wayland 1986
Religious Dress, CEM 1978
J Solomon, *Wedding Day*, Hamish Hamilton 1981
Understanding your Neighbours series, Lutterworth: *Understanding Your Jewish Neighbour* 1974; *Understanding Your Muslim Neighbour* 1976; *Understanding Your Hindu Neighbour* 1977; *Understanding Your Sikh Neighbour* 1980

1 Advent and Christmas

The aim of this unit is to help children see that for **Christians** the birth of Jesus has a universal meaning. The unit examines the observance of Advent and the celebration of Christmas by Christians all over the world.

Information

The *annual* celebration of an event focuses people's lives in a dynamic way on ideas of crucial significance. This is given a ritual context both in the calendar and in customary celebrations.

Advent

In churches which observe the Christian year it begins with the first Sunday in Advent, which occurs on the fourth Sunday before Christmas Day. The season of Advent (coming) as a preparation for Christmas seems to have originated in Gaul in the sixth century CE. To begin with, the length of the period varied. The four Sundays now observed in the West date from the time of Pope Gregory the Great (died 604 CE).

Advent is meant to be a sombre but hopeful season. The first Sunday is sometimes observed with a solemn procession in a darkened church illuminated only by the candles carried by the attendants to the clergy and choir. There are readings from the Old Testament which are identified by the Church as foretelling the coming of a saviour, and hymns and carols appropriate to the season are sung.

In some churches in Europe there is the custom (also taken up by some churches in Britain) of the 'Advent crown'. The crown is made up of evergreen foliage with four candles fixed in it. On each of the four Sundays in Advent a candle is added and lit. This symbolically indicates the increase of light as the festival approaches. A fifth candle is lit on Christmas day. The date of the celebration of Christmas was deliberately chosen to coincide with the winter solstice when days are darkest. From this point on, the days become longer.

The season is one of expectation. However, it is often overwhelmed with anticipations of Christmas both commercially and in religious services. If teachers can give the children a taste of the mood of quiet expectation which is represented by Advent, they will be restoring an element frequently absent.

Christmas customs

The name 'Christmas' derives from the Old English *Cristes Maesse*, Christ's Mass, and has become the customary English title for the feast. However, other languages preserve the reference to 'birth' (eg Spanish *Natividad* and Italian *Natale*).·

The custom of Midnight Mass, which was originally for Easter Eve, has been widely adopted for Christmas. Again this emphasises the theme of light and darkness.

St Francis of Assisi, in Greccio, Italy, in 1223 CE used a life-size crib in celebrating the Christ child. (See section 3, pages 103–104 for the story.) The building of a model crib at Christmas has become a universal custom since then and most churches have a ceremony of blessing the crib, which is set in a stable with the figure of Mary the mother of Jesus, and Joseph her husband, together with animals such as an ox and an ass. This image comes from the account in Luke's gospel of the announcement by angels of the birth of Jesus to shepherds in the fields and the story of the birth at Bethlehem. In Luke's account Jesus was born in a stable or cattleshed because there was no room in the inn. His cradle was a

manger (Luke 2:1–18). In Germany and elsewhere the carving of Christmas crib figures developed into an art form.

The account in Matthew's gospel tells of the coming of wise men from the East, often referred to as kings or magi, who followed a star which stood over the place where the young child was. They brought the symbolic gifts of gold, frankincense and myrrh. Gold for a king, incense for a god, and myrrh foretelling his suffering (Matthew 2).

Many customs derive from the dating of Christmas on the winter solstice (now 21–22 December): Christmas has taken over the symbolism of many pre-Christian celebrations. Midwinter was always a time of great merrymaking and giving of presents. The Yule log and the decorating of houses with mistletoe and other evergreens come from Teutonic midwinter rituals.

Of course, the dating of Christmas was decided in the northern hemisphere and the symbolism of the winter solstice is lost in the southern hemisphere where in fact it occurs in the middle of summer. Australians nevertheless keep the customs of the northern winter Christmas, although Christmas lunch is usually a picnic!

The music of Christmas, as represented by carols, also shows the influence of secular practice. Carols were originally songs for dancing to and that is why many of the older ones are very rhythmic and cheerful. Some others are in the style of madrigals.

If possible the children should be helped to distinguish between the secular celebration of Christmas and the religious observance. The two things of course overlap. And it is clear why some of the Reformers (Calvin and Knox for instance) wished to abolish the celebration of Christmas because of what they felt to be its overwhelming pagan character.

Santa Claus and Father Christmas

The celebration of St Nicholas of Myra on 6 December was very popular in the Middle Ages. The saint was supposed to visit children with rewards and punishments according to their desserts. This legend is still acted out in several countries. In Britain and many other countries the St Nicholas tradition has been assimilated into the Christmas festival and in the form of Santa Claus (from the Dutch *Sinter Klaas*) he has become a legendary figure who is supposed to bring presents to children on Christmas Eve.

In Holland on the last Saturday of November St Nicholas arrives in Amsterdam accompanied by his servant Black Peter. They bring with them not only sacks of presents but also birch rods to chastise those who have been naughty. You might feel this is not very laudable, but it is still re-enacted in fun. St Nicholas' Day is 6 December and on that day, in his bishop's mitre and robes, he rides on a white horse to the royal palace. Similar customs are observed in Austria and Germany.

Sometimes he is simply called Father Christmas, and a whole folk tale has grown up around him rather different from the Santa Claus tradition. His home is said to be in the North Pole and he has a magical sledge drawn by magical reindeer.

St Lucia

In Sweden the Christmas festivities begin on the feast of St Lucia on 13 December. By custom a daughter of the family dresses in white and, wearing a crown of evergreens and some lighted candles, she serves coffee and buns to the rest of the family.

Notice the use of evergreens here and elsewhere. These represent eternal life. Sometimes, as in the case of holly, they are given special significance in relation to Christ. The holly's white flower is said to represent the purity of Mary. The prickly leaves are reminders of the crown of thorns put on Jesus' head before he was crucified. The red berries are the drops of blood and the bark 'as bitter as any gall' represents the bitterness of Jesus' suffering on the cross. (See the carol, 'The Holly and the Ivy'.) In fact the name 'holly' probably comes from the word 'holy'.

The Christingle

Another tradition from Scandinavia which is now practised in Britain is the Christingle. The Christingle is an orange representing the world. A candle is inserted to represent Christ, the light of the world. At Christingle services each child is given a Christingle, usually also decorated with dried fruits or sweets on sticks.

Approaches

1 It might be useful to begin by establishing what the pupils know about Christmas. If they are unfamiliar with the story it could be read in the Luke and Matthew versions in one of the collections made for children (Alan Dale, John Bailey, Jack Priestley).

2 The children may be learning carols. Choose a suitable example and explore with them the story the carol tells.

3 Make an Advent crown (see section 1, pages 9–10 for details) and if you are already within four weeks of Christmas, light one of the candles and indicate that one more will be lit each week until Christmas week.

4 Discuss the celebration of birthdays. Why are birthdays celebrated? (One of the more subtle reasons is that on a birthday the person's place in the community is recognised by everyone else. It is a new idea to most that birthdays are also important for the *group*.) This leads on to the idea of celebrating the birth of Christ to give him his place in the life of the Christian community.

Note that we sometimes speak of the birth of 'Christ'. 'Christ' is a title meaning 'Messiah'. It is because of belief in him as the Messiah or 'Saviour' that his birth is considered universally important. 'Jesus' is the name given to him by his earthly parents.

Activities

1   Advent

The class might develop a ceremony reflecting the idea of light overcoming darkness and the quiet expectation of an Advent service.

This could be done either as a version of a church Advent service with readings from Isaiah or others concerned with the theme, in a candlelit room, or as a more abstract celebration using music and movement to convey the mood. A third alternative might be a combination of music, movement and words. The class could design simple costumes to wear. The ceremony would try to avoid the more gaudy type of Christmas celebration and concentrate on inner feelings of quietness, confidence and expectation. The music could be specially composed and performed where the facilities exist; or could be chosen with help from the teacher and recorded in sequence on tape.

Here are some suitable readings from the book Isaiah.

52:7–10	55:6–10	40:3–5
40:6–8	11:1–2	9:2
9:6–7		

Here are some suggestions of suitable music for listening.

Handel, The Pastoral Symphony from *Messiah*
J S Bach, 'Sheep may safely graze'
Dvorak, Largo from the 'New World' Symphony
Mozart, Adagio from the Clarinet Concerto

2   The Christmas Crib

There are many ways in which this theme could be developed. What is important is that that the project should grow in dialogue with the pupils.

The children might enjoy examining some examples from the past and present. The cattleshed or stable can be constructed from cardboard, or, following the 'cave-like' tradition, it could be built of wire netting and papier-mâché. The figures can be modelled from clay or plasticine or be simply dressed wooden peg figures, depending on the abilities of the children. On the whole it is better not to place ready-made figures as this does away with the need to reflect on their significance. The whole crib should be large enough for two or three children to have access at once, but not so big as to become a threat to the teacher's sanity! It would be a good idea if a place could be found in the school where the class's work could be appreciated by others. It is better not to put the 'wise men' in the ensemble until Epiphany (6 January). This gives the project a link with the next term for a short period.

Where it is suitable the Christmas crib might be incorporated into an assembly.

Note that the use of model infant figures features in other religions, notably in Hinduism, where Krishna's birth (see section 3, page 128) is celebrated by devotion to the baby in a cradle, and at the celebration in Japan of the birth of the Buddha (Hanamatsuri) where the infant image is anointed with fragrant tea.

Celebrating the feast of St Lucia in Sweden.

Resources

Books

Pauline Baynes, *Good King Wenceslas*, Lutterworth 1987 (attractive book, tells the story behind the carol)
I Fedrigotti, *The World of Christmas*, Macdonald 1986
See also the list on page 11 of section 1.

2 Easter

Aims
The aim of this unit is to help children understand the *religious* meaning of Easter for **Christians** by looking at some of the customs associated with the festival. Pupils cannot be expected to understand the theological explanation of Easter, but the ideas which the unit aims to suggest are the Christian beliefs that there is life after death and that the death of Jesus contains within it triumph over evil and the conquest of death.

Information

The Messiah

It is important in Christian understanding that Jesus enters the history of the world in a natural way. He does not arrive like Superman diving in from the heavens. He is born among a people who in various ways are expecting God to raise up a saviour from among them. Jesus becomes recognised as a rabbi and his teaching develops both in conformity with, and in contrast to traditional Jewish teaching. In the end his death occurs at a time when according to Christian tradition it is closely associated with the symbolism of Passover.

That symbolism is transferred to Jesus who in Christian devotion is referred to as the Lamb of God. The burden from which he provides salvation is human sinfulness and the consequence of it, namely (spiritual) death. The Book of Revelation greatly extends the symbolism of the lamb in relation to Jesus (see Revelation 5, 6, 7, 14, 15, 19, 21).

'Messiah' in its Greek form, *Christos*, has come in English to be 'Christ'. Thus in Christian thought the idea of the Messiah, God's chosen saviour, is extended in Jesus. Of course these issues cannot be directly conveyed to children of 7–9. However, it is important for the teacher to have some recognition of the weight attached by the Christian churches to this event. It is the key event of *all* Christian teaching and contains the message on which the Church was founded. If we teach about Christmas and leave out Easter because it's too 'difficult' we distort the substance of the Christian religion.

The Paschal candle

The ceremony of the Paschal candle has been celebrated in many churches for centuries. It has been adopted by many more churches in recent times. Its symbolism is very direct. Briefly, on Easter Eve the people assemble in a completely darkened church. In the porch a new fire is struck (some do this with flint and tinder) and a fire kindled. From the fire the priest lights the Paschal candle, which is simply a large candle easily visible. As he enters the church he sings 'The light of Christ' on one note and the people answer 'Thanks be to God'. This he does three times as he moves up the church, each succeeding time on a higher note. The candle is placed on a special stand and it is inscribed with a cross, the letters Alpha and Omega (which, being the first and last letters of the Greek alphabet, the beginning and the end, stand for God) and the year (Western dating is from the birth of Christ). Then five grains of incense are inserted to represent the five wounds of Christ (feet, hands and side; see John 19:34). The incense grains are nowadays often represented by five large-headed nails.

The congregation then have their own candles lit from the Paschal candle.

The service continues with the blessing of the baptismal water and the first celebration of the Eucharist. The candle burns all night and is lit for all services until Whitsun (Pentecost).

This description is given only to provide the teacher with the background to the activity below (no 1).

The Eastern Orthodox churches add other customs at Easter. The discovery of the empty tomb is re-enacted, as is the search for the body of Jesus. As a sign of 'dying with' Jesus and rising again to new life, a representation of the crucified Jesus is laid on a table and the faithful will pass *under* it.

Approaches

Easter does not occur in school term time and unlike Christmas it cannot really be celebrated in advance. However, there is no reason why the festival should not be considered *after* the Easter vacation, in the summer term. Most church calendars continue the season of Easter for five weeks after the day itself.

1   The study could become an extension of a programme on spring. Associating Easter and the coming of new life in spring is already suggested as a theme for the 5–7 age range (see section 1, page 12) and there are good grounds for picking up the theme here again.

2   One universal feature of confectioners' shops at Easter (and long before) is chocolate Easter eggs. There could be some discussion as to why eggs are a symbol of Easter. This could lead to discussing the custom of rolling eggs in this country, and decorating eggs (see section 1, page 13) in Central Europe, and cracking eggs in Greece—all of course hard-boiled! Perhaps there are local customs in your area.

3   It is important to ensure that the pupils know the story of Jesus' rising from the dead and his appearances. The study could begin with a short account like the one which follows.

According to Luke's gospel (chapter 24) some women came to the tomb on Sunday morning. (They had of course rested on Saturday, the Sabbath day.) They brought with them spices and perfumes to prepare Jesus' body for burial. However, on arrival at the tomb they discovered that the stone covering the entrance had been rolled away. They went inside and were surprised to find no body. Two men in dazzling clothes said 'Why do you look for a live person among the dead?' At this the women returned and reported what they had seen to the disciples. Their names are given as Mary of Magdala, Joanna, and Mary the mother of James. The apostles would not believe them.

The same day two disciples were walking to a village called Emmaus about seven miles from Jerusalem. They were talking about what had happened. As they talked they were joined by someone else, who was Jesus himself but they didn't know it. He asked them what they were talking about. One of them, Cleopas, was surprised that he didn't know what had been happening these last few days. They told him about Jesus and how he had been crucified. They had hoped he was going to be the liberator of Israel. They also spoke of the women going to the tomb. The stranger told them that the Messiah had first to suffer before 'entering upon his glory'. Later, when they reached the village, they were sitting at supper and Jesus broke the bread and offered it to them. When he

Note the A and Ω, the first and last letters of the Greek alphabet, on this Paschal candle. This is the symbol for God. The cross is the mark for Christ, and the five grains of incense represent his wounds (his hands, feet and side). The candle's light represents the risen life of Christ and the date shows the belief that he is alive *now*.

did this they suddenly recognised him and at that moment he vanished. They immediately rushed back to Jerusalem to tell the others. They were met with the news that Jesus had appeared to Peter and they then gave their account of the meeting on the road to Emmaus.

As they were talking, Jesus appeared in the midst of them and ate a piece of fish before their eyes. He then taught them the meaning of his death and resurrection and instructed them to be witnesses. He promised they would receive power from above.

Then he led them out to Bethany and left them there.

Later, in the Acts of the Apostles, Luke describes how Jesus was finally separated from his disciples when he ascended into heaven, and how they received the Holy Spirit on the day of Pentecost. (See also Mark 16:1–8, Matthew 28:1–20, John 20 and 21, 1 Corinthians 15:1–7.)

Sometimes, in order to cope with the mystery of the story, teachers are tempted to offer explanations. But the gospel stories are explicit in asserting that Jesus rose from the dead and this is important in Christian theology. Christians may disagree about the literal truth of the events. But if teachers try to give natural explanations then the dramatic significance of the event is lost. Quite aside from the starkness of the accounts themselves, it would naturally be appropriate for teachers to discuss the mysteriousness of the event as described. The focus however should be on the meaning, as adopted by the Christian churches.

4   Discuss with the children why we don't come to school on Sunday. Sunday is the first day of the week and the reason Christians have celebrations on Sunday is because it is the day on which Jesus rose from the dead. It is a kind of weekly Easter celebration.

From this you could then explain the meaning of the word Easter. Easter comes from an Anglo-Saxon word (*eastre*) for a dawn-goddess. So the English word recalls a feast of sunrise. Perhaps the discussion could continue about feelings linked to 'sunrise'. This could lead to the making of Easter posters incorporating the idea of the dawn of a new day.

5   C S Lewis's *The Lion, the Witch and the Wardrobe* (Puffin 1950) describes the death and rising again of Aslan the lion (pp 147–151). This whole story of Aslan is a way of retelling the story of Jesus (he comes to a land where it is always winter and never Christmas, and so on). Reading the appropriate portion could be a useful beginning.

Activities

1   The class could prepare for an adapted form of the Paschal candle ceremony. At the ceremony itself, the teacher should try to have the room darkened (total darkness is not, of course, necessary). Prayers can be invented or adapted from one of the forms of service. The ceremony should begin with the striking of new fire. It is a matter of choice whether you experiment with striking flints, but most are content with a cigarette lighter or matches. Lighting fires is dangerous and should only take place outside the building (if this is too complicated then you can proceed directly by lighting the candle). Large Paschal candles are somewhat costly and it is probably better to compromise with a smaller one. Many specialist shops have such candles. The lighted candle can be carried into the classroom. The person carrying it stops at the back, then middle, then front of the room, saying 'The light of Christ', and so on as described above. When the Paschal candle is installed in a specially prepared holder, then one person lights a candle

from it; from that one another is lit, and so on until the whole class is holding lighted candles and the whole room is aglow with its warm light. The preparation needs to be very careful and it is essential to have cardboard hand guards on each candle. These are made by cutting a cross in the centre of a small circle of cardboard and pushing the candle through.

Children can be very excited holding lit candles and it is probably safer for this part of the proceedings not to last very long. Extinguishing candles must also be done carefully to avoid hot wax being blown on to hands and arms. Instruction on blowing out a candle (by holding one hand on the other side of the flame and blowing gently) should be given in advance.

The room can now be lit normally by pulling aside curtains. The ceremony then proceeds to the readings which should be short. You can choose abbreviated statements from the prophetic readings, or use a collection of quotations made over a period of time about Jesus' resurrection. It is important that you construct and adapt the proceedings to suit the particular circumstances of your class. The ceremony could of course be an assembly for the whole school.

It is important to involve the children in the planning and preparation of the event and not to present them with a 'ready-made' happening. What is described here is a Christian ceremony based on a church ceremony. It could, if appropriate, be accompanied by an explanatory commentary.

Here is a selection of suitable readings from the Easter Vigil to choose from.

Genesis 1:1–5; 26–31
Psalms 23; 42:1–7; 46
Isaiah 55:6–11
Matthew 28:1–10 ⎫
Mark 16:1–8 ⎬ *one* of these
Luke 24:1–12 ⎭

It is helpful to include some suitable music, including perhaps hymns such as 'Hail gladdening light . . .' or 'Morning has broken . . .'

2 An enjoyable activity is the decoration of Easter eggs. The eggs are hard-boiled in advance and they can be carefully decorated with poster paints (and perhaps a fixer sprayed on afterwards). Try to encourage the use of careful patterns. The preliminaries will include a discussion of the meaning associated with eggs at Easter (symbols of new life; rolling associated with the rolling aside of the door of the tomb).

3 As a separate activity or in association with no 1 above, children could reproduce the marking on the Paschal candle, together with an explanation of the meaning of each part. The symbols of Christ's wounds on the symbol of resurrection are particularly significant: 'glorious scars' as one hymn calls them. Children are also intrigued by the statement 'I am Alpha and Omega, the beginning and the end'.

4 We are quite accustomed to the idea of Christmas cake, perhaps less so to Easter cake. However, there are traditional Easter goodies and it would be appropriate to engage in their preparation where circumstances permit—including the hot cross buns which are traditionally meant for Good Friday, the spices recalling the 'bitterness' of the day (see section 1, page 13). The buns are nonetheless a celebration of the good consequences of that sacrifice, represented by Easter.

5 Build an Easter garden. This does not have the same tradition as a Christmas crib, but it allows the introduction of spring flowers which are the symbols of

An Easter garden

Easter. An Easter garden includes primarily an empty rock tomb with a cover rolled away. Sometimes three small crosses are placed at the back as a reminder of the events of Good Friday. The rest should consist of flowers planted in earth or concealed water holders. Try to make it as lovely to look at as possible. Again, involve the children as far as possible in thinking about what should go into an Easter garden.

6 This unit could be studied in conjunction with pages 76–79 on the Passover, and the number of Passover ideas that have found their way into Easter could be emphasised: the idea of being delivered from tyranny; the idea of being a people chosen by God; the idea of the Passover sacrifice with which Jesus is identified in Christian teaching. (Note that the Jewish sacrifice of a lamb no longer takes place, and has not taken place for centuries—since the destruction of the Temple in Jerusalem. At the Passover *seder*, the reminder of the Paschal lamb is in the form of the lamb bone.)

Care should be taken not to treat Passover just as a preliminary to Christ's coming, but simply to show the context of much of the language used about Christ in his resurrection.

Resources

Books

J Chapman, *The Great Candle Scandal*, Hodder & Stoughton 1982 (fun story about making a huge Paschal candle)

N Fairbairn, *Living Festivals* series: *Easter*, RMEP 1982

Lent, Holy Week and Easter: Services and Prayers, Church House, CUP and SPCK 1984

J Priestley, *Living Festivals* series: *Holy Week*, RMEP 1984

See also the list on page 13 of section 1.

3 Wesak

The aim of this unit is to increase pupils' understanding of the importance of the **Buddha**. It is also designed to help them acquire some understanding of the message and appeal of the Buddha.

Information

The festival

Wesak is the day on which the Buddha is celebrated. Most Buddhist commemorate the Buddha's birth, enlightenment and death on the same day. There are variations in China and Japan where these events are commemorated separately.

All Buddhist festivals are based on the lunar calendar and Wesak is no exception. As is often the case the name is also the name of the month in which it falls (May). *Wesak* is the Sinhalese name. It is called *Vaishakha* in India. The local temple is decorated and in particular lamps are lit because the main emphasis is placed on 'enlightenment'. Wesak lanterns are made of thin paper pasted over a light wooden frame. Every temple has a 'Bodhi tree', that is, a tree which is said to be the offshoot of the original tree in India under which Gautama Buddha found enlightenment. There is usually also a *stupa* containing a relic of the Buddha, which becomes the centre of reverence. These are often ringed with little oil lamps. People may send Wesak cards to their friends. Apart from these the same customs are observed as for all Buddhist festivals: abstaining from agriculture or any occupation which might harm living creatures; visiting the temple; feeding monks (bringing them food!); listening to sermons.

Buddhist teaching

You can read about Buddhist teaching elsewhere (eg *Religions*, Longman 1988) but so far as the children are concerned it is important to understand something of the 'feel' of the Buddhist stance. Here are some indications.

> Buddhists hope one day to achieve 'enlightenment'; that is they will see everything clearly as it really is and when they die they will pass to a state called *nirvana*.
>
> The Buddha gave instructions on the kind of training which will help people to achieve *nirvana* eventually. This includes instruction about good behaviour, having compassion for others, and meditation.
>
> Buddhists believe that we are constantly reborn into this life if we do not achieve *nirvana*, and it is not expected that we will achieve this in the course of *one* lifetime.
>
> In most Asian countries the practice of Buddhism is led by *bhikkhus* (monks) who belong to the community called the *sangha*.
>
> Buddhism has many forms but the basic teaching about *nirvana* is the same. Ordinary Buddhists often use words known as the three 'refuges':
>
> I go to the Buddha for refuge;
> I go to the Dharma for refuge;
> I go to the Sangha for refuge.

Dharma (Sanskrit. *Dhamma* in Pali) is both the teaching of the Buddha and the law of the universe.

> Buddhists also keep simple rules of conduct and undertake the 'five precepts':
>
> to keep from harming others;
> to keep from taking what is not given;

to keep from wrong sexual conduct;

to keep from lying;

to keep from alcohol and drugs because they cloud the mind.

Unselfishness and kindness are encouraged and selfishness and greed are discouraged. Speaking the truth and keeping the mind clear are essential if one is to achieve enlightenment. Because Buddhist teaching is against killing and because it is believed that all living creatures are in some sense 'one', there is a spirit of non-violence to humans and an ecological concern in Buddhism. Buddhists believe in *karma*—that all actions have consequences and those consequences are inevitable. This has its positive side in that ordinary Buddhists feel that they can build up merit by good activities which will help to bring them to a higher level in their next life. One way of gaining merit is letting birds go free. It is almost a ritual act at Wesak. Unfortunately, unscrupulous traders simply capture the birds in order to sell them for freeing again.

Buddhists do not have a dynamic belief in 'God' and it is a little misleading to present their activities as 'prayer' or 'worship'. Reverence is paid to the Buddha, the refuges are chanted and some people practise meditation. Nevertheless some Buddhists also believe in spirits or in the powers of special beings.

Approaches

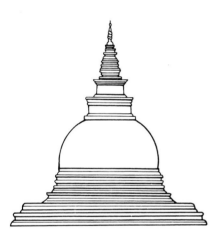

The style of stupa typical in Sri Lanka, called a dagoba

1 If the children have learned the outline of the story of Gautama (section 1, page 22), you could begin by recapitulating this story.

2 Show the children a picture of the seated Buddha to elicit questions and discussion.
Points of note:

expression on the face;

top knot (the Buddha cut his hair on abandoning his princely life, leaving a top knot);

ushnisha (this is a bump indicating wisdom);

long ears (tradition has it that princes and monarchs have long ears);

in warm country (because of dress).

3 Look at some pictures (or use a set of slides) of Buddhist monks, and discuss what kind of religion they follow. You might combine these with pictures of *stupas* or *pagodas* in Thailand or Burma. The idea is to stimulate the awareness of whole cultures which focus on the Buddha's teaching as their dominant philosophy. Communal celebrations can then be seen in that context and the role of Wesak can be studied in relation to the celebrations which figure in calendars in this country.

4 Identify by the calendar or by preliminary observation the full moon of May. Discuss the origin of the word 'month' and the names of the months. Explain that other people have different names and why for Buddhists in Sri Lanka the month Wesak is particularly important.

Activities

1 Make Wesak cards with birds and flowers or with scenes from Buddha's birth or enlightenment.

2 Make a model *stupa* and place a ring of oil lamps around. Commercial 'night lights' placed in five cake holders would do, or simply small cake candles.

3 If an image of the Buddha is available, set up a small shrine with offerings of flowers before it and perhaps burn a few incense sticks to help create the atmosphere.

4   Make a 'puja crown'. You will need three rings of cardboard of increasing size each on a base. Fill the largest with rice and items of low value such as iron and tin. Place the next size on top of this and fill with rice and moderately precious things (crystals, small coins). The smallest ring goes on top, filled with rice and precious things such as brooches, flowers and pound coins. The three rings represent three levels of existence: EARTH, HEAVEN and NIRVANA.

(from *Topic Pack*, Junior Education—October 1987)

5   Make coloured 'lanterns' with tissue paper or balsa wood. These could be hung in groups or strung out across the classroom or carried on a stick. Of course it is out of the question to put actual burning lights in these in a classroom.

The Buddha preaching

6   There are practising Buddhist monks in this country and if there is a group near your school you might invite one to come and talk to the class about the Buddha.

7   Ask the children to sit cross-legged on the floor and try to adopt the position of meditation, with backs straight, eyes open and quietly concentrating on one thing—perhaps a lighted candle on a low table. There are no doctrinal implications to this exercise—it just gives some sense of the still quiet side of Buddhism.

SECTION 2: FOR 7–9 YEAR OLDS

Resources

Books
A Bancroft, *The Festivals of the Buddha*, RMEP 1984
D and U Samarasekara, *I am a Buddhist*, Franklin Watts 1986
J Snelling, *Buddhist Festivals: Festivals* series, Wayland 1985
See also the list on page 23 of section 1.

4 The Christian Calendar

Time and the passage of time are mysteries for us all. This unit is to help children see how we divide up time and how we use the cycle of the seasons to provide some stability.

Information

People everywhere celebrate within time things which have a timeless reference. For example, Christmas comes and goes each year, but the thing it refers to is presented as an eternal truth.

It will be for individual teachers to decide which examples of feasts and festivals the children should be able to give an account of, but an ordinary diary might indicate those which should be understood at an early stage.

A deeper level which perhaps should be touched upon, is the way in which the festivals of a particular religion bring out the basic pattern of the religion.

This unit relates to the 'festival' units in this section (eg 2, 3, 9, 15) and it could therefore be the underlying unit for all of these. For that reason, more information is provided than might normally be the case.

Calendars

There are two bases for calculating calendars.

One is the *phases of the moon* (four seven-day periods). This is the basis of the Muslim and Jewish calendars, for example. The Jewish calendar inserts a 'corrective' month when necessary so that the same months occur approximately at the same season.

The other is the cycle of the *earth's movements round the sun* causing the seasons of spring, summer, autumn, winter. The West has adopted the Gregorian calendar which varies the length of months, and adds a day to February every four years. This means using months (phases of the moon) but imposing a solar pattern so that the months always come in the same season. (In Islam the months move through the seasons.)

Teachers who find the finer details fascinating will find them described in good encyclopaedias, but for the most part it is sufficient to see that the sun and moon are key features in marking out time and that they are not exactly in step.

The Christian calendar

Sunday

The seven-day week was already in use by the time the Christian Church was established. Sunday, the *first* day of the week became the regular day when Christians assembled for worship. Sunday was observed because it was the day of the week when Jesus Christ is reported to have risen from the dead. So for Christians every Sunday is a celebration of the resurrection of Christ. When Christianity was loosened from its Jewish context Sunday took with it some of the features of the Jewish Sabbath. Observance varies widely among Christians. In some Protestant churches Sunday is meant to be observed not only by attendance at worship but also by abstaining from work and secular recreation.

Saints and Martyrs

In the early centuries of the Church's life, there was much persecution, and local churches would adopt the custom of commemorating annually the deaths of their own martyrs and saints. The intensity of their faith is shown in that their commemorative days were sometimes referred to as the saint's 'birthday'.

The two cycles

Apart from the fixed days of commemoration, the Christian year is based on two cycles—one 'solar' and one 'lunar'. The solar is related to Christmas and the lunar is related to Easter.

The Christmas cycle

Since the Gregorian calendar used in Western countries is designed to keep to one whole circuit of the sun, it is a *solar* calendar and Christmas is always on 25 December and always, in the northern hemisphere, in winter. The date of Christmas fixes the dates of the four Sundays before Christmas which make up the season called Advent. Most modern calendars provide a longer period of preparation for Christmas, beginning with the ninth Sunday before Christmas.

There are then two Sundays after Christmas preceding 6 January, which is Epiphany.

The number of Sundays after Epiphany depends on the date of Easter (see below).

So this is the Christmas cycle:

9th Sunday before Christmas
8th Sunday before Christmas
7th Sunday before Christmas
6th Sunday before Christmas
5th Sunday before Christmas
1st Sunday in Advent (4th before Christmas)
2nd Sunday in Advent (3rd before Christmas)
3rd Sunday in Advent (2nd before Christmas)
4th Sunday in Advent (1st before Christmas)
Christmas Eve 24 December
CHRISTMAS DAY 25 December
1st Sunday after Christmas
2nd Sunday after Christmas
Epiphany 6 January
Six possible Sundays after Epiphany (depending on the date of Easter)

SECTION 2: FOR 7–9 YEAR OLDS

The Easter cycle

The first (Jewish) Christians simply added the celebration of the resurrection of Jesus Christ to the celebration of the Passover which took place at the first full moon of the first month of spring (the night of 14–15 Nisan in the Jewish calendar). Since it was known that Jesus rose on the first day of the week, the feast was eventually transferred to the first Sunday *after* Passover. The date can vary between 27 March and 20 April. Christians also adopted the fifty days from Passover to Pentecost. Pentecost is the Jewish harvest festival which is also the commemoration of the revelation of the Torah (Law) to Moses. In the New Testament Acts of the Apostles it is recorded that it was on the day of Pentecost that the followers of the risen Christ received the Holy Spirit. In English-speaking countries, Pentecost is often called Whitsunday ('White'-Sunday).

Early in the Church's history the period before Easter became a period of training and discipline, called in English 'Lent'. Lent begins with *Ash Wednesday* and is immediately followed by the six Sundays in Lent. The Sunday following is *Easter*. (Pancake Tuesday is a secular festival on the day before Ash Wednesday—called 'Mardi gras' in other countries.)

So the Easter cycle is as follows.

Ash Wednesday
Six Sundays in Lent (the 4th is called 'Mothering Sunday', the 6th is called 'Palm Sunday')
Holy Week (the week before Easter; the Friday in Holy Week is called Good Friday)
EASTER (21 March—20 April, depending on the moon, but always a Sunday)
Ascension (Thursday after the 5th Sunday after Easter)
Sunday after Ascension
Pentecost (7th Sunday after Easter)
Trinity (Sunday after Pentecost)
Sundays after Pentecost (depending on date of Easter, between 18 and 23)

Note: the teacher can find further information in *Festivals in World Religions*, Shap Working Party (Longman 1986). Eastern Orthodox churches have different dates. Greek Orthodox calculate Easter in a different way which sometimes varies from the Western Church. Some others work with the Julian calendar which is now thirteen days behind the Gregorian.

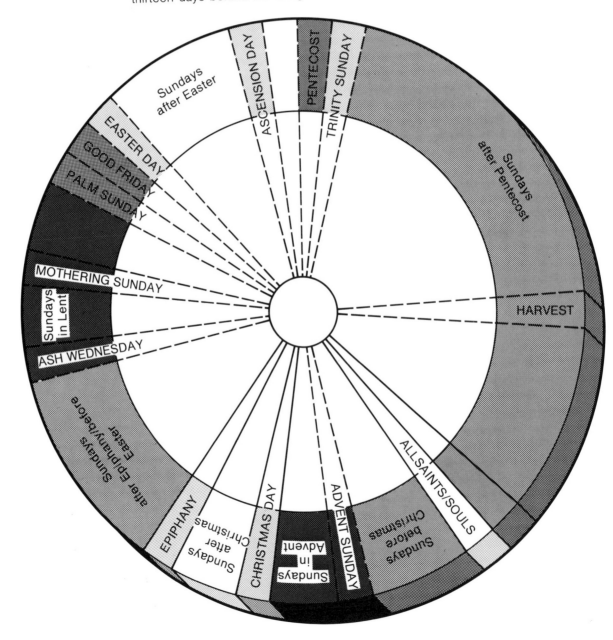

Feasts of the Blessed Virgin Mary

It is important to realise that some Christian churches lay little or no stress on calendrical observances whereas for others (such as the Eastern Orthodox) it is an integral part of their observance.

In churches where she plays an important role there is a cycle of observances related to the Blessed Virgin Mary. For example, in the Roman Catholic calendar:

8 September	The Nativity of the Blessed Virgin Mary
8 December	The Immaculate Conception of the Blessed Virgin Mary
25 March	The Annunciation of the Lord
31 May	The Visitation of the Blessed Virgin Mary
15 August	The Assumption of the Blessed Virgin Mary
1 January	The Solemnity of Mary, Mother of God

Approaches

1 The class might have been concerned with a theme on 'time' in another context, such as the clock with hours and minutes. This could be extended to consider 'a day', 'a week', 'a month'. Some observation work on the phases of the moon will lead to an understanding of the word 'month'.

2 Some work on the 'school year' and the way children feel their lives to be divided between school and holidays, winter and summer can lead to direct work on the construction of a calendar.

3 The unit could begin by asking questions about any festival observed in the year.

What does it celebrate? Why is it celebrated on that day? How is that day celebrated?

4 The names of the days of the week. One is named after the sun, another after the moon. The remainder are named after ancient gods.

Sunday:	The Sun's Day
Monday:	The Moon's Day
Tuesday:	Tiw's Day
Wednesday:	Woden's Day
Thursday:	Thor's Day
Friday:	Freya's Day
Saturday:	Saturn's Day

Compare the names in French—these are named after Roman gods: Dimanche (Lord's Day), Lundi (Lune = Moon), Mardi (Mars), Mercredi (Mercury), Jeudi (Jove), Vendredi (Venus), Samedi (Saturn).

Why are there *seven* days? (A week is a month divided into four, but the year does not fit exactly, so, apart from February, the months are longer than 28 days.)

Activities

1 The phases of the moon waxing and waning can be shaped and cut out and covered with foil or painted white.

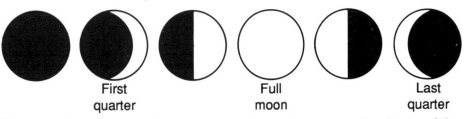

First quarter   Full moon   Last quarter

These can be suspended from the ceiling. Many diaries have the phases of the moon marked. Some direct observation to confirm these could be encouraged.

Extensions of this observation of the moon:

all Islamic festivals depend on *seeing* the moon;
connections between the moon and tides;
folklore about connection with the moon (Chinese, for example);
all Buddhist observances are related to phases of the moon and festivals are
   often named after the month.

2   Make a circle with four quadrants and find a way of symbolising the seasons
of the Northern Hemisphere.

3   Draw up a calendar for display, setting out all the religious observances possible during the term (the Shap Calendar will help, and many ordinary diaries
include all the Islamic and some of the Jewish and Sikh dates). Try to represent
pictorially the meaning of each of the dates represented.

4   Find some of the stories connected with some of these: for example Baisakhi
(for Sikhs), Sukkot (for Jews), Pentecost (for Christians), Janamashtami (for
Hindus), Al Hijrah (for Muslims). (Baisakhi is the day of the founding of the Khalsa,

Here is a page from a combined Islamic
and Gregorian calendar showing June
1985. You can see how the lunar months of
Ramadan and Shawwal overlap the month
of June.

Sukkot is 'Tabernacles' and is celebrated with the building of 'booths', Pentecost is the day when the Holy Spirit is said to have descended on the disciples of Christ. Janamashtami is the birthday of Krishna. Al Hijrah is the Muslim New Year and commemorates Muhammad's migration from Mecca to Medina.) Note: teachers may introduce others which they know better, but this is an opportunity to explore some lesser known festivals.

Find some way of presenting a chosen story to the class.

5 List the main festivals of the Christian year, beginning with Christmas and ending with Pentecost. Alongside, show what they commemorate. This can lead to some discussion about what is important to Christians about Jesus.

For example:

Christmas (25 December):	Jesus is born
Epiphany (6 January):	Jesus is baptised
Candlemas (2 February):	Jesus is presented in the Temple
Ash Wednesday (first day of Lent):	Jesus in the wilderness
Annunciation (25 March):	Angel Gabriel announces to Mary the coming birth of Jesus
Palm Sunday:	Jesus enters Jerusalem before his crucifixion
Maundy Thursday:	Jesus celebrates the Last Supper with his disciples
Good Friday:	Jesus is crucified
Easter:	Jesus rises from the dead
Ascension:	Jesus ascends into heaven
Pentecost:	The Holy Spirit is given to Jesus' disciples

Resources

Shap Calendar of Religious Festivals, published annually by the Commission for Racial Equality (obtainable from Shap Working Party, National Society's RE Centre, 23 Kensington Square, London W5 8HN)
Shap Working Party, *Festivals in World Religions*, Longman 1986

5 The Life of Jesus

Aims

It is assumed that the children will have learned piecemeal of some of the life and teaching of Jesus. In this unit the emphasis is on the life of Jesus, so that the children have a clearer picture of Jesus as a person who was born, and who lived and died at a specific time and place, and why he is an important person for **Christians**.

Information

Sources

In fact we know very little about the *life* of Jesus. The gospels are 'proclaiming' documents, that is, they are more concerned to show Jesus as Messiah or Saviour and Lord than to give a careful account of his life. By far the largest portion is given over to the last week of his life because his sufferings and death were and are of great importance in Christian theology. Much of his direct teaching was preserved because it was memorised by disciples and passed on to converts. There are many indications that the early Christians expected the world to end and the kingdom to come quite soon and they had little idea that they might be presenting details for their successors 2,000 years or so later!

Nevertheless there is much that can be deduced, for we know that Jesus was a Jew born in the province of Galilee and so we can assume that his upbringing

Village scene in Palestine

was in the Jewish tradition. His earthly father was a carpenter, which gives us some idea of his domestic circumstances. And the many references in his teaching to the natural world, birds, sowing the seed and so on, and to domestic matters like grinding the corn, sweeping the home, leavening the dough, give clues to his way of life.

Many details we should love to know are missing and it is only the last three years of his life that are to any extent documented. There is just one incident from his childhood which is preserved: the visit to Jerusalem when he was about 12 years old.

Teaching the life of Jesus

1   It is best to make the account as vivid as possible and provide as many aids to the imagination as possible. Some books in the past have rather overloaded learning about life in first-century Palestine—almost to the point where the importance of Jesus was overlooked. However, as long as the teacher doesn't insist on the learning of every detail, it can be a help to be able to 'paint in' some background. Perhaps it would be a good idea to begin with some modern photographs and maps of present-day Israel so that the children understand that you are discussing a place which is still there today.

Some incidental details which could be included as they arise in particular narratives are for example: the flat-roofed houses (as in the account of lowering the sick man through the roof), the treasure chest (as referred to in sayings about laying up treasure on earth), the way in which bread was cooked, and so on. The children will need some explanations why the Romans were there and about the Jewish practice of attendance at the synagogue and what a synagogue is. This kind of information is readily available from many sources eg *Life in the Time of Jesus* by Michael Keene (Oliver & Boyd 1987). It is more a matter of the teacher requiring the background to enliven the narrative than teaching these things for their own sake.

2   The story can be divided into:

> (a) birth in Bethlehem
>   (flight into Egypt)
> (b) residence in Nazareth
>   (childhood)
> (c) baptism by John the Baptist
>   and early ministry; call of the disciples
> (d) journey to Jerusalem
> (e) the last week
> (f) crucifixion and resurrection

It is best not to attempt any account of the more subtle divisions perceived by scholars in their analysis of the gospels.

It is not possible here to give a full account of the possible content. Teachers are directed to useful outlines such as Trevor Shannon's *Jesus* (Lutterworth Press 1982) or N Martin's *The Life of Jesus* (Wayland 1986).

You will need to be selective. However, it is important that some of what you teach is taken *directly* from the Bible, in some simple version. Do not dwell on the birth narratives since they can form a unit on their own (see section 3, page 102). Most important is to try and re-create the normal boyhood of Jesus in his parents' home at Nazareth. Next you should indicate the cultural religious context (visit to Jerusalem), how he was called to be a religious teacher and how, when he was baptised by John, there was a growing consciousness of a specific task. Take then some examples of his teaching, some parables, part of the Sermon on the Mount. Indicate how he gathered together a band of assistants who followed him everywhere and shared some of the preaching, announcing the

SECTION 2: FOR 7–9 YEAR OLDS

coming of the kingdom. Show how there was growing hostility and opposition and how this eventually focused on his arrest in Jerusalem by the Temple police after the Last Supper with his disciples. Give an account of his trial and crucifixion and the narratives of his resurrection and the beginnings of the Christian Church. Talk about the idea of the *Christ*.

3 Chronology. As already indicated, it is difficult to establish an exact chronology for the life of Jesus, but most scholars accept that his public ministry began when he was 30 years old and that the crucifixion took place three years later. (Contrast this with the Buddha, whose ministry lasted forty years and who died at the age of 80.)

Western Christian dating is AD (Anno Domini), that is, from the birth of Jesus. However Dionysius Exiguus who introduced this dating in the sixth century got it wrong by several years! King Herod the Great died in 4 BC and Jesus' birth was probably at least two years before that, in 6 BC. It is difficult to explain that Jesus was born six years before the date assigned! That is another good reason for abandoning the expressions AD and BC and using CE, meaning 'in the Common Era', and BCE, meaning 'before the Common Era, especially as the present dating system is adopted by many others besides Christians.

Approaches

1 Pick up some aspects of the story from Christmas or Easter through exploring questions like, Where was he born? Begin to set out on the quest for the whole story.

2 Begin with personal biographies, including date of birth, place of birth, present residence, brothers and sisters. Children could be asked to fill up a questionnaire with the help of their parents. Can we do the same for Jesus? We must here discover that we cannot do the same for Jesus. We do not have these details and yet he continues to be remembered. Trevor Shannon's *Jesus* suggests a way to proceed.

3 Try to discover how much the children know about Jesus. It could all be noted in abbreviated form on the board. Then eliminate what is in fact inaccurate and tell the class, we are going to put all this information together and in order. Pick out points from the list which provide useful starting points.

Activities

1 Ask the children to imagine Jesus Christ coming today. You could encourage thinking about the sort of things he would teach about, or, alternatively, the circumstances in which his birth and life would occur. Individual writing or a short play with the title 'If Jesus came today' could be attempted. The aim is to stimulate a *contemporary* focus rather than a historical one.

2 Re-enact some of the incidents from the life of Jesus, or mime them to a narrator; eg:

> feeding the five thousand
> call of the disciples
> call of Zachaeus
> healing of the blind man
> entry into Jerusalem
> the trial before Caiaphas and/or Pilate

3 Arrange an antiphonal verse-speaking of the Sermon on the Mount (Matthew 5:1–16). Antiphonal means having two groups reading a verse alternately. Divide the class into two.

4   Imagine you are on television and conduct an on-the-spot interview of those who witnessed the healing of the man let down through the roof. Perhaps a group could prepare it for presentation.

5   If there is a suitable church with many carvings and/or stained glass, a visit could be made to identify what incidents in the life of Jesus are recorded.

The entry into Jerusalem from a stained-glass window in Chartres Cathedral.

SECTION 2: FOR 7–9 YEAR OLDS

Resources

Books
Lion Encyclopaedia of the Bible, Lion 1978
B D Pitman, *Getting to know about: Houses and Homes in the Lands of the Bible*, Denholme
  House Press 1974
T Shannon, *Jesus*, Lutterworth Press 1982
J A Thompson, *Handbook of Life in Bible Times*, IVP 1986
See also page 21 of section 1 and page 125 of section 3.

6 Moses

Aims
For the **Jewish** people, Moses is the great leader, prophet and lawgiver who shaped the character of the Israel which was to come. The aims of this unit are to identify Moses as a key figure in Judaism and to note how important certain historical figures are in the future of a people.

Information

It is important to present Moses as one who saw himself, and was acknowledged as, acting on God's commands.

The most effective sequence is likely to be a chronological story:

birth and upbringing
the Burning Bush and call
leading out of Egypt, Passover, the plagues and the parting of the Red Sea
the wanderings in the wilderness
the experience on Mount Sinai
the tablets of stone and the Ten Commandments
the Tabernacle
Moses' death before he entered the Promised Land

It is important for the children to know that Moses is held to be the author of the first books of the Bible, called by Jews *Torah*. The Torah is seen as the authority for all Jewish teaching and it is read daily in synagogues. A section on the Torah will help to focus the continuing religious significance of Moses. The scroll of the Law is kept in a rich cloth in the ark in the synagogue. (For more information see page 66 and section 3, page 170.) Use photographs or slides to show Torah scrolls in the synagogue.

The scroll of the Torah

Approaches

1   Perhaps some of the children will have heard of the Ten Commandments, even if they don't know what they are. Looking them up in Exodus chapter 20 could provide the starting point for a study of Moses.

2   Read the story of Moses in the bulrushes in a simple version (Exodus 1:6–10, 16; 2:1–10; Acts 7:20–22) and then build up a picture of the Hebrews in slavery in Egypt.

3   Start by asking the children to give the names of any great leaders whom they know about and anything they can remember about them. From there begin the study of a great Jewish leader who lived about 3,500 years ago but whose words are remembered today.

4   It might be effective to begin with the children learning a spiritual such as 'Go down, Moses' and, when they have learned to sing it, to ask them if they know what the song refers to.

Activities

1   Make for display a scroll from Alan Dale's version of the Ten Commandments.

2   If there is a synagogue near to you, visit it—with the permission of the secretary and the rabbi.

3   Examine the words on a Hebrew Bible and perhaps copy a few words, remembering it goes from right to left.

4   Act out some of the narrative of the Exodus, or the call of Moses at the Burning Bush.

SECTION 2: FOR 7–9 YEAR OLDS

Resources

Books
M and M Doney, *Moses, Leader of a Nation*, Hutchinson 1980
A Dale, *Winding Quest*, OUP 1972

7 Sacred Writings

Aims

This unit seeks to provide some general knowledge of important religious writings and their use in public worship.

Information

Most religions have important writings. This unit selects the following for consideration.

1 Torah	— Judaism
2 Bible, Old and New Testaments	— Christianity
3 Qur'an	— Islam
4 *Bhagavad Gita	— Hinduism
5 Guru Granth Sahib	— Sikhism
6 *Dhammapada	— Buddhism

As a preliminary it is important to try and obtain examples of these six. Hebrew Bibles (no 1) are fairly readily obtainable. The Qur'an (no 3) is not so easy since Muslims are reluctant to sell copies to non-Muslims. If you do have access to an Arabic copy of the Qur'an remember to treat it with reverence so as not to offend. The Guru Granth (no 5) is perhaps even more rare in a portable version. However, where copies of the actual book are not available try to ensure that you have at least photographs or slides. Of course paperback versions in English are easier to find and are useful in seeking out suitable quotations.

In each of the religions mentioned—Judaism, Christianity, Islam, Hinduism, Sikhism and Buddhism—authoritative scriptures play an important part and in the case of the first three and Sikhism they are a central focus in the public acts of worship because they are seen in some sense to be 'the Word of God' and therefore a means of communication between God and man. And because the scriptures have this role they are given a context in which they are shown reverence.

The Torah

'In the beginning God created the heaven and the earth. . .' (Genesis 1:1). The Torah is written in Hebrew.

The great scroll is kept in the ark, a special container with pride of place in the synagogue, usually with a curtain across. At the appropriate moment the scroll is removed and first carried round the synagogue before being carefully laid and unwound for the reading of the appropriate portion. The scrolls used in the synagogue are always hand-copied and there is a pointer (a *yad*) to follow the text so that the reader avoids touching the text. The scroll itself is kept in a richly decorated cover and sometimes with silver ornaments on the projecting rods. A breastplate is hung round it recalling the breastplate once worn by the high priest in Jerusalem. Of course the Torah is also printed, but the one used ceremonially in the synagogue is always the hand-copied scroll described above.

If you can obtain some miniature scrolls it helps in an explanation to the children. The Torah consists of the first five books of the Bible (which Christians call the Old Testament). It contains the foundation history of the Jews and the Law received from God. As it is read in the synagogue, Jews are constantly reminded of their relationship to God as a people and of their obligations.

The Torah is read through annually in portions each Sabbath in the synagogue. Simhat Torah is the festival which celebrates the end of the reading of the Torah

* It is difficult to designate *one* authoritative scripture in Hinduism and Buddhism. These are chosen as examples greatly treasured by followers.

and the beginning of the next cycle of readings. There is a joyful procession round the synagogue seven times.

The Jewish Bible also has two other parts which are called the 'Prophets' and the 'Writings' and these are also read in the synagogue. But nothing is given the same degree of reverence as the Torah. (If a Torah scroll is damaged it is placed carefully in a box and buried in a grave or cave.) The whole Hebrew Bible is sometimes called 'Tenak', from T for Torah, N for Neviim (Prophets), K for Ketivim (Writings).

The Qur'an is written in Arabic.

The Qur'an

As an object the Qur'an is not generally given prominence in the mosque but mosques are often decorated with calligraphy giving quotations from the book and it is reverently studied in the mosque. There is also a definitive version of the Qur'an both in content and appearance which is diligently copied. Muslims hold that the words of the book are God's revealed message and it is only authoritative in Arabic: to quote a translation is not to quote the Qur'an.

The Christian Bible

The Bible incorporates the contents of the Jewish Bible, which are referred to as the 'Old Testament', and the writings which are called collectively the 'New Testament'. It is important *not* to refer to the Jewish Bible itself as the Old Testament. For Jews the Bible (Tenak) is the continuing valid guide for today and in many instances the understanding of the text is quite different from that of the Christians. Therefore, although the words are the same, the book functions differently in each tradition. The Bible holds an important place in Christian worship where it is always read: usually a reading from the Old Testament and a reading from the New Testament and always at the Holy Communion a portion from one of the gospels.

The Guru Granth Sahib

This occupies the most important place in the Sikh gurdwara: on a raised platform under a canopy and always attended by a Sikh holding a *chauri*—a handle with hairs attached, which was waved by a servant for an important person to help keep cool. In no other religion is the scripture treated so much like a person. For Sikhs the Adi Granth is the eleventh guru. When the tenth guru, Guru Gobind Singh, came to appoint a successor, he told his followers that the book would be their guru from now on.

The Guru Granth Sahib

In some gurdwaras there is a special room where the book is 'put to bed' at night in rich coverings, and from where it is carried in the morning into the temple. It is always carried on the bearer's head. Devout Sikhs make gifts of beautiful coverings for the book with which it is draped when not in use. The Adi Granth consists mainly of prayers and hymns written by Guru Nanak and his successors, and is heard usually by being sung by performers, although there are also direct readings.

The Bhagavad Gita

This is one of the most popular of all Indian sacred writings. The title means 'The Song of the Lord' and it is a section of the sixth book of a huge epic called the *Mahabharata*.

It is a poem which takes the form of a dialogue between the prince Arjuna and his charioteer who is the god Krishna in disguise. The dialogue takes place just before a battle in which Arjuna with his four brothers is about to engage with their enemies the sons of Dhritarashtra. Beginning with the question about engaging in killing, the discussion soon moves on to many other topics. It is Krishna's answers which provide many of the best known texts in Hinduism (see section 3, pages 126–131).

Hindu worship is diverse, but the Gita is frequently used for meditation and its verses chanted. For many, the authoritative scriptures are the four Vedas and these are often found in temples. However, they are usually only read by scholars or chanted in specific rituals by priests.

The Bhagavad Gita is written in Sanskrit.

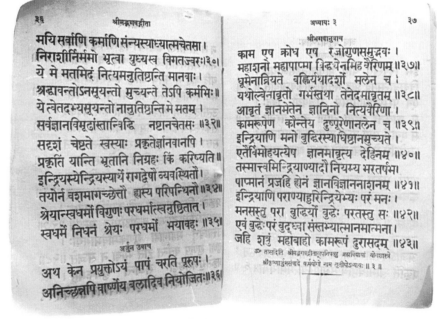

The Dhammapada

Buddhist views on the extent of what constitutes the authoritative scriptures vary somewhat. Most would accept what is called the *Tri-pitaka* (the three baskets) consisting of the *Vinaya* (monks' rules) the *Sutra Pitaka* (the Buddha's teaching) and the *Abhidharma Pitaka*. The content of the last varies with Buddhist schools. However the Dhammapada, 'teaching verses', is one of the best known books in Theravada Buddhism and contains much of the Buddha's teaching in shortened form.

Theoretically Buddhists do not take the same view of authoritative scripture as other religions since theirs is a journey to 'enlightenment' rather than obedience to revelation. Nevertheless verses of scripture are chanted at Buddhist gatherings, particularly by monks (*bhikkus*).

Approaches

1   A visit to a church or other place of worship (see section 3, pages 168 and 178, and section 2, page 92) might be the starting point for a particular consideration of sacred books, because of the prominence of for instance the lectern, or the ark in a synagogue or the Guru Granth in a gurdwara.

2   Use a small section out of a video showing worship in progress (eg Videotext, or 'Christianity through the Eyes of Christian Children'—CEM PEP) where the reading of scripture is taking place. Draw attention to the way in which scripture is being used and invite comments about what the children know about such books.

Pictorial Charts Educational Trust produce useful sets of pictures which show reading occurring in a number of ritual situations: *Holy Books 1* and *Holy Books 2*, and another called *Holy Writings*, which shows the actual text of each.

3   Discuss with the children the idea of 'important books'. 'Do *you* have a special book?' 'Why is it special?' 'Do you know of books that are special to a lot of people?'. . .

4   Another approach is to go further back and make this unit the follow-on from a topic on writing. What are the resources for recording in writing and why do some books become especially important for people?

Activities

The potential and scope of this unit is very wide and teachers must decide in the light of their own circumstances how many examples of sacred scriptures in use they will investigate with their class. At least *three* should be included. The purpose here is to show these scriptures in ceremonial or ritual use, demonstrating that they hold an authoritative place in the practice of each religion. Resist any temptation to investigate the contents of these books exhaustively. That is another kind of study entirely.

1   Tell the story of Guru Nanak (see *Stories from the Sikh World*, Macdonald 1988) and the succession of nine other gurus and how Guru Gobind Singh decided that the book with hymns and prayers should be the next guru for the Sikhs. So the book is always spoken of as Guru Granth, sometimes with 'Sahib' added. (Granth means 'collection' and 'Sahib' is an expression of deference to someone important—'Lord', 'Eminence'). Use pictures or slides to show the situation of

SECTION 2: FOR 7–9 YEAR OLDS

The Dhammapada is written in Pali.

the book in the gurdwara. Explain how costly it is. People sometimes 'borrow' one to celebrate an important occasion such as a wedding.

When choosing a baby's name, the book is opened at random and the name chosen must have the first letter on the page as the initial. (The children could experiment by doing this with any book.)

Copy out in English Guru Nanak's first hymn the 'Mool Mantra':

> There is One God,
> Eternal Truth is his name;
> Maker of all things,
> Fearing nothing and never at war with anything,
> Timeless not born in a human way,
> He is of his own Being.
> Made known to men by the grace of the Guru.

If this is too long, the first two lines could be used.

Copy the symbols **ੴ** = *ik onkar* which is the first line in the language of the Guru Granth. It is often seen on Sikh gurdwaras. It could be prepared in a poster size for display.

2 Show some slides of a mosque and of people reading the Qur'an. Give some outline of Islam. There are many children in Britain and all over the world who worship God whom they call *Allah*. They are called *Muslims* and their special book is called the *Qur'an* given to them by Allah through the great teacher *Muhammad*. The Qur'an says that you should not use any pictures of anything in worship; that is why there are no pictures or sculptures inside the mosque. (This can be extended at discretion to *Minaret, Muezzin* and the Call to Prayer.)

If possible pass round a copy of the Qur'an, but first explain that everyone must have clean hands (pass round moistened tissues) and that there must be a clean place on the desk (paper or cloth or a stand). If you have the means, prepare a cut-out from which a small stand can be made. You may have a child who can recite a little of the book.

Have some magnified examples of Arabic script available for examination; explain how it is read from right to left.

Prepare outlines of the word Allah in Arabic (see section 3, page 139—right-hand word. Ignore smaller writing.) and have the children colour and decorate it with patterned borders. Choose a text from an anthology and prepare it for display. Note that the problem of bringing an Arabic Qur'an into the classroom might prove to be too great. In that case an English version can be substituted but treated in the same way and backed up with some examples of Arabic script. Do not ask the children to draw pictures of Muhammad or the angel.

(You could include the story of Muhammad receiving the words of the Qur'an from the Angel Gabriel but care must be taken to emphasise that for Muslims the book comes from God; see section 3, pages 132–133.)

3 Discuss how the Torah is used in the synagogue (see above). Obtain and show the children a *mezuzah* which is fastened to the doorposts of Jewish homes. Look up Deuteronomy chapter 6 verses 4–9. Copy out the words of verses 4 and 5, called the *Shema* because in Hebrew that is the word with which it begins ('Hear'). The copies should be in small writing and rolled up into a tube. Make small *mezuzahs* out of cardboard and place the text inside.

Children could make scrolls with decorated covers and some Hebrew writing.

4 A small project on the different languages used in scriptures, and what they look like, could be pursued. See Pictorial Charts Educational Trust *Holy Writings* posters (commentary by Martin Palmer).

A mezuzah

5   The Christian Bible consists of the Old Testament originally written in Hebrew and the New Testament originally written in Greek. A historical approach could be used since copies of the ancient documents showing portions of the Bible are readily available from the British Museum.

How far you base activities on the Christian Bible will depend on how it has figured in other parts of your RE teaching. Another emphasis here is to show how it has been held in reverence by believers. The material used therefore would relate to the way in which it has been copied (eg, Book of Kells) and children should be encouraged perhaps to copy some words and illuminate them themselves.

6   Again in considering the Bhagavad Gita, illustrated copies will demonstrate the reverence in which the book is held. There should be some study of Indian worship in temple and home. Choose an extract which will be easily understood (see example below) and again make an illuminated version.

7   The story of the Buddha (see section 1, page 22) and his first sermon in the deer park are a good introduction to the Dhammapada. It contains the Four Noble Truths and the Noble Eightfold Path. It is important that children *know* about these even if further analysis has to wait until later.

Some quotations
Gita 9.6

> When you offer with love a leaf, a flower, or water to me, I accept that offer of love from the giver who gives himself.

Dhammapada 1

> Hatred does not cease by hatred at any time;
> Hatred ceases by love—this is an old rule.

Guru Granth Sahib—the beginning of the Japji

> There is but one God whose name is true, the Creator, devoid of fear and enmity, immortal, unborn, self existent;

Qur'an—*surah* 1

> Praise be to God, the Lord of the Worlds!
> The compassionate, the merciful!

Torah—Deuteronomy 6:4–5

> Hear, O Israel, the LORD our God is one and you must love the LORD your God with all your heart and soul and strength.

New Testament—John 6:35

> I am the bread of life. Whoever comes to me shall never be hungry and whoever believes in me shall never be thirsty.

Resources

Books
P Bahree, *The Hindu World*
A Bancroft *The Buddhist World*
A Brown, *The Christian World*   } Macdonald 1982–86
D Charing, *The Jewish World*
R Tames, *The Muslim World*
D Singh and A Smith, *The Sikh World* }

The Good News Children's Bible, Collins 1986
J Mayled, *Holy Books*, Wayland 1986

AVA
Holy Books 1 and *2*, Pictorial Charts Educational Trust
Holy Writings, Pictorial Charts Educational Trust

SECTION 2: FOR 7–9 YEAR OLDS

8 Stories with Meaning

Aims

The purpose of this unit is to introduce pupils to the use of stories in religion. Later, children often become more analytical and are more concerned with literal interpretation than with meaning. It is important that early on they become accustomed to asking the question of what the story *means*.

Information

Every religion has its 'story' or 'stories' and firmly embedded in each story is a meaning for that religion. In some religions it is a key story which dominates. In Christianity for example the key story is the story of Jesus. Without that story there is no Christianity. In some religions there is a great wealth of stories. Hindu religion is preserved and practised in terms of its myths, that is, its stories.

It is said by some scholars that religion cannot really exist without using the form of a story. This is because religion is trying to capture some eternal truth in the passing world of time and this can only be done in a narrative.

Religious stories are usually about the beginning of something—a creation, for instance, or how a big change is brought about by a saviour.

Above all it is essential that the children should enjoy the story for its own sake. The teacher should indicate that it is one that is of importance to a particular religion, but the degree to which the meaning can be drawn on will vary with the age and specific abilities of the children.

Here are some stories which could be used.

A Hindu creation story

In spite of the many gods mentioned in Hinduism, most Hindus believe only in *one* supreme God, and think of all others as forms of the one God. The introductory note is important to this story because it is an attempt to represent the repeating cycle of creation and it shows how all the universe is thought to come out of God himself.

Note: for Hindus the universe is created and destroyed again in a series of repeating cycles. These cycles are called *kalpas* and each one it is believed lasts 4,320 million years by human reckoning. Each *kalpa* is considered to be only *one day* of Brahma, the creation god. At the end of the day of Brahma everything is destroyed and disappears into the night of Brahma. The night of Brahma is the same length of time as the day of Brahma.

For many Hindus the supreme god is called Vishnu. He is sometimes shown, in art, as asleep on the coils of a many-headed cobra called Ananta. *Ananta* means 'without end'. The snake is itself floating on a great ocean. This picture represents a time when the world does not exist. That is called the night of Brahma. At the end of this night, Vishnu decides to produce the world again.

He first gently stirs the waters of the great ocean and in between the ripples a space grows. This space carries the sound of Vishnu which is the rushing of the wind. The wind blows and suddenly a flame comes alight. The fire burns away some of the water and heaven comes into existence. Then Vishnu concentrates his mind and out of his stomach comes a single lotus. The lotus is a water

Note that Brahma holds in his hands a book which is a copy of the four Vedas of Hindu scripture. These are considered to be eternal and contain the words to create the universe again.

lily and is an important symbol in Indian thinking. It represents what is pure and perfect. This lotus from the body of Vishnu has a thousand petals of pure gold. Seated on the lotus is Brahma who will create the whole world. Brahma has four faces. Each one controls a quarter of the universe.

A story from ancient Egypt

Many of the stories of the gods of ancient Egypt have been pieced together from carvings and inscriptions in the pyramids, the tombs of kings, and temples. These had remained hidden for centuries and only came to light during the archaeological excavations of the nineteenth century. Ra, the Sun god, was the first and most important of the gods.

Before the land of Egypt rose out of the waters at the beginning of the world, Ra the Shining One came into being. He was all-powerful, and the secret of his power lay in his Name which he has hidden from all the world. Having this power, he had only to name a thing, and that thing too came into being.

'I am Khepera at the dawn, and Ra at noon, and Tum in the evening'—and as he said it, behold he was the sun rising in the east, passing across the sky and setting in the west. And this was the first day of the world.

When he named Shu, the wind blew. The rain fell when he named Tefnut, the spitter. After this he spoke the name of Geb and the earth rose above the waters of the sea. He cried 'Nut!'—and that goddess was the arch of the sky stretching over the earth with her feet on one horizon and her hands on the other. Then he named Hapi, and the sacred River Nile flowed through Egypt to make it fruitful. Then Ra went on to name all things on earth, which grew into being in his words. Last of all he spoke the words for Man and Woman, and soon there were people dwelling throughout the land of Egypt.

After this Ra himself took on the shape of a man and became the first pharaoh of Egypt. For thousands of years he reigned over the land, and there was peace and plenty. The Nile rose each year and flooded the fields; then it sank back into its channel, leaving the rich coating of mud which made sure of fine crops as the cool spring turned into the baking summer.

There were no lean years when the Nile did not rise high enough; nor were there any years when the floods rose too high or lasted too long. It was the golden age of the world, and ever afterwards the Egyptians spoke of the good things which happened in the time of Ra.

(from 'Ra and his Children' in *Tales of Ancient Egypt* by Roger Lancelyn Green, The Bodley Head 1967)

Khepera means 'he who becomes'. It is also the word for 'scarab'. *Khepera* is Ra as the rising sun. *Tum* is Ra as the setting sun.

Ra is represented in many different ways but perhaps most commonly as a man with the head of a falcon and above his head the solar disc surrounded by the sacred asp Uraeus. Uraeus spits flame and destroys the gods' enemies. In his left hand Ra holds the sacred *ankh*—the symbol of life.

Discuss how the ancient Egyptians might have thought of their pharaohs if these were all sons of Ra.

Notice too that Ra creates by speaking the *word*. Compare 'God *said*, ''Let there be light'' ' in Genesis. Speaking the 'word' to create is common in creation stories.

The Genesis Story (Genesis 1:1–2:4)

More stories can be found in the Hamlyn series of mythologies and in *Looking at Myth* by John Rankin (Lutterworth 1979).

Approaches

1 Begin with a discussion of the children's most popular fairy stories or hero stories; then explain that many religions have stories which contain ways of trying to understand the world, and that you are now going to look at some of these stories.

2 You may prefer to begin with the question of how the world was created and then look at a number of creation stories from different religions.

3 Begin with one of the stories quoted above simply as a story.

Activities

You should try to ensure in the first instance that the children enjoy the story and the purpose of the subsequent activity should be to indicate that the story has *meaning*.

Other activities can be designed to help retain some features of the story or extend the exploration into other directions.

1 Some stories—such as the story of Rama and Sita (in the *Ramayana*)—lend themselves to being re-enacted by the class. Alternatively a sequence of movements with rhythms or music can be used, say, for the Genesis story.

2 Drawing some features can also help to fix the story more clearly. The *ankh* symbol from Egypt is easy to copy, for example.

3 Encourage the children to use their own imagination and describe their idea of heaven or invent a story to explain the creation of the world.

4 Ask the children to imagine they believe in rebirth and try to describe what they think a previous life might have been like or what they would like their next life to be like.

SECTION 2: FOR 7–9 YEAR OLDS

Resources

Books

N J Bull and R J Ferris, *Stories from World Religions*, Oliver & Boyd 1982
H Cherry and K McLeish, *In the Beginning*, Oliver & Boyd 1982
J Mayled, *Creation Stories*, Wayland 1987
N Shelley (retold by), *Legends of the Gods*, Angus & Robertson 1976

9 Passover

Aims

Passover is the **Jewish** festival which commemorates the exodus of the Hebrew people out of slavery in Egypt, and this unit is designed to bring to the children a sense of the strong community identity felt by Jews and to help them experience the importance of this kind of ritual observance and the use of symbols.

Information

The festival of Passover is a particularly appropriate subject to explore with young pupils because its celebration within the Jewish tradition actively involves children. Indeed, the youngest member of the family plays a central role in the *seder* meal by asking the four questions. As a result, making Passover a topic in the classroom involves a variety of practical activities including songs, art, cookery and, perhaps most important of all, fun!

Passover is of central importance to Jewish belief and practice. Judaism generally does not lend itself to the production of creeds. Although beliefs are obviously implied, Judaism nevertheless is a religion which is expressed primarily in actions. So that celebrating Passover is not to be seen as a kind of 'commentary' on belief but as 'acting out' what you are. All the important elements in Judaism appear in the Passover celebrations: the Jews' understanding of their history, the importance of the Torah, the role of the family, and so on.

The foundation story of the Passover is Exodus chapter 12.

The Ten Commandments in Exodus 20 are introduced with the words 'I am the Lord your God *who brought you out of Egypt, out of the land of slavery.*' This shows the fundamental importance of this event in the Jewish consciousness.

The story

The 'story' which is used in the Passover meal is called the Haggadah and it must be remembered that the ritual of Passover has evolved over the centuries and only in principle corresponds to the instructions of Exodus 12. Some children may not be aware of Judaism as a contemporary religion with its evolved practices, and it is important that they learn to think of it not simply as a religion read about in the Bible.

Passover is a week-long festival celebrated from the 15th or 16th to the 21st or 22nd day of the Hebrew month of Nisan. The first and last days are days of rest; no work may be done and there are religious services.

In their hurry to escape from Egypt, the Israelites did not wait for dough to rise in their bread-making but simply baked flat loaves, *matzot* (plural). As a reminder, Jews eat *matzah* (singular—unleavened bread) in the *seder* (order) of the Passover meal, and throughout the week-long festival they do not eat or drink any form of *hametz*, that is, food which needs fermentation or leaven, such as 'ordinary' bread, biscuits or cakes—or beer or whisky.

Passover (*Pesah* in Hebrew) is also the Spring festival when everything must be cleaned up and cupboards and pockets turned out. All the *hametz* must be eaten up or taken outside in the evening before Passover. On the morning of Passover the last bits are burnt or thrown to the wind or water. The idea is that symbolically one must be *entirely* free from slavery. The focus of Passover celebrations is the Passover supper.

The Supper

The table set. Note the *seder* dish and the *matzah*.

There are three vital elements of the *seder*, or 'order': the *zeroa* (bone), *maror* (bitter herbs) and *matzah* (unleavened bread). On the table at the supper is the *seder* dish on which are placed

zeroa: a piece of lamb shankbone (which is not eaten) in memory of the ancient Temple sacrifice of a lamb. It is also connected with the use of lambs' blood in saving the Israelites in Egypt.

beytza: a roasted egg, also not eaten, and symbolising other sacrifices.

karpas: a spring vegetable or greenery, usually but not necessarily, parsley. This is indicative of the time of year and early on in the ceremony is dipped in salt water, for a taste of the Israelites' tears and sweat.

maror: bitter herbs or plants, such as radish, horseradish, chives. *Maror* symbolises the bitterness of Egyptian slavery and must be eaten at the *seder*, however unpleasant.

haroset: a paste of grated apple, ground nuts, cinnamon, honey and wine. It symbolises the mortar used by the Israelite slave builders.

Near the *seder* plate will be three *matzot* (pieces of unleavened bread) representing the 'bread of affliction'. Of the middle *matzah*, one half is used for the blessing and the other is hidden for the *afikomen* (dessert): it will be the last bite to be eaten that night so the lingering taste will be of *matzah*. A popular diversion of the children towards the end of the meal is 'hunting the *afikomen*': finding it is said to enable the second part of the *seder* to take place and the finder usually wins a reward.

It is the duty of every man and woman on the first night of Passover to drink at least four glasses of wine. Each glass is poured or refilled at a specific point during the *seder* and it is understood that each one represents a phrase describing redemption:

I shall liberate you from bondage;
I shall bring you to the land;
I shall deliver you from Egypt;
I shall take you home as a people.

The Passover table. Remember the ceremonies take place in the context and atmosphere of a 'party meal'.

Because there is a fifth one, 'I shall redeem you from servitude', there arose the custom of the fifth glass of wine—the cup of Elijah filled between the third and fourth glasses and never drunk. Elijah, according to legend, never died and is thought to be the forerunner of the Messiah who will remove suffering and usher in the world to come. The doors are opened at this point, symbolically to let Elijah enter.

Early in the meal the youngest present asks the four traditional questions (really exclamations) about why this night is different from every other night. 'For on this night we eat *matzah*; on this night we must eat *maror*; on this night we dip green herbs in salt water; on this night we all recline' (a reference to the style of a Roman banquet).

The answers begin with 'We were slaves and our ancestors were idol worshippers' and the rest of the story narrates the liberation from Egypt, including the recitation of the plagues. This emphasises that Passover is the reiteration of God's intervention on behalf of the Jews.

At the recitation of the ten plagues everyone spills a drop of wine (from the second cup). This is because, although these plagues killed the oppressors, sadness should still be felt at human suffering: the cup of joy cannot therefore be full.

It should be noted that the Passover supper is a *supper* at which other food is eaten, to which these symbolic elements are added. It is a time when joy and happiness should prevail and songs are sung together.

(much of the detail above is drawn from *Festivals in World Religions*, Shap Working Party, Longman 1986)

Approaches

1 Study of the Passover could be part of a wider topic study on homes and families. The observance of the *seder* meal provides an example of specific religious practice at home.

2 The unit could be one of a series on festivals, and Passover as a unique kind of celebration. Some factors exist in common with other festivals: sharing food at a special meal, singing particular songs, dressing up and making preparations. Passover however is particular in the way in which part of the meal is carefully prescribed.

3 Passover could be part of a topic on spring since it always occurs at springtime and has the characteristics of clearing away the rubbish from the path of happiness, new life, freedom and hope. A Passover topic fits best in the spring term and could culminate in some special activity.

4 Begin with a reading of the Passover event in Exodus. Discuss this with the pupils, bringing out what they know about Jews today and the way in which Passover is observed.

Activities

1 Look at a picture of a *seder* plate, or better still borrow one from a Jewish friend (or perhaps the local RE or teachers' centre may have one).
Consider the symbolism of each of the items on the *seder* dish.

2 Perhaps instead, or as a preliminary to number 1 above, the class could assemble the various items for the *seder* plate and the *matzot*. Packets of 'matzos' are to be found in supermarkets and delicatessen. Try to find ones approved (or *kosher*) for Passover.

Here is a recipe for **haroset**.

> 1 grated apple
> 4 tbsps ground nuts (eg hazelnuts, walnuts or almonds)
> 1 tsp cinnamon
> A little wine (or raisin juice)
> 1 tsp honey (optional)
> Mix together to make a sweet, sticky paste.

This (and bitter herbs) could be tasted by the class with a small piece of *matzah*.

3   Songs and games associated with Passover could be learned.

4   A good way to complete a topic on Passover would be to simulate a Passover *seder* in the classroom. This involves a good deal of preparation and organisation. The guidance of *The Seder Handbook* and *Matza and Bitter Herbs* by Clive Lawton would be particularly helpful.

It must be emphasised with the pupils that you are engaged in a *simulation*. If you can enlist the help of Jewish friends it will make the task easier. Don't forget details like 'spring cleaning' the classroom and checking that all the *hametz* is outside.

SECTION 2: FOR 7–9 YEAR OLDS

Resources

Books

L Hannigan, *Sam's Passover*, A & C Black 1985 (an attractive book for children which will help the teacher with many ideas)

C Lawton, *Matza and Bitter Herbs*, Hamish Hamilton 1984 (clear illustrations of the *seder* dish and the table set for the Passover meal)

C Lawton, *The Seder Handbook*, Board of Deputies of British Jews 1986 (a teachers' guide)

R Turner, *Jewish Festivals*, Wayland 1985

AVA

Useful materials can be purchased from the Jewish Education Bureau, 8 Westcombe Avenue, Leeds LS8 2BS.

10 Christian Holy Places in Britain

Aims

This unit is concerned to acquaint children living in Britain with some of the ancient centres of worship and devotion in the United Kingdom, and help them perceive the importance attached to the 'sacred place' by many people.

Information

The unit can relate to the general history in the school curriculum because these sacred places are always associated with some historical event.

This unit has links with those on journeys (section 1, page 36) and pilgrimage (section 3, page 156). The practice of religion expresses itself not only through symbolism, ritual acts and sacred texts but also through sacred places. This is less apparent on the grand scale in Britain since the Middle Ages. Places like Mecca and Lourdes, Jerusalem, Rome, Benares are often well known and recognised for their religious focus. Less well known are Iona, Canterbury, Lindisfarne, St David's and others in Britain.

If there is in your vicinity a location associated with some important religious event in the past, some study of it should be included in the unit, and indeed may become the main focus.

Iona

Iona is an island of the Inner Hebrides off the larger island of Mull. Iona is about three and a half miles long and about one and a half miles broad. Yet it is perhaps the most sacred spot in all Scotland. There is evidence that it was a Celtic holy place even before St Columba landed from Ireland in 563 CE. It became the most famous centre of Celtic Christianity from where missionaries were sent to convert Scotland and northern England. A Celtic monastery consisted of a church

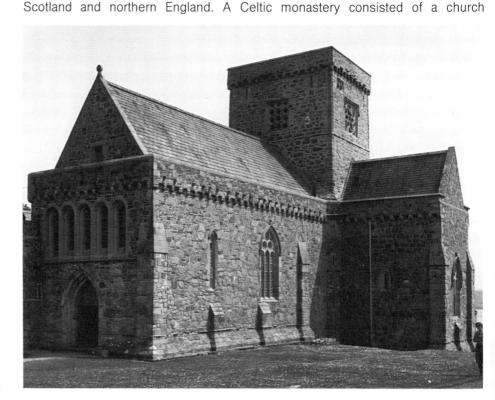

Iona

surrounded by a cluster of individual monks' cells. After St Columba's death his relics remained on the island until the ninth century when they were removed to Ireland. Pilgrims came from far and near to be in the holy place of St Columba and the bodies of important people were brought here for burial. In the eleventh century the monastery was restored by Queen Margaret, wife of Malcolm Canmore, King of Scotland. In 1213 a new Benedictine monastery was built. This monastery was dismantled at the Protestant Reformation in Scotland.

In the 1930s George McLeod took unemployed men from the Govan shipyards to Iona and began to rebuild the ruined abbey. He also formed the Iona Community. Members do not live all the year round on Iona but pledge themselves to a religious rule wherever their place of work. It is intended to be a group of Christians pledged to work for peace and responsible living. The community numbers about 150. Thousands come to visit Iona every year. For more information about Iona see Alan Brown's *Christian Communities* (Lutterworth 1982).

Canterbury

Canterbury is well known for its cathedral and because it is the centre of the Archdiocese of the Southern Province of the Church of England. However, two historical points are of especial importance.

1 St Augustine, the first Archbishop of Canterbury was sent by the pope, Gregory I, to lead a mission to England in 596 CE. He landed at Thanet with his companion monks in 597 CE, and was received well by King Ethelbert of Kent who gave them a place to live in Canterbury. Christianity was already present in England and Celtic Christianity had been established in Ireland and the north of Britain some time before. In 601 the pope made Augustine archbishop and gave him authority over all the churches in Britain. St Augustine built the first cathedral in Canterbury.

2 The murder of Thomas à Becket on 29 December 1170 took place in the cathedral. He was Archbishop of Canterbury and had quarrelled with the king (Henry II, his friend in youthful years). Impatiently Henry suggested that he would be glad to be rid of him. Certain knights set out to please the king. Becket met his murderers bravely. After his death Canterbury became a great centre of pilgrimage. Henry II himself came to do penance in 1174. He received five strokes with a rod from every bishop and abbot present and three from each of the monks! The pilgrims to the shrine of Thomas à Becket are celebrated in Chaucer's *Canterbury Tales*.

Approaches

1 Stonehenge is probably a monument known to many, and showing a good-sized picture of it could open the introductory discussion.

Stonehenge was built in three successive stages from about 2000 BCE. There is no writing to tell us with certainty what this monument was built for. It seems, nevertheless, to be related to observations of the sun and moon. Later, when the Celts came to Britain, they treated the stone circles with great reverence and used them for their own worship led by the Druids.

All through history human beings have, it seems, recognised certain places as being very special—where spiritual 'other worldly' things can happen. In Christian times we know why some places became special: either because some great event occurred there or because the remains of a holy man or woman (a saint) are kept there.

2 Show a picture of the Church of the Holy Nativity in Bethlehem. Begin with the question 'Why do you think the Church of the Holy Nativity in Bethlehem should be a very special place?' Hopefully you can elicit the birth stories and the life of Jesus. With pictures of the particular sites in Israel, indicate how they have

The murder of Thomas à Becket

become special and sacred, and how, because Christians didn't like these places being ruled over by non-Christians, many set out from England and elsewhere in Europe on the Crusades. We have sacred places in Britain too, not because Jesus lived or died here but because some other events took place there. However, in legend Jesus is said to have come to England with Joseph of Arimathea and from this arose the story of the Glastonbury thorn supposed to be sprung from the staff of Joseph of Arimathea. It is to this legend that William Blake refers in his poem 'Jerusalem':

> And did those feet in ancient times,
> Walk upon England's mountains green,
> And did the holy lamb of God . . .

However, we are more sure about the coming of Christian teachers to Britain in Iona (St Columba), Canterbury (St Augustine), and Lindisfarne (St Cuthbert).

3   One of the best known of Christian places of pilgrimage is Lourdes in south-west France. This could also be a starting point in a similar way to number 2 above. Thousands of Roman Catholics flock to Lourdes every year, hoping principally for the healing of illness by bathing in the water which is held to be miraculous. Many miracles are said to have occurred there. Tell of the simple peasant girl Bernadette Soubirous who, last century, had a vision of the Virgin Mary who told her that the waters would bring healing to those who came in faith.

4   England has many great cathedrals. If your school is within reasonable distance of one, the unit could begin with some discussion of when it was built and how big it is and something of its history. Most are medieval and these always have an association with some great saint of the past whose relics originally were kept there. So the site of a special holy place may be in your locality as a starting point.

5   If you know a place which is 'atmospheric' it might be good to make some direct experience the starting point. Take the pupils to a place where they can *feel* something impressive in the surroundings and perhaps be asked to be quiet there. Then tell them something of the history connected with the place and discuss the effect of that history on their feelings.

Activities

1   Clearly the most useful activity, when it can be arranged, is a visit. For the majority, the visit cannot be made to the major traditional holy places. However, most schools are within reasonable reach of some locally known place which has some renown in religious history. Note that this visit can coincide with a church visit (see section 3, page 181), although the aims in the two units are somewhat different. However the visit is arranged, the historic associations of the 'holy place' will be emphasised. Some school visitors to Jarrow, for example, prepared beforehand by learning about the Venerable Bede and medieval monks, and wearing simple approximations to the monks' robes re-enacted the monks' day (somewhat compressed of course!).

2   Retell and act out the particular story of the place. Perhaps the story will lend itself to the making of a collage.

3   Remembering that one of the purposes is to understand the way in which sacred places are important to some people, activities should be found in which the pupils experience something of the feeling of a sacred place. Perhaps it is possible to create a 'shrine' in part of the classroom which includes references to the holy place being studied. *As a make-believe*, the pupils might be asked to treat the shrine with reverence.

4   The pupils in groups might make up a play of several characters on a pilgrimage to the chosen sacred place, in which they discuss the past history of the place and why it has become so special. This could become the basis of an assembly presentation.

SECTION 2: FOR 7–9 YEAR OLDS

Resources

S Perowne, *Holy Places of Christendom*, Mowbray 1976

11 Sacred Places: Benares

Aims

The aim of the unit is to widen pupils' knowledge and understanding in developing awareness of places sacred to people in another part of the world.

They will also learn some basic aspects of **Hinduism** such as the sense of God being everywhere; the idea of rebirth and how that relates to funeral ceremonies; and perhaps a simple idea of *moksha* (liberation or salvation).

Information

It is important to encourage children to 'move out' in their thinking from their immediate environment, and a *place* is something concrete which they can easily focus on.

As a sacred place, Benares (Varanasi) is the greatest centre of pilgrimage in India. Many things can make a place sacred. For the people who come, it is

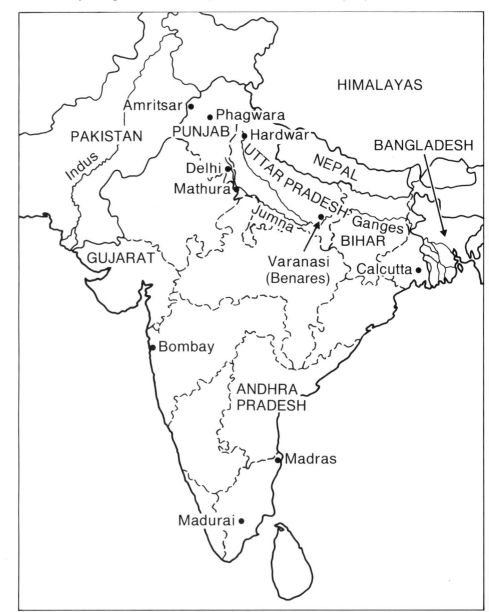

Note the varied spellings. Benares is called Varanasi on modern maps. It is the Indian form of the name.

The *ghats* at Benares on the Ganges

because they feel it to be a place where heaven and earth come together and therefore where they can more easily renew themselves spiritually. It is principally the river Ganges which makes Benares sacred, for Ganges is held to be a goddess. (See section 1, page 29.) Not only is Benares thought to be a good place to renew oneself but it is an especially good place to send one's dead relatives on their spiritual journey from earth.

For pupils of Indian/Hindu origin, the study will be an acknowledgement of their cultural inheritance.

Note that for this unit it is essential to obtain pictures of Benares. These are to be found in most books on India. The pictures should show the *ghats* (steps) on the river, both those used for bathing and those for cremation.

Benares is for millions of Hindus the most sacred city in India. It lies in the northern plain of the left bank of the river Ganges, on a great curve of the river. The Ganges is a sacred river itself. For a Hindu, to visit Benares is to be cleansed of the sins of thousands of past rebirths. Devout Hindus would choose to end their days here. To be cremated in Benares, the crossing place between heaven and earth, and to have one's ashes scattered on the Ganges, is thought to ensure an end to the constant round of rebirths.

Two important elements in Hindu worship are much in evidence here, fire and water.

Benares is not only sacred to Hindus however. Near the city the Buddha preached his first sermon (in the deer park at Sarnath) and Mahavira the founder of the Jains also came here.

The scope of the study is very wide. You will have to judge how much of Hindu beliefs and practice it is appropriate to explain in the circumstances of your class. However it will be necessary to explain the following.

1   Hindus worship many gods, although these are seen as expressions of one all-inclusive transcendent 'Brahman'.

2   Gods are usually 'paired' male and female:

Shiva—Parvati
Vishnu—Lakshmi

Vishnu has nine *avatars* or incarnations. The most famous are Krishna (—Radha) and Rama (—Sita). The river Ganges is itself a female goddess.

3   Hindus in common with many others believe in rebirth, that is, that when we die our soul takes on another birth. This, it is taught, happens thousands and thousands of times. However, the aim is to find one's way out of this cycle of rebirths by various means, one being by the faithful performance of ritual acts.

4   Death rites are by cremation. The body is burned on a funeral pyre of wood. This can be an expensive investment for poor people. The steep sandy river banks are made firm with huge stone platforms and flights of steps (*ghats*) down to the water. There are more than 50 of these, some up to 15 metres high. It is on the platforms of certain *ghats* that cremations take place. The 'burning *ghats*' are maintained by a traditional community called the Doams.

5   Bathing in the river Ganges is considered to be beneficial to the soul and pilgrims come from all over India (and the world) to bathe here. Dawn is considered the best time. All bathe together, men and women and whatever their caste or position in society.

'More than thirteen languages and an unaccountable number of dialects fill the air with a babble that is comforting in its passive tone. Here Brahmins in dazzling white *dhotis* bathe alongside lepers, bloated merchants next to high court judges and doctors. Here are villagers, workers in coal mines and steel plants, beggars, Hindus from north and south, and from overseas. Side by side they submerge themselves in the Ganges, performing a regular ritual or realizing the dream of a lifetime'. (Henry Wilson, *Benares*, Thames and Hudson 1985, p 15)

Approaches

1   The unit could be an aspect of a geographical study of India. In this case one would move from the physical feature of the river Ganges to its religious significance and the specific manifestations of Benares.

2   Every book on Hinduism or on India which has pictures will have a picture of the *ghats* at Benares. Some of the most impressive photographs come from this fascinating spot. So a beginning could be made by studying a picture or a poster of Benares and trying to see how much can be elicited by the pupils' own observations.

3   Some teachers have hesitations about initiating discussions about death in the classroom, and indeed it is necessary to be sensitive about this. However, many have discovered that their pupils are eager to discuss it and are more matter of fact than older people.

Hindus believe we all have an eternal soul which, when we die, is reborn again in another body and that we bring with us the consequences of our previous lives. The ceremony of cremation and the spreading of the ashes on the sacred river are related to this understanding. Discussion of this can lead to a look at Benares itself.

4   This unit could be related to the notion of a pilgrimage or making a journey (see section 1, page 36 and section 3, page 156), Hindus travel vast distances just to be able to visit Benares and bathe there in the Ganges.

Activities

1   When dealing with a place which is far away, it is advisable to develop the children's use of maps. It is sometimes said that children find it difficult to understand a map. Some may, but there is everything to be gained from trying to develop their understanding. So, placing Benares on a map of India has its value. The spot could be surrounded by some illustrations of activities which take place there.

2   One way of gaining a sense of where it is might be to find out how to get there—to plan the route and timetable as if one were a travel agent.

3   If the resources are available, some work could be done on Hindu gods—on Vishnu or the goddess Ganga. Alternatively a project on the river Ganges including some reflections on the value of a river might be interesting.

4   Some art work on the elements of fire and water would focus on two major aspects of the rituals at Benares.

SECTION 2: FOR 7–9 YEAR OLDS

Resources

Books
L Bolwell, *A Journey down the Ganges*, Wayland 1985
R Singh, *Benares: Sacred City of India*, Thames & Hudson 1987
H Wilson, *Benares*, Thames & Hudson 1985 (a large reference book to borrow from a library)

12 Guru Nanak and the Sikhs

Aims

The aim is to acquaint children with the outstanding personality of Guru Nanak. They should learn that he is the founder of the **Sikh** religion and is much venerated by Sikhs.

Further, study of Guru Nanak should help in the formation of some basic understanding of Sikh religious teaching:

the oneness of God;
the equality of all people;
the duty of service;
the obligation of hospitality;
the duty to defend the weak;
(the symbols of the Khalsa).

Guru Nanak

Information

Nanak is the acknowledged founder of the Sikh religion. In terms of the world's population Sikhism is not the religion of a large number. However, Sikhism is well represented in Britain and Britain has the largest single population of Sikhs outside of India.

Guru Nanak is known to Sikh children by means of a large number of stories told about him and these stories can be transferred directly to the classroom.

Guru Nanak was born on 15 April 1469 CE and died on 22 September 1539 CE. His father was a revenue superintendent for a Muslim, Rai Bular who was the landlord of a village called Talwandi. He was brought up as an orthodox Hindu although there were both Hindus and Muslims in the area.

There is no straightforward account of his life and as is often the case we have to rely on stories written by devout people. These are called *janam sakhis* or 'life evidences'.

Nanak grew up a devout person interested in religion and it is said he learnt Sanskrit, Persian and Arabic. He seems to have been dissatisfied with his formal Hindu upbringing.

At the age of 16 he was in the service of the ruler of Sultanpur who was also a Muslim.

It is reported that he was a spiritual teacher from an early age and performed ritual prayer and ablutions regularly. Ablutions were performed at the river and one morning Nanak didn't come back as usual. His clothes were on the bank and most people thought he must have drowned.

However, after three days Nanak reappeared, but remained silent. The next day he made a strange pronouncement: 'There is neither Hindu nor Muslim, so whose path shall I follow? I shall follow God's path. God is neither Hindu nor Muslim and the path which I follow is God's.'

When he explained what had happened, he said he had been taken into God's presence, where he had been offered a cup of *amrit* (nectar) to drink and was given the command to preach and teach in God's name.

So Nanak condemned the divisions between faiths because there was only one God. He was about 30 years old when he received his call and he then made a series of journeys to the main centres of Hinduism and Islam as well as to Sri Lanka and Tibet. He was accompanied by Mardana, a Muslim disciple and musician who is important because Nanak was a poet and all his messages are delivered in songs which he composed accompanied by Mardana on a stringed instrument.

There are many stories in the *janam sakhis* associated with these journeys. Here are three of them.

SECTION 2: FOR 7–9 YEAR OLDS

---

1 During a visit to Mecca Guru Nanak lay down to rest in the colonnade near the Ka'ba and went to sleep. When it came to the time for evening prayer a worshipper scolded Nanak because his feet were pointing towards the Ka'ba.

'Do you call yourself a man of God, yet stretch your feet towards the house of God?'

The guru replied, 'Turn my feet towards a point where the house of God is not!'

The man dragged his feet round, but as he moved them the Ka'ba also moved!

2 On another occasion at Hardwar he saw Brahmins throwing water eastwards towards the rising sun as an act of worship on behalf of their ancestors. Guru Nanak began to throw water in the opposite direction. 'If the water you throw can reach your ancestors then I'm sure the water I throw can reach my fields near Lahore which is quite near!'

3   Once when visiting the city of Lahore, Guru Nanak was entertained by a wealthy banker called Duni Chand. He provided a magnificent banquet in his honour. Afterwards Duni Chand said to the guru, 'I am a wealthy man, if there is anything I can do for you, please tell me.'

Guru Nanak thought carefully and took a case from his pocket containing a needle. He held up the needle and said 'I would like you to keep this needle for me and give it back when we meet in the next world.' Then he left the feast.

Duni Chand was delighted with the important task he had been given and took the needle to show to his wife. To his astonishment she laughed and said 'I should hurry and ask Guru Nanak how you can take the needle to heaven with you!' So Duni Chand ran after him and asked 'Guru Nanak, please tell me how I can take this needle with me when I die?' Guru Nanak replied, 'If you cannot take such a tiny needle when you die, how are you going to take all your riches? You will only be remembered for the good things you do in this world when you go to the next.' From that day on Duni Chand and his wife used their wealth to help the poor.

About 1521 CE, when Nanak was 50 years old, he ceased his journeys and settled with his family at Kartarpur. A community formed around him. He built a place of worship, a hostel and a hall for teaching (the precursor of the gurdwara). Worship consisted of meditation and the singing of the guru's hymns. Of these, 974 are preserved, and these were eventually the basis of the book which was to become the Sikh scriptures.

Guru Nanak prepared his successor, who was one of his disciples, Guru Angad.

Approaches

1   The most likely starting point is in the story which can be read in *Guru Nanak* by G S Sidhu and others (see Resources).

2   You might start with questions about Sikhs and Sikh religion leading to the question of how the religion began.

3   There are many traditional portraits of Guru Nanak, although very idealised and with a halo. Examination of a picture and speculation from the pupils about the person depicted can arouse interest in his origins. If there are Sikhs in the class they may have a considerable repertoire of tales of Guru Nanak.

Activities

1   Central to the teaching of Guru Nanak is that God is One. This is represented by the *ik onkar* symbol ੧ੴ . It means, roughly, 'one being'. This could be copied and accompanied by the opening words of the Sikh morning prayer:

> There is one God
> Eternal truth is his name.

2   In order to help obtain a clearer understanding, some work could be done on the geography of northern India and the Punjab, particularly with reference to the climate and farming.

3   Your school may be close enough to a gurdwara to organise a visit or at least to invite a Sikh to come and talk about Guru Nanak.

4   Pictures of Guru Nanak are fairly easy to obtain and should be displayed in the classroom. Further study might be pursued if appropriate (see section 3, page 162).

If there is a sufficient variety of pictures available, children could be encouraged to write about the different ways he is represented.

5   The children could be asked to make their own picture of Guru Nanak. This could include collage techniques.

6   The children could make **festival garlands**.

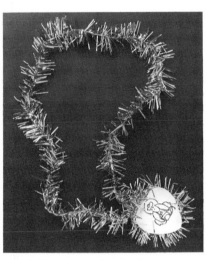

A Guru Nanak festival garland

You will need cardboard, felt-tipped pens, gold foil, adhesive, tinsel, and a picture or artefact showing Guru Nanak.

Cut two pear or heart shapes from the cardboard, about 17 × 15 cm. Draw and colour Guru Nanak on one piece.

Cut a piece of tinsel about 60 cm long and attach both ends to the back of one of the cardboard shapes with adhesive.

Glue the second piece of cardboard on to the back of the first to hide the tinsel ends.

Cut a similar shape from gold foil about 23 × 20 cm. Remove the centre, leaving a border of 3 cm.

Fringe to 1 cm of the inside edge with cuts into the paper.

Glue the uncut centimetre on the inside and stick over the cardboard garland on the right side.

(from *Topic Pack*, Junior Education, October 1987)

SECTION 2: FOR 7-9 YEAR OLDS

Resources

Books
M Davidson, *Guru Nanak's Birthday*, RMEP 1982
W O Cole, *A Sikh Family in Britain*, RMEP 2nd ed 1985
G S Sidhu *et al*, *Guru Nanak*, Sikh Missionary Society, 20 Peacock Street, Gravesend
D Singh and A Smith, *The Sikh World*, Macdonald 1985

13 The Mosque

The unit will help the pupil to identify the specific features of a mosque and thereby to begin to understand some basic elements of **Islamic** teaching.

Information

Here are some features of a mosque which could be incorporated into your lesson(s).

1 Many mosques have large domes. They are intended to amplify sound and increase the sense of space and the limitlessness of God.

2 The minaret was originally built in order to give the *muezzin* (the one who calls to prayer) a good vantage point from which to be heard all around. Nowadays of course the message is more likely to be relayed on loud speakers! Further minarets would be built just to balance the first one until sometimes they became a decorative feature in themselves.

3 Running water is always provided at a mosque because worshippers always wash ritually before prayer. These ablutions are called *wudu*. First, the worshipper washes the hands up to the wrists three times. Next he rinses his mouth three times. Then he rinses his nose three times and then his face. Next he washes his right arm and left arm up to the elbow three times. He passes his wet hands over the head, ears and neck, and finally he washes the right foot and then the left foot to the ankle three times. The rules of *wudu* apply to both men and women.

Children are often interested in the ritual detail and it should not be quickly passed over. They are usually intrigued by the fact of washing before prayer and this can be a fruitful source of discussion.

4 The inside of the mosque itself is empty and this emphasises that nothing comes between a person and God: there are no intermediaries. The floor is usually

In the mosque worshippers stand side by side.

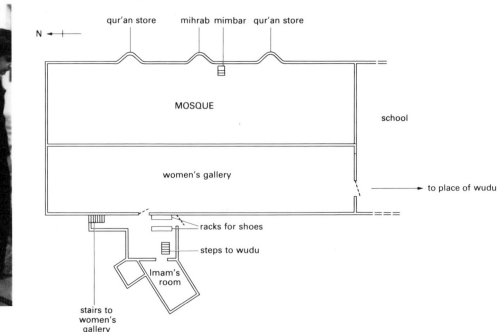

carpeted and worshippers must leave their shoes outside. (When praying elsewhere, a Muslim will use a small carpet, a kind of portable mosque.) The only furniture is the pulpit (*mimbar*) where the *imam* preaches on Fridays. (The imam is the man who leads the worship in the mosque. He is a teacher and leader by reason of his learning. There is no ordained ministry like priests.)

5   Although the walls inside are often beautifully decorated there are no pictures of human beings. Decoration is either abstract patterns (and some of these are beautiful and intricate) or stylised calligraphy with verses from the Qur'an. Those not acquainted with it are often not aware that they are looking at Arabic script.

6   On one wall of the mosque there is a niche (*mihrab*) which marks the direction (*qiblah*) of the *Ka'ba*, the house of God in the sacred city of Mecca.

When Muslims pray they stand side by side in rows facing the direction of Mecca. In the mosque the prayers are led by the imam. When travelling to different places, the worshipper will need the help of a compass to locate the direction of Mecca. (Some children might be able to work out the direction from the classroom to Mecca with the help of an atlas and a compass.)

7   On Fridays, the imam will always preach a sermon to the congregation.

8   Often, at the entrance to the mosque is the list of times of prayer for that day. A Muslim is expected to pray five times a day.

From the mosque pupils will learn that Islam forbids the use of images. From the sheer spaciousness they will learn of Islam's teaching about the greatness of God. From the use of calligraphy they will learn of the supreme importance of the spoken word, especially the Word of God. They will also learn about the central role of Arabic in the practice of Islam. From the *mihrabs* they will learn of the focus of Mecca. From the practice of prayer they will learn of the centrality and particular style of prayer in Islam. And they will learn of the solidarity and brotherhood experienced by Muslims.

In their own study, pupils should gain a respect for the religion of Islam and its followers. Hopefully they will think about the sense of awe and subjection to God reflected in the mosque. They will also perhaps recognise the value placed on regular discipline. Some may also come to appreciate aesthetic elements in the creation of mosques.

Note, however, that in this country mosques have often been created out of rooms in a house. It will be of interest to see how the 'classic' elements of a mosque are translated into this setting.

Approaches

The most appropriate beginning to the study depends on the particular context of the school and the class. Here are some suggestions.

1   Study of the mosque could form part of a small teaching unit on buildings in general, in which case some pictures of mosques and the invitation to make an initial response would be appropriate.

2   If your school has some Muslim children then you might begin by asking them about the mosque. You will know your pupils well enough to know whether this is an appropriate beginning or not.

3   A variation of number 1 above is to use one good picture of a mosque (including if possible a fountain) and to see how much the class can deduce simply by observation. For this you need a *large* picture or perhaps a projected transparency.

SECTION 2: FOR 7–9 YEAR OLDS

4 Play a brief part of the Muslim call to prayer. (Some children like to learn the words. They could at least learn *'Allahu Akbar'*—'God is the greatest'.) 'God is the greatest' is repeated four times. It goes on: 'Bear witness that there is no God but Allah [twice]. I bear witness that Muhammad is the messenger of Allah [twice]. Come to prayer [twice]. Come to security [twice]. God is the greatest [twice]. There is no God but Allah [twice].' For morning prayer, after 'Come to security', 'Prayer is better than sleep' is inserted, repeated twice.

The amount of this used must be at your discretion. However, the call to prayer can be discussed usefully. Muslims consider it especially appropriate that the human voice should call people to prayer *with words*. This discussion will lead to the question of the place of prayer. Not everyone can come to the mosque to pray, but if they can they should, and especially on Fridays at midday.

Activities

1 Best of all, of course, is to arrange a visit to a mosque. If it is possible, try to create sufficient quiet and attention so that something of the wonder and simplicity is felt.

2 As already mentioned, the children could try to find out the direction of Mecca and at least line up facing that direction. Perhaps they could also try out the prayer positions described in several books. Care must be taken, however, not to suggest that they are *actually* performing Islamic prayer.

3 Below is an example of Arabic calligraphy. Some children might like to copy this and display it. Arabic script is written from right to left.

"In the Name of God, Most Gracious, Most Merciful"

4 Mosque shapes are not difficult to draw and the children could be invited to make an outline representation of a mosque they have visited or one they have been shown in a picture. Some might be capable of modelling a simple shape.

5 If appropriate, the children can be invited to compare a mosque with another religious building which they know.

6 The children could make **minarets** as part of a mosque model.

For a large minaret you will need: three strong cardboard cylinders or one cut into three lengths, two 30 cm long and one 20 cm long (note: the centres of toilet rolls are not suitable); a circle of stiff card 16 cm in diameter; a selection of margarine tub lids; a small plastic mousse-container; strong adhesive, white matt emulsion paint.

Use a tub lid to join the two longer cylinders together and glue them in place (figure 1).

Cut four arch shapes from the shortest cylinder (figure 2). This should be done with a Stanley knife and great care.

Mount the cylinder on to a tub lid which has the same diameter and then on to one slightly bigger, then on to a circle of card (figure 3).

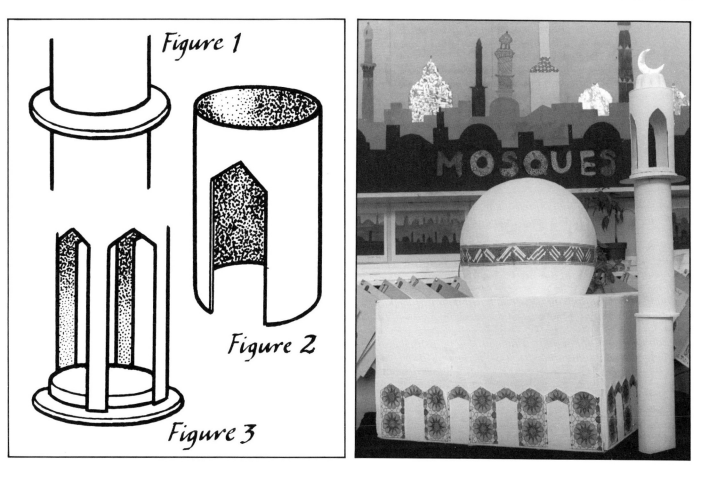

Mount this on to other cylinders with the large card circle making the base of the top section.

Glue the mousse tub on to the top of the model and paint the whole minaret with white emulsion paint.

(*Topic Pack*, Junior Education, October 1987)

Resources

Books

M Aggarwal and Abu Bakar Nazir, *I am a Muslim*, Franklin Watts 1984

O Bennett, *Festival! Ramadan and Eid-ul-Fitr*, Commonwealth Institute & Macmillan Educational 1986

R Kerven, *Festival! Ramadan and Eid-ul-Fitr*: Teachers' notes and pupils' worksheets, Commonwealth Institute & Macmillan Educational 1986

R Protheroe and R Meherali, *Visiting a Mosque*, Lutterworth 1984

R Tames, *The Muslim World*, Macdonald 1982

D Wade, *The Islamic Colouring Book*, Wildwood House 1976

AVA

Wallet on the Mosque—£3 from Primary RE Materials Project, Westhill College, Weoley Park Road, Birmingham B29 6LL

14 Baptism (and Confirmation)

Aims

Most religions have rituals of initiation which establish the newcomer as a member of that community. The aim of this unit is to help pupils understand the symbols of **Christian** initiation.

Information

Baptism has become customary for infants but in recent years adult baptisms have become more common. Baptism means literally 'washing' and it was practised before the time of Christ as an initiation ceremony. However, the Christian Church made it the regular means of entry and gave it a stronger meaning. Baptism is seen as symbolically having one's sins washed away. It is also seen as symbolically dying and rising again; as 'applying' the death and resurrection of Jesus to a person. It is also understood as incorporating people into the Church; making them members of the body. Usually at baptism candidates are asked to renounce evil and declare their faith in God. They then have water poured over their heads.

Because baptism signifies being adopted by God into the Christian family, a name is given. That is why a Christian's forename is called a 'Christian' name. In the ancient Church the newly baptised were also given a new white garment to wear and a lighted candle: the first signifying the new purified life and the second the life of Christ. The candle is a continued custom in many churches. The most usual words accompanying the act of baptism are 'I baptise you in the name of the Father, and of the Son, and of the Holy Spirit'.

Infant baptism

It is the custom in most churches to baptise children. In this case adults are asked to speak for them.

For some Christians (notably Baptists), infant baptism is considered wrong because the children cannot answer for themselves. In these churches only adult baptism takes place. Those who allow infant baptism would argue that it has happened throughout the Church's history and it is simply anticipating what the child must obviously want when nurtured in a Christian home.

Total immersion

Baptists and others favour total immersion in water, and their churches have large baths for this purpose.

Note that the Eastern Orthodox churches also practise total immersion, but with infants. Those who favour total immersion would say that the symbolism of dying and rising again is more forcibly seen in this way.

Children will need to know that baptism is given both to infants and adults.

Confirmation

In some churches, notably the Anglican church, initiation is completed by the ritual of confirmation when the person is old enough to answer for himself or herself. Adults usually proceed directly to confirmation after baptism. Note that in the Roman Catholic church, 'First Communion' is seen much more as the conscious initiation into the Church.

Confirmation in Anglican churches involves the 'laying on of hands' by a bishop and it is taught that the person thereby receives a gift of the Holy Spirit. There is usually a period of instruction preceding this event. In the Roman Catholic church confirmation is by anointing with oil. The oil is blessed by a bishop on another special occasion.

Children will need to know simply that there is an opportunity to take on the promises of baptism, when the baby is grown up.

Other churches have similar ceremonies of 'joining' as adults.

Fonts Traditional churches have a font where baptisms take place and it is significant that the font is near the *entrance* to the church. Baptism is the beginning of the Christian journey.

Content The teacher is the only one who can judge the degree to which Christian teaching on baptism can be elaborated in a particular class context. However, the essential elements are as already stated: that the pupils should know and understand the symbolic acts of washing and acceptance, and gain some sense of the pleasure of a family at baptism and the way in which it is felt that baptism makes the baby an acknowledged member of the family. (Just as it is intended that the newly baptised becomes an acknowledged member of the church.)

Approaches 1 If there has been a recent baptism in the family of one of the pupils, some brief discussion of what happened and what it meant can provide the way into the topic, and some basic ideas will begin to emerge.

2 The concept of initiation could be picked up through discussion about becoming a member of a Scout Cub pack or Brownie Guide group or some other organisation. The ideas of 'belonging' and 'commitment' should emerge.

3 The unit could be part of a much wider topic on Water. This topic is often studied in schools and has many interesting facets. Here one can explore the ritual function. The association is twofold—with *washing* and with *refreshing*. It is important to make this symbolic connection because all too frequently pupils find difficulty in handling spiritual ideas, simply because they have no experience in the use of symbols or symbolic language. (See section 3, pages 188–189)

4 The unit may develop from a church visit and the study of the font.

5 Begin with 'names' and what their purpose is and how we come to have them.

Activities 1 Pictures or slides of baptism will help to focus the context of baptism and will usually help to draw out some participation from the pupils.

2 If the pupils have seen a font in church, some might like to draw it, with some words from the baptismal service added: 'I baptise you in the name of the Father, and of the Son, and of the Holy Spirit.'

3 If there has been a recent baptism in the family of one of the pupils, perhaps there could be a baptism cake shared in the class, wishing the baby well. French baptism parties always have sugared almonds!

4 Visit a local church specially to look at the font and talk with the minister. (If it is an Anglican or Roman Catholic church, look at the 'bishop's chair' too.)

5 Simulate a solemn 'laying on of hands' without the accompanying words. Encourage the children to talk about how they felt.

SECTION 2: FOR 7–9 YEAR OLDS

Resources

Baptism and Confirmation in the Church of England (leaflet available from National Society's RE Centre, 23 Kensington Square, London W8 5HN)
O Bennett, *Colin's Baptism*, Hamish Hamilton 1986

15 Eid-ul-Fitr – a Muslim Festival

Aims

Eid-ul-Fitr is a **Muslim** festival celebrating the end of Ramadan, the annual month of fasting during daylight hours. The aim of the unit is to enable the pupils to understand the celebration enjoyed by Muslims and to acknowledge the festival if it takes place in the school year.

Information

Eid-ul-Fitr is one of the two major festivals celebrated by Muslims. *Eid-ul-Fitr* means 'Festival of Fast-breaking' and is celebrated directly after Ramadan, the month of fasting. The other main festival is Eid-ul-Adha which marks the culmination of the *hajj*, the pilgrimage to Mecca.

Ramadan and the Five 'Pillars'

Before exploring Eid-ul-Fitr it is important to understand the significance of fasting during Ramadan. Fasting (*siyam*) during the month of Ramadan is one of the five basic rules or laws to which adherents of Islam are expected to respond. These are known as the Five Pillars of Islam. The other four are *shahadah* (a Muslim's affirmation of faith), *salat* (prayer five times a day), *zakat* (obligatory almsgiving) and *hajj* (a Muslim's pilgrimage to Mecca).

Fasting

During the month of Ramadan, Muslims are required to abstain from eating, drinking and smoking during daylight hours (daylight hours being when one can distinguish between a white and black thread in natural light). The requirement, however, is not made of the sick, the old, pregnant women or young children, for it is not intended to be punishing in any way. Fasting is considered to be a source of delight for it gives the faithful the opportunity to follow the directions laid down in the Qu'ran, the Holy Book of Islam, and to practise self-discipline as witness of allegiance to Allah.

Lailat-ul-Qadr

Towards the end of Ramadan falls the important time when Muslims remember the revelation of the Qu'ran which was communicated to Muhammad by the Angel Gabriel. This has become known as the 'Night of Power' and many Muslims offer extra prayers and spend more time studying the Qu'ran in honour of this event.

The new moon

On the last day of Ramadan great excitement is sensed in Islamic countries as people anticipate sighting the new moon. Muslims follow a lunar calendar and watch for the coming of the new moon to mark the end of Ramadan and the start of the month of Shawwal when the festival of Eid-ul-Fitr can be celebrated.

Zakat-ul-Fitr

But before celebrations can begin, Muslims must attend to *zakat-ul-fitr*. *Zakat*, being one of the Five Pillars of Islam, requires believers to give a proportion of their income to the poor. This ensures that all Muslims, rich or poor, are able to break their fast at the end of Ramadan and share in the festivities. It also reminds adherents that all are equal in the eyes of Allah. The shared fasting and shared giving strengthens feelings of fellowship among the faithful.

The celebration

When the new moon is sighted celebrations can begin, and naturally food plays a major role in the festival of fast-breaking. Special food will have been prepared and is shared with families and friends.

New clothes play a significant part in the festival. They add a sense of 'occasion' and prestige to the event, so Muslims will wash and attire themselves in preparation for the celebrations.

An important event of the first day will be a visit to the mosque. At other times of the year, most of those attending the mosque are male, but on the occasion of Eid-ul-Fitr women and girls join in the worship. Mosques become very crowded, so much so that people often gather in the open air outside to pray. There is a great sense of togetherness and geniality towards one another on this special day; goodwill abounds. Then the visits to friends and relatives begin. Disputes can be ironed out, forgiveness sought and arguments forgotten. Greetings cards with '*Eid Mubarak*' (Happy Eid) are sent or delivered. Gifts are exchanged too, often in the form of cakes or sweets. Money or other gifts are given to children, who look forward to the event with eager anticipation.

The celebration of the festival lasts for three days and the celebration will continue. Special food and feasts naturally play an important part in the festivities after the fasting of Ramadan, but there are also parades, fairs and parties to enjoy.

Muslims are of many nationalities and though they share the same faith and celebrate the same festivals, cultural differences are very evident. 'Stereotype Muslims' should be avoided when introducing children to Eid-ul-Fitr. Not all Muslims wear the same style of clothes or eat the same type of food for example. Care must be taken to illustrate cultural differences and varieties, remembering to point out that Muslims celebrate Eid-ul-Fitr in Great Britain too.

Approaches

1 Feasts and fasting

The subject of food is near to children's hearts and provides opportunities for contributions from many areas of the curriculum. A suitable starting point might be to explore familiar special occasions when food is shared, such as parties, weddings and anniversaries. Pupils might then discuss 'religious' feasts such as Christmas or Easter and the preparations and rituals which accompany them. Here children might be introduced to Eid-ul-Fitr and its importance to Muslims.

Pupils might also discuss the value of fasting and its purpose. Perhaps there have been occasions when they have abstained from certain foods or activities themselves for a particular purpose. Muslim children are not required to fast in the same way as adults during Ramadan, but many will practise fasting for shorter periods during the day or for a few days at a time.

2 Giving presents

All pupils will be familiar with present-giving. Encourage discussion about their responses to giving and receiving gifts. List the different kinds of occasions on which it is done. Relate this to the giving of presents during Eid-ul-Fitr.

3 Celebrations

Discuss the preparations made for a party, such as decorating the room, preparing food, making hats, writing and sending invitations and cards and so on. Then plan and prepare an Eid-ul-Fitr party with your class.

4 Time

This unit could follow from unit 4 of this section, where time and calendars are discussed. Comparisons could be made between the development of the Western calendar and the lunar calendar of Islam. Pupils might note the changes of the moon (on clear nights!) and record them on a chart, perhaps relating them to a chart of the full Muslim year.

Interesting comparisons can be made between the ways in which years are counted. Muslims count their lunar years from the first day of the year on which the Prophet Muhammad migrated from Mecca to Medina (in the year 622 CE according to Western calendars).

SECTION 2: FOR 7–9 YEAR OLDS

Eid sweets (vermicelli sweetmeat)

You will need:

Measuring cup	½ cup vegetable margarine
Teaspoon	2 cups water
Large spoon for stirring	¼ cup sugar
Saucepan	¼ cup raisins
Serving dish (½ litre size)	¼ cup flaked almonds
2 cups vermicelli broken into small pieces	½ tsp vanilla essence
	glacé cherries for decoration

What to do

1 Wash your hands.
2 Put the broken vermicelli into the saucepan with the water.
3 Bring it to the boil.
4 Turn the heat down.
5 Stir the vermicelli occasionally to stop it sticking to the pan.
6 Continue cooking on a low heat until all the water has evaporated (about 8 minutes).
7 Remove the saucepan from the heat.
8 Add margarine, sugar, vanilla essence, almonds and raisins to the vermicelli.
9 Stir until the margarine has melted and all the ingredients are well mixed.
10 Turn into the serving dish.
11 Smooth the top and decorate with glacé cherries.
12 Leave until completely cold before eating.

Activities

1 Hold an Eid party

a Make Eid-ul-Fitr cards as invitations to the party. They should open from right to left as Muslims learn Arabic which reads in that direction. Write inside 'Eid Mubarak' (Happy Eid). Decorate the cards with Islamic patterns (duplicate for younger children to colour in) or birds, flowers or mosques. The human form is never represented in Islamic art, so direct the children away from drawing people on their cards. Send the invitations to another class or to parents.

Typical Islamic patterns and calligraphy. Patterns express a sense of order in God's creation.

Eid-ul-Fitr cards

b With your class, make special food such as cakes or sweets for the party. Remember that there are cultural differences in the food prepared for Eid-ul-Fitr. Children may like to prepare simple food from various Muslim countries and label it for the party.

c Decorate the classroom with banners saying *Eid Mubarak*. Older children may try their hands at copying Islamic calligraphy designs, or writing *Eid Mubarak* in Arabic script.

d Make tissue-paper garlands and hats or badges for your guests. Although this is not an Islamic tradition, it is important to remember that new clothes are a feature of the celebrations, so garlands and hats should add to the occasion.

e Prepare the class to give a small presentation to the guests explaining the significance of Eid-ul-Fitr and Ramadan.

f Find a selection of music which could be played at the party, from Saudi Arabia or Pakistan for example.

2 Clothes

A topic on clothes offers plenty of scope for various areas of the curriculum. New clothes for Eid-ul-Fitr are important. Show slides or pictures of typical dress from a few Islamic countries.

In groups the children may draw around the outlines of a boy and a girl and design life-size new clothes for Eid according to the style they have selected. Coloured fabric or paper may be stuck on for the clothes.

Duplicate outlines of a variety of styles of Muslim dress for younger children. They may colour in new clothes for Eid and cut out the outlines. Stick the outlines on card and hang them from the ceiling in groups according to their national dress.

SECTION 2: FOR 7–9 YEAR OLDS

Resources

Books

M H Ashan, *Muslim Festival*, Wayland 1985

O Bennett, *Festival! Ramadan and Eid-ul-Fitr*, Commonwealth Institute & Macmillan Educational 1986

R Kerven, *Festival! Ramadan and Eid-ul-Fitr: Teachers' notes and pupils' worksheets*, Commonwealth Institute & Macmillan Educational 1986

1 Christmas

Aims

This unit aims to help pupils become aware that Luke's gospel and Matthew's both tell of Jesus' birth, but each in its own way; it explores the appeal of the stories and ways in which **Christians** have responded and do respond to them.

Information

Christmas was not celebrated as a major feast in the Christian Church before the fourth century CE. Central to the earliest teaching of the Church was Jesus' death, and the 'Easter' faith that God raised Jesus.

Putting 'the Christmas story' in context

Mark's gospel, usually held to be the earliest of the four gospels, contains no story of Jesus' birth. John's has no 'story' either, but a profound poem—traditionally read at Christmas—which explores and affirms 'who Jesus is'. (John 1:1–18). Matthew and Luke also wanted to explain 'who Jesus is', but they have done so in stories about Jesus' birth. *The* Christmas story as presented by schools, media, children's books, nativity plays and Christmas cards is frequently a mix of Matthew's and Luke's stories.

Each of the birth narratives, Luke's on the one hand and Matthew's on the other, is a collection and sequence of stories. If you read Luke 1:5—2:40 and Matthew 1:18—2:23 you will see that the 'popular' story of Christmas with which some children will be familiar is very selective, probably comprising only the birth of Jesus in Bethlehem (Matthew and Luke), the visit of the shepherds (Luke) and the magi or wise men (Matthew).

A note on Luke's story— Luke 2:1–20

Luke wants to tell his readers that, in the birth of Jesus in Bethlehem, prophecies of Jewish scripture are fulfilled, there is hope. He believes that, in the birth of Jesus, God is acting 'now': the date (verse 1) is as much a theological statement—it's *now* that God is taking action—as a historical one. He also wants to show that all this is taking place among the poor and the humble: Jesus (note that the name means 'Saviour') is born among the poor, he is born in the manger; shepherds are the first visitors. The angels announce the birth and mark out a new era of God's communication with humankind, and of peace.

Luke's writing echoes passages from Jewish scripture such as Isaiah 9:2–3, 6, which speak of a future ruler (Messiah). Like Matthew, Luke knew that the Messiah (see page 44) would be born in Bethlehem; so Bethlehem is another clue about 'who this baby is'. Bethlehem was David's birthplace: the Messiah would be a descendant of David.

A note on Matthew's story— Matthew 2:1–12

Matthew agrees that Jesus was born in Bethlehem and he quotes a text from Jewish scripture to show that the Messiah was expected to be born there. Using texts to make a point is a feature of Matthew's writing. Notice too how people are 'warned' in dreams, for Matthew an indication of events taking place which are part of a divine plan.

And what about the wise men led by the star? What does their story tell the reader? Notice they go to Jerusalem, the city where you might expect to find a descendant of King David. Prophecies of the future had spoken of other kings and nations coming to Jerusalem when the Messiah came: so Matthew's wise men go there first. Notice how from earliest times these wise men became 'kings' in popular stories, and in pictures were shown to be of different races. Perhaps Matthew is saying that this birth is of universal significance.

There are then many levels of meaning within the stories. They are 'good' stories, but there is a lot to be discovered below the surface too.

Approaches

Three lines of approach are suggested here: they are complementary but could be followed at different times.

Handling the stories

If children are not familiar with the stories, tell Luke's story, and Matthew's story. You might decide to use Luke's story first, and introduce Matthew's, which includes the wise men, later—possibly after the Christmas holiday to coincide with 7 January, Christmas in the Russian Orthodox church, and the Feast of the Epiphany, 6 January, in Roman Catholic and Anglican churches, celebrating the coming of the magi.

1 Enjoyment of and engagement with the story
Allow the story to 'speak' in its own right, finding resonances in the hearer's experience, concerns and feelings. Young children might focus on the birth of a special baby (cf section 1, page 9). An older group, exploring Luke, might think about living under an alien rule and people's hope for a different future; or of a difficult journey for a pregnant girl. There is a human element with which the reader can identify, and a note of hope, the message of peace.

2 Asking 'What did the writer want to say?'
In the case of the birth stories this will mean asking 'What did the writer want people to understand about Jesus?'

3 Asking 'How does the writer convey meaning?'
Sometimes the language of poetry or symbol is used. Angels, stars, dreams, names, for example, can be seen as symbols rather than as literal events.

Matthew and Luke also echo Jewish scripture in what they write. This would have been significant for their first readers, but of course it is more difficult for people to see today, let alone primary school children! (Note of course that theirs is a Christian interpretation of Jewish scripture, and is not accepted by Jews.)

Keeping the story alive

Discuss with the children the ways in which stories, and these stories in particular, are kept alive. Plan to introduce one way in which the story of Jesus' birth has been preserved and passed on: the custom of the Christmas crib. In many churches the crib is at first empty and the infant Jesus is placed in it at a special service, or at the beginning of Midnight Mass on Christmas Eve and the 'kings' shouldn't really arrive until January! The idea of the crib obviously echoes Luke's gospel, but its introduction as a 'focus' for the Christmas season is attributed to St Francis, whose story might be told.

The First Crib

In 1223 Francis wanted to celebrate a beautiful Christmas. It was to be a Christmas which would make him 'feel he was really there in Bethlehem and see with his own eyes how much the child had had to suffer: and how he was laid in the manger and how he was laid down between the ox and the little donkey'. So the first crib was made because of Francis's longing. The scene has been described in a very simple moving way by someone who was there: 'The day of gladness was drawing near. The friars together with many other men and women, gathered from all parts: each one, feeling full of joy, prepared torches and candles to light up that night. What happened on Christmas night was to light up the coming centuries of time like a glittering star. The Saint of God [ie St Francis] finally arrived: he saw that everything had been prepared and he was glad. The manger was made ready; it was filled with hay and the ox and little donkey were led to it. The night was very bright with all the lights and it was a delight for both the people and the animals. The friars with their sacred songs gave God the praise due to him. Then they celebrated Mass at the manger and the Saint who was assisting as deacon that night, put on the vestments and sang the Gospel. He preached then to the people about the birth of the King who became poor, and he spoke of the tiny village of Bethlehem where he was born.' His words were so vivid that the crowd of worshippers believed they were in Bethlehem. One of those present 'saw in the manger the child lying as if he were lifeless. The Saint came towards him to awaken him.' This was a vision of what St Francis had done: because the Child Jesus had been forgotten in many hearts and he was revived in these hearts by St Francis.

(adapted from *The Life of St Francis* by A Ghilhardi (trans. S Attanasio), Paul Hamlyn 1967, p 56)

Francis's living representation of the story evoked a response among the poor of Greccio.

Responses to 'the story'

Above and opposite:
Present day interpretations of the stories of Jesus' birth from Africa (the Shepherds) and Latin America (The Wise Men) complement traditional Western representations and point to the continuing vitality of the story among Christians.

Within the birth narratives of Matthew and Luke the theme of response is already there; it isn't alien to the stories. But the stories have themselves evoked responses and some of these may be used. Four kinds of 'response' are suggested here. Each might become the subject of a Christmas topic in its own right, but the first two might be used to supplement the gospel stories, allowing time to enjoy them and reflect on them.

1 The work of artists showing the birth of Jesus
You will need to gather your own collection of pictures; postcard prints and accumulated Christmas cards are useful. Don't always go for the 'Great Masters' either. Recent Oxfam, Christian Aid and Cafod cards give contemporary pictures of 'the Christmas story' and usually take it out of a European setting.

2 Music
This may 'respond' by trying to encapsulate both the spirit of the story and the celebration of the festival. There is inevitably an element of personal choice here, and teachers may simply decide to share a piece of music which *they* find expresses something of, or about, 'the story'.

Bach's *Christmas Oratorio*, Charpentier's *Midnight Mass for Christmas Eve* and Palestrina's *Hodie Christus Natus Est* all provide moments which might be shared with some children by some teachers in appropriate contexts. But the clue is to search out those which *you* can use.

3 Stories
The pervasiveness of 'the Christmas story' and its meanings may be discovered in a wealth of stories meant for telling at Christmas which explore some of the themes of the gospel stories, or which have taken features of those stories and woven them with other tales, or created new stories that still carry something of the spirit of the Christmas stories. The two BBC Radiovision productions

Baboushka and *Salinka and the Golden Bird* (see Resources) would be useful here. G C Menotti's *Amahl and the Night Visitors* (Faber & Faber 1986) would offer the opportunity for exploring story and music.

4 Social concern

A different kind of response is that of groups who try to live out the 'good news for the poor' of Luke's birth story. Older children might find out, for instance, about the work of the Salvation Army and discover how they celebrate Christmas in their locality, and how they serve those who are lonely and in need.

Activities

1 For this activity you will need copies of the two stories and a collection of Christmas cards.

a Read the two stories—Luke 2:1–20 and Matthew 2:1–12.

b Look at Christmas cards, find one which is Luke's story, one which is Matthew's. Do some mix up the stories?

c Begin to distinguish the two from each other by drawing up two simple lists 'Only in Luke' and 'Only in Matthew'. Explore what they agree about too (Bethlehem, Mary, Joseph).

d Make two collages: Luke's story and Matthew's story. What needs to go in each collage? For example:
Luke: *Mary*, Joseph, Jesus, shepherds, angel choir, message of peace
Matthew: *Joseph*, Mary, Jesus, star, three wise men

Discuss what Luke wanted to say about Jesus' birth. Did Matthew have a different message to give through his story?

2 A variation of the above activity would be to collect pictures with contrasting portrayals of the Christmas story. Allow children time to talk about them. Who is shown in the pictures? What kind of scene do they show? In what ways is it like/unlike Matthew's and Luke's stories? Which pictures do the children like/dislike and why? Notice different cultural settings (which speak of the story's popularity and responses to it). The emphasis here is on exploring *responses* to the story.

3 Design a card which a *Christian* might send at Christmas based on Luke's story, or Matthew's. (Note that some children may not wish to do work which involves representing the human figure. Allow for calligraphy—of a significant verse or key words, or perhaps a star design for Matthew.)

4 Take a number of themes from the Christmas stories of Luke and Matthew and explore them further with the children (eg Peace, Goodwill to all, Homelessness, the Poor, Hope, Gifts, Journeys, Searching).

Resources

Books
Celebrating Christmas, 2nd ed, CEM 1979 (for teachers, article on the New Testament narratives and approaches)
P Egan, *The Christmas Road*, Church House Publishing 1986 (collection of readings and poems about the meaning of Christmas from a Christian source)
D Kossoff, *The Christmas Story in Masterpieces*, Collins/Phaidon Press 1977 (provides a range of visual material)

AVA
Baboushka and *Salinka and the Golden Bird*, BBC (Radiovision), Longman (2 filmstrips—with notes—each with a story for Christmas)
Christian Festivals, E745, Pictorial Charts Educational Trust (4 posters: Christmas, Easter, Whitsun and Harvest)

SECTION 3: FOR 9–11 YEAR OLDS

2 Easter

| Aims |

The aims of this unit are that children should become familiar with the stories which the first Christians told of Jesus' resurrection, and begin to understand them as stories in which **Christians** continue to find meaning for their lives.

Information

For Christians Easter is the 'Feast of Feasts'. 'Eastertide' is celebrated for 50 days, right through to Pentecost (page 116). Add to this 40 days of Lent (excluding Sundays!) as a time of preparation for the festival, and you have a clear indication of Easter's importance in the Christian calendar. Each Sunday of the year too is in essence a celebration of Jesus' resurrection: this was the day of the week when the first Christians met, celebrating because it was the day when they believed Jesus was raised from the dead.

Easter experience

For Christians, the resurrection of Jesus celebrated at Easter is not simply a past event, but a present reality. It is the sense that Christ is the person who, having adopted the human state, overcame all its ills, including death itself. And the benefits of this victory are offered to believers in response to their faith in him.

Stories of the resurrection

It is probably Paul who gives the oldest written account of Jesus' resurrection, in 1 Corinthians 15:1–11. Here he makes it clear he is handing on information he himself had received about Jesus' resurrection: 'I delivered to you . . . what I also received' (1 Corinthians 15:3). This suggests a chain of witnesses.

The four gospels of course have their stories to tell too: it is useful to read through the stories listed in the chart. Those passages not included—Mark 16:9–20 and John 21—are missed out deliberately since many scholars see them as later additions to the respective gospels.

STORY	MATTHEW	MARK	LUKE	JOHN
The 'empty tomb' (but with varying detail)	28:1–10	16:1–8	24:1–11(12)	20:1–10
An 'appearance' to Mary Magdala	—	—	—	20:11–18
The bribing of the guards	28:11–15 (a sequel to 27:62–66)	—	—	—
An 'appearance' in Galilee	28:16–20	—	—	—
The road to Emmaus	—	—	24:13–35	—
'Appearance' to the disciples in Jerusalem	—	—	24:36–49	20:19–23
Jesus 'appears' to Thomas	—	—	—	20:24–29

Christians and the stories

Apart from the stories mentioned above, the first Christians consistently expressed their conviction about Jesus' resurrection in a clear and simple way. Look at Peter's words in Acts 2:23–24, 'God raised him from death'. It is a claim often disputed. Acts 17:22–34 reports that the Athenians mocked Paul on this point.

Christians differ in the ways in which they approach the matter of the resurrection of Jesus. Here are some viewpoints.

1 The Church has traditionally affirmed the physical resurrection of Jesus, and the stories of the empty tomb and the appearances should be accepted as they stand.

2   What matters is that Jesus 'lives on' in those who choose to follow his teaching and example. His bones may be buried, but this is not important. It was the quality of his life and manner of death which triumphed and lived on in spirit.

3   The disciples did in some way *experience Jesus' presence* among them; this was such a profound experience it changed their whole outlook, and led to their preaching about the risen Christ.

4   The resurrection experiences arose in the experience of the sacrament of the Bread and Wine of Communion and it is in that shared fellowship that the risen Christ is best understood.

Certainly the resurrection of Christ is a great mystery and speculation about the resurrection body is perhaps interesting but probably not very profitable, since 'resurrection' removes the story out of the objective historical arena.

Stories conveying meaning

The Chichester Project book *Christmas and Easter* by T Shannon (Lutterworth Press 1984) begins by talking about 'Matters of Life and Death'. Belief in Jesus' resurrection influences the way Christians think about their own deaths: death is not an end. Many Easter hymns have the theme of death being conquered. Death may be seen as entering on new life; it's a beginning. Some Easter hymns celebrate the newness of springtime, comparing it with the new life and hope which Christians believe Jesus' resurrection brings.

Approaches

1   Provide a context for the resurrection stories by exploring the disciples' experiences during Holy Week. This could perhaps be done in school before the Easter holidays. Follow it up after the holiday with the stories of Jesus' resurrection and the responses of the disciples. (It might be helpful to look at the topic on Pentecost (page 116) here too.) Find the contrast between the dejected state of the disciples at the time of the crucifixion and their joyful state when they are convinced that Jesus is alive.

2   Provide the children with the opportunity to engage with *one* of the stories of the resurrection. Use for example Alan Dale's *New World* (OUP 1967), and the story he calls 'On a country road', or read the biblical account in Luke 24:13–35.

The story itself conveys much of what the earliest Christians believed about Jesus (eg, that God vindicates the righteous sufferer; that Jesus fulfilled the prophecies of Jewish scripture; that he is present with his followers when they break bread together). Let the children raise their own questions about the story; these can then be explored. Or decide to focus on particular points; for example:

Who are the 'characters'? What is known about them? Why were they leaving Jerusalem?
What did the stranger explain to them?
How did they come to recognise him? What event might it have reminded them of?
What was their response?

A key issue in this story is *recognition*: why was Jesus not recognised at first? The children may have their own ideas here.

Note that in line with approach number 1 there is again a focus on the disciples' experience.

3   Using the Emmaus story may also 'open up' some of the questions which may be asked of the *other* stories, and which suggest a detective approach to the stories in the chart opposite:

Who saw Jesus?   Where did they see him?
When did they see him?   What happened on that occasion?

Different stories could be given to groups of children and the answers to these questions carefully recorded in a simple matrix.

In discussion the constant factors—empty tomb, appearances, 'mysterious' nature of the appearances—should emerge as well as the divergences which the accounts show. Each of these factors can be simply discussed.

Activities

The approaches above all suggest activities, but some activities which are not so dependent on the text are suggested below (2 and 3):

1 Plan a series of 'news bulletins' based on the work you have done on the stories of the resurrection. These could be presented in assemblies over a short period after the Easter holidays.

2 Explore what the resurrection stories might mean for Christians today (and in the past) when they face death. One top junior class explored a local graveyard very carefully as part of a local church topic. They collected 'texts' as well as inscriptions and phrases which suggested a particular attitude towards death; for example, 'Fell asleep', 'Only sleeping'. This led to discussion of death—is it an end, or does something lie beyond death? (Obviously this topic calls for sensitivity to the personal and individual circumstances of the children.)

3 Plan to decorate the classroom for Easter, basing the decorations on 'Now the green blade riseth', 'Lord of the Dance', or another hymn/song that Christians sing at Easter which would provide an adequate stimulus for the activity.

Now the green blade riseth

Now the green blade riseth, from the buried grain,
Wheat that in dark earth many days has lain;
Love lives again, that with the dead has been:

> Love is come again,
> Like wheat that springeth green.

In the grave they laid him, Love whom men had slain,
Thinking that never he would wake again,
Laid in the earth like grain that sleeps unseen:

> Love is come . . .

Forth he came at Easter, like the risen grain,
He that for three days in the grave had lain,
Quick from the dead, my risen Lord is seen:

> Love is come . . .

When our hearts are wintry, grieving, or in pain,
Thy touch can call us back to life again,
Fields of our hearts, that dead and bare have been:

> Love is come . . .

(from *The New English Hymnal*, The Canterbury Press 1986)

Now the green blade riseth—old French melody
Harmonies by Martin Shaw (1875–1958)

Resources

Books
R Gregory (Ed), *Sixty Bible Stories*: Bedfordshire RE series, TMRS (Russell House, 14 Dunstable Street, Bedford MK45 2JT) (useful reference book for teachers; identifies main themes of stories and explores a little of what biblical scholarship can contribute to understanding the stories)

T Shannon, *Jesus*, Lutterworth Press 1982

T Shannon, *Christmas and Easter*, Lutterworth Educational 1984 (both of these Chichester Project books provide useful background information)

R Walton (Ed), *A Source Book of the Bible for Teachers*, SCM Press 1970 (sections on biblical material are still useful reference for teachers; those on 'teaching' are somewhat dated)

AVA
For those who want to link the gospel accounts of Holy Week and Easter with the celebrations of Christians today, the following will be useful.

Festivals, Westhill Regional RE Centre, Mary Glasgow 1984 (an expensive but useful pack of 5 filmstrips, cassettes and detailed notes. Covers Passover, Easter, Ramadan and Divali and has an introductory filmstrip to festivals)

Palm Sunday and Maundy Thursday, S1473, Slide Centre

Good Friday and Holy Saturday and Easter Day, S1475, Slide Centre (packs of 18 and 12 slides respectively, with notes for the teacher)

And for a presentation of the stories which children might view after working on the slides above, see:

Zeffirelli, *Jesus of Nazareth*, Precision Video (the well known film available on 4 video cassettes)

3 Hanukah

Aims

Children will have the opportunity to explore the symbolism of light; to encounter **Jewish** religious commitment and to be aware of the ways in which festivals keep alive the memory of the past and enliven the present.

Information

Hanukah is one of the minor festivals of **Judaism**, observed on eight nights in the month of Kislev which in the northern hemisphere falls at the darkest time of the year. The motif of light, coming from the lighting of the *hanukiah* (an eight-branched candlestick or lamp used for the festival) and deriving from the story behind the festival, has led to the frequent association of this festival with others in which light is a symbol; for example, Divali (section 1, page 14) and Christmas. Whilst the symbolism of light is present for exploration by children, other themes are also of importance. Hanukah means dedication; with this may be linked themes of commitment and faithfulness, and in particular of 'holding fast' to these under persecution. Hanukah is also a story about a struggle for freedom. The power of story in religious traditions is also clear from this festival as well as its reliving and recalling through symbolic actions and foods.

The story of Hanukah

The story of Hanukah is about the Jewish people's struggle to keep their identity and religious freedom in Israel in the second century BCE. At the time the country was under the rule of Antiochus Epiphanes. The Jews worshipped *one* God who could not be represented by any image or by any human form. Refusal to compromise by worshipping Greek gods, or indeed Antiochus himself, led to the oppression of the people. It was hard too to keep other commandments, such as observing the Sabbath and keeping special food regulations, and difficult to celebrate festivals, or even to study the Torah.

The story of the people's struggle in one village—Modin—to keep their way of life, and what happened, is found in the Apocrypha in 1 Maccabees 1:41—4:61. The 'great miracle' of the light is not found in Maccabees but is found in later Jewish writings. Below is a brief version of the story.

Note: The Apocrypha consists of late Jewish writings which are not included as part of the authoritative Jewish Scriptures.

Hanukka—the feast of lights

Many, many centuries ago, the powerful King of Syria, Antiochus Epiphanes, tried to make the Jews renounce their faith. He forbade them to worship the one God or to read and study the holy books. They were not allowed to observe their holidays or to abide by the laws of their fathers. Antiochus was a cruel king, and his army was strong. If any of the Jews dared disobey his orders, he had them put to death. Even the temple at Jerusalem was shamelessly desecrated. The Jews were distressed. What were they to do? Where were they to turn? Some took to the hills to live according to their religion, but even there they were never safe from the king's soldiers. Then the high priest Mattathias Maccabee and his five sons joined the fugitives and persuaded the Jews to make a stand against the Syrians. Mattathias' eldest son, Judah, gathered together a small army, and three years to the day after Antiochus had issued his decree the Jews fought a victorious battle against great odds. The Maccabees entered the ransacked temple and threw out the pagan idols; then they prepared it for reconsecration. At last all was ready except for the lighting of the temple lamp with its seven branches. But for this they needed specially consecrated olive oil, of which they could find only one jar. It was not enough, for the lamp must never be extinguished, and the oil from one jar was only enough for one day. But the Jews lit the lamp just the same. In its light they prayed to God, giving thanks that they were again free. Then a miracle took place. The lamp, filled with the oil from one small jar, burned not one day, but two, three, and in the end a whole eight days—long enough for the priests to prepare new oil.

It is in memory of this that the Jews keep the feast of lights, Hanukka. The holiday is especially dear to children. They get presents, and eat potato cakes called latkes and doughnuts called savganiyot. But most of all they look forward to lighting the candles. On the first day they light one, on the next day two, and so on until the eighth day the *hanukkiya*, the eight-branched lamp, is all lit up.

(from 'The Glow of the Hanukkiya' in *Jewish Tales: the Eight Lights of the Hanukkiya* by Leo Pavlat, Beehive Books, London 1986)

Celebrating Hanukah

A *hanukiah*, clearly showing the eight candleholders and the additional place for the *shammas* or serving light

Light

During Hanukah, public candelabra may be lit; they may be lit also in the presence of a congregation in the synagogue, but this Jewish festival, like others, has a focus in the home, where a flame will be lit each evening when the family are gathered together. Traditionally when lit the lights are placed in the window to 'witness' to passers-by.

A *hanukiah* may be designed to hold candles, or to burn small wicks placed in olive oil. Electric candelabra are frowned upon. There will be places for eight lights and a *shammas*, or serving light. Where candles are used the *shammas* is first placed in position; the other candles will be lit with this. Each night an additional candle is placed in the holder, always moving from right to left. By the final night all eight are in position. Candles are traditionally lit from left to right, so the newest candle is always burning first. Prayers accompany the lighting of the candles, and there may be readings and traditional songs.

A Hanukah prayer

We kindle these lights on account of the miracles, the deliverances, and the wonders You performed for our fathers, by means of Your holy priests. During all the eight days of Hanukkah these lights are sacred, and it is not permitted for us to make any use of them, but only to look at them, in order that we may give thanks unto Your Name for Your miracles, Your deliverances, and Your wonders.

(from *The Hanukah Book* by M S Rockland, Schocken Books 1975, p 29)

The symbolism of light is very rich and worth exploring with children in the context of the Hanukah story (see Activities). Children will have their own ideas about possible meanings of the lights, but here are some suggestions: light and hope in the darkness of winter; victory against great odds; plenty when there had been want; freedom; the success of a few against many.

SECTION 3: FOR 9–11 YEAR OLDS

The lights used to recall the miracle are for pure pleasure and not for utilitarian purposes. You can watch the light and shade, the flickering, and enjoy its play on the hands and around the room, but don't use the eight lights, for example, to read! Rather they should 'rekindle' the story and let its themes live.

Stories and songs

As well as the story behind the festival, other stories relating to the themes of Hanukah, or to Hanukah celebrated in the absence of freedom, may be collected and told. Biblical stories may also be told—that of Daniel for example would be appropriate to the season (see Resources)—and songs are sung. *Ma'oz tzur*, recalling God's help to his people, is traditional for some whilst others recite Psalm 30 which is called 'A song at the Dedication of the House'.

Ma'oz tzur

Ma - oz tzur ye - shu - a - ti le - kha na - eh le sha - be - ah
Rock of Ag - es, let our song praise Thy sav - ing pow - er;

tik - kon bet te - fil - la - ti ve - sham to - dah ne zab - be - ah le-
thou a - midst the rag - ing foes wast our shelt' - ring tow - er.

-et ta - khin mat - be - ah mi - tzar ham - nab - be - ah
Fu - rious they as - sailed us, but Thine arm a -' vail - ed us,

az eg - mor be - shir miz - mor ha - nuk - kat ham - miz - be - ah.
And Thy word broke their sword when our own strength failed us.

(from M S Rockland, op cit, p 30)

Games

Chess (Maccabeans v. Syrians) and cards, also adapted to the Hanukah story, have been among the games played at the festival, but *dreidel* (Hebrew: *sevivon*) is probably the best known game for Hanukah. (The *dreidel* is a four-sided spinning top, marked with Hebrew letters.) The tradition of playing games has even been linked with the origins of the festival. It is said by some that those who continued Torah study after it was banned by Antiochus Epiphanes kept games close at hand. And if Antiochus' soldiers appeared, then gambling was the apparent reason for the meeting!

Dreidel was probably a popular secular game, which was given the dignity of carrying a religious message. The four letters are also understood as standing for Yiddish words, indicative of how the game might be played: 'n' = *nehm* (take) or *nichts* (nothing); 'g' = *gib* (give) or *ganz* (all); 'h' = *halb* (half); 's' = *shtel* (put). In playing the game each player puts an agreed number of items, for instance sweets or nuts, into a kitty. Each spins the *dreidel*. When it falls, the letter uppermost indicates the action to be taken. Thus in one version of the game, נ indicates nothing happens and the player passes; ג entitles a player to everything in the kitty; ה means that the player receives one half of what is in the

Playing *dreidel*

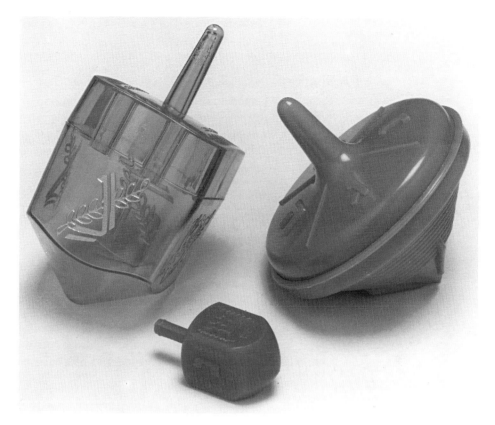

'A great miracle happened there'. *Dreidel* come in different shapes and sizes but have in common the four Hebrew characters.

kitty; whilst ‭ש‬ means that something must be put in the kitty (to be agreed before the game starts). The hidden message of the letters is given alongside.

Gifts
Hanukah '*geld*', a gift of money, would seem to be an old custom of Eastern European origin. Children may receive a present on the final night, or perhaps a small gift for each day of the festival.

Food
Foods cooked in oil have become popular, for obvious reasons. Potato *latkes* and doughnuts are favourites. Taste too serves as a reminder of the great miracle.

Approaches

1   Let children look at a *dreidel* and pick out its features, especially the letters ‭נ‬ *nun*, ‭ג‬ *gimmel*, ‭ה‬ *he* and ‭ש‬ *shin*. Which alphabet/language do they come from? What do they stand for? (*Nes gadol haya sham*, 'A great miracle happened there'.) Lead into the story; promise to return to the game later.

2   Begin (ideally on the first day of Hanukah when it falls in termtime) by introducing the *hanukiah* with its eight branches for candles (or burners for wicks and oil) and its *shammas*, or serving light. Possibly show pictures of *hanukiot* (plural); with the differences in style and decoration, note the constancy of *eight* places for a light to burn. Why? Lead into the story. Plan to light the *shammas* and the first candle (cf Activities).

3   Talk about families and customs; identify some. What about 'larger groups' of people? Do they have customs which belong especially to them? Discussion may elicit such items as special foods, dress, special days, special places to worship, special stories that are told. Introduce Hanukah in this context.

4   Talk about freedom. Encourage children to think about all the things they are free to do. How would they feel if they were suddenly forbidden to do them? What

would life be like? Lead into the Hanukah story, a story about people who had lost their freedom.

Activities Involvement of children (and adults!) in Jewish festivals helps to ensure the handing of belief and practice from one generation to another. Books abound with practical activities in marking this and other Jewish festivals. If you can get it through an RE centre, *The Hanukkah Book* by M S Rockland (Schocken 1975) is worth consulting, as is the volume *Step-by-Step Hanukah* in *Hanukah: A Family Learning Kit* (Everyman's University, Israel, 1982).

If you have no such opportunity, here are some suggestions for Hanukah activities:

Plan a Hanukah week in school (especially if the festival falls in term time). Let activities such as the following culminate in a special school assembly.

1 Create enough time at the end of each day, for eight days, to light the Hanukah lamps/candles.

2 Involve children in making simple Hanukah lights of their own. Decide that each candle must symbolise the story of Hanukah or its 'spirit' in some way. For example, short phrases might do: 'good wins through', 'freedom for all human-kind'. Or light each candle to recall the life of one person who is not free today.

3 Plan a Hanukah party. Prepare invitations with suitable symbols: make decorations and prepare to play *dreidel*; decide to do some cooking. Share in making potato *latkes*, but take care with the frying!

Potato latkes
1 lb potatoes, peeled and finely grated
1 egg beaten
1 tbsp SR flour or matzo meal
Salt
Pepper
Oil for frying

Squeeze the potatoes until they are dry.
Mix in the egg, flour and seasonings. Heat
about half an inch (1 cm) of oil in a frying pan
and fry spoonfuls of the mixture until they
are brown on the underside. Turn and brown
on the second side. Drain on absorbent paper.
Serves 3–4.

(from *The Gourmet Guide to Jewish Cooking* by B Carr and P Obermann, Octopus 1973)

4 Prepare a wall newspaper of events in Modin, through the persecution up to the rededication of the Temple. Remember to allow for:

'on-the-spot' reports;
interviews;
editorial comment;
a religious column.

You will find 1 Maccabees useful for information here.

5 Explore some of the themes of Hanukah—'dedication', freedom, courage—in children's writing. Perhaps design a series of posters where children complete the sentences:

Freedom is ....

Courage is ....

6 Learn some songs for Hanukah. A good collection can be found in J Gilbert's *Topic Anthologies for Young Children: Festivals* (OUP Music Dept 1986).

The last night of Hanukah

Resources

Books

L Berg, *Celebrations: Hanukka* (Ginn Reading Level 10), Ginn 1985

B Hollyer, *Daniel in the Lion's Den*, Macdonald 1983

R Kozoday, *The Book of Jewish Holidays*, Behrman House 1981

M Schlein, *Hanukkah*, Behrman House 1983

(these two books are written from within and for the Jewish community; they are available from the Jewish Education Bureau, 8 Westcombe Avenue, Leeds LS8 2BS)

L Scholefield, *Chanukah*, RMEP 1983

R Turner, *Jewish Festivals*, Wayland 1985

AVA

Video *Living Festivals Video 1*: Chanukah and four other festivals, CEM/PEP

Posters *Jewish Festivals*, E746, Pictorial Charts Educational Trust

SECTION 3: FOR 9–11 YEAR OLDS

4 Christian Celebration of Pentecost: Whitsunday

Aims	Children will learn about the story of Pentecost and discover some of its meanings for **Christians**.

Information

Festivals have become a very popular topic in RE—but some festivals are more popular than others! Pentecost or 'Whitsun' doesn't seem to belong to this category! Yet in Christianity it ranks in importance with Christmas and Easter, and as we shall see it completes the Easter story.

Like other festivals it has some basic ingredients: story, symbol and celebration interweave, together conveying meaning and finding resonances in human experience. Unlike other festivals it does not seem to have a 'popular' dimension.

Pentecost in a Jewish context

In Acts chapter 2 the writer tells that the Holy Spirit 'came' to the apostles on the day of Pentecost. Pentecost comes from a Greek word meaning 'fiftieth day'. In the Jewish calendar it defines the time, after the celebration of Passover, of one of the pilgrim festivals (when people would go to Jerusalem) in celebration of the wheat harvest. The festival was and is known as the Feast of Weeks or *Shavuot*, referring to its occurrence seven weeks after Passover (see Deuteronomy 16: 9–10).

As well as the wheat harvest the festival marked the beginning of a new agricultural season when the first fruits of the land were brought to the Temple; each farmer would bring his 'first fruits' as they ripened. This could be any time up to the autumn festival of Sukkot which marked the end of harvest.

For Jews the festival also came to commemorate the giving of the Torah to Moses on Mount Sinai; its continued celebration today recalls this as well as picking up its harvest themes.

In the first century CE Jews from many of the Mediterranean countries could in fact make the journey to Jerusalem for this 'pilgrim festival', travel at this time of year being easier than at the earlier spring festival of Passover. Acts 2 paints a picture of the cosmopolitan atmosphere in Jerusalem at the time of Pentecost!

Pentecost as a Christian festival

Pentecost for Christians probably at first referred to fifty days which celebrated the resurrection of Jesus. In time it became a one-day celebration which marked both Jesus' ascension and the coming of the Holy Spirit. Then by the end of the fourth century CE two celebrations had emerged: Ascension Day, forty days after Easter, and Pentecost or Whitsunday, ten days later. These festivals bring the Easter period of celebration to an end.

The story: Acts Chapter 2: 1–13

Luke's Gospel ends with Jesus parting from his disciples, having told them to wait in Jerusalem where they will receive 'power from on high'. The Acts of the Apostles (thought to be by Luke too) begins with two vivid stories in which these two themes—Jesus parting from his disciples and their receiving 'power from on high'—are developed. It is the second story which is told here:

The empty cross signifies Christian belief in Jesus' resurrection. The flame here symbolises the Holy Spirit and Christian belief in God's continuing presence.

The coming of the Holy Spirit

While the day of Pentecost was running its course they were all together in one place, when suddenly there came from the sky a noise like that of a strong driving wind, which filled the whole house where they were sitting. And there appeared to them tongues like flames of fire, dispersed among them and resting on each one. And they were filled with the Holy Spirit and began to talk in other tongues, as the Spirit gave them power of utterance.

Now there were living in Jerusalem devout Jews drawn from every nation under heaven: and at this sound the crowd gathered, all bewildered because each one heard his own language spoken. They were amazed and in their astonishment exclaimed, 'Why they are all Galileans, are they not, these men who are speaking? How is it then that we hear them, each of us in his own native language? Parthians, Medes, Elamites; inhabitants of Mesopotamia, of Judaea and Cappadocia, of Pontus and Asia, of Phrygia and Pamphylia, of Egypt and the districts of Libya around Cyrene; visitors from Rome, both Jews and proselytes, Cretans and Arabs, we hear telling in our own tongues the great things God has done.' And they were all amazed and perplexed, saying to one another, 'What can this mean?' Others said contemptuously, 'They have been drinking!'

(from the New English Bible, British and Foreign Bible Society 1972)

Celebrating Pentecost

In the churches, Pentecost is celebrated with appropriate readings and hymns. Acts 2 is a key reading, whilst Old Testament readings may include the story of the Tower of Babel (which is about languages dividing people) or Moses at Sinai (picking up the Jewish celebration).

Hymns draw on a number of themes: they may in part tell the story of Pentecost; or they may take the form of a prayer in which Christians pray for the Spirit's presence in their own lives.

Other hymns take their themes from Christian understanding of the 'fruits of the Spirit'—the qualities which take root and grow in the Christian's life as a result of the Spirit's presence. Many of these hymns are based on the writings of St Paul; 1 Corinthians 13 often lies behind the hymns, and also Galatians 5:22–23.

> The fruit of the Spirit is love, joy, peace, patience, kindness, goodness, faithfulness, gentleness, self-control.

Easter and Pentecost in the early Church were the two occasions in the year for baptism and confirmation, and church membership is still associated with this time of year. The Anglo-Saxon name Whitsunday is really 'White Sunday' and refers to the white robes put on those who were newly baptised.

The symbol of the Holy Spirit is the dove. It is used to symbolise the presence of the Spirit at Jesus' baptism (Luke 3:21–22). Fire and wind are also used as symbols of the Spirit and God's presence.

One popular custom which has survived in some places is the 'Whit Walks' or processions of Christians—perhaps wearing white—bearing witness to their faith.

SECTION 3: FOR 9–11 YEAR OLDS

117

Approaches

1   It will be for the teacher to decide how far it is possible to discuss the meaning of 'Spirit' as a power which Christians believe is available to them as the gift of Christ to sustain them, but pupils can become acquainted with the story. Study could then proceed to the discussion of the 'fruits of the Spirit' as in Galatians 5:22–23.

2   Pentecost or Whitsunday is sometimes called the 'birthday' of the Church. A study of the spread of the Church from a small beginning in Jerusalem might indicate more clearly than anything else that something decisive occurred at Pentecost. You could concentrate on how Christianity reached a specific country (or, if it is possible, even how it reached the town where your school is!).

3   The Pentecost experience brought about a change in the disciples. Pentecost could be approached through Peter's story: from his denial of Jesus (Luke 22:54–62), through to the discovery of the empty tomb (John 20:1–8, Luke 24:1–12) and the day of Pentecost (Acts 2).

4   Link work on Pentecost with work on symbols (see page 185). Explore the symbols of wind and fire. Think about the 'qualities' of wind and fire. These ideas are those of a group of eleven and twelve year olds:

Wind

Power
Strength
Invisible, but you
know it is there.
You cannot control it.
It's like breath—life.

Fire

Warmth—comforting
Fire is essential to life.
It can give protection.
It can show the way,
light up darkness.
It purifies.
It can stand for happiness.
It softens metals—they can be re-formed.

The children went on to discuss whether these symbols were a 'good' way for Christians to speak of God's presence and activity.

Activities

1   Design posters for the period in the Christian calendar from Ash Wednesday to Pentecost, using symbols as the basis for the posters. You will need to include Ash Wednesday, Maundy Thursday, Good Friday, Easter Day, and Pentecost. Alternatively, design a good poster for Pentecost alone.

2   Following up the 'fruits of the Spirit' approach, some children might write short stories about characters named after them, eg Mrs Joy, Miss Peace, Mr Patience.

3   As an outcome of the study of the spread of the Church, a world map could be marked with the sequence of the gradual expansion.

4 Allow time for reflection. Listen for example to the beginning of Haydn's *Creation* or listen to Christians at Taizé quietly singing a prayer for the Spirit's presence, like this one:

Veni Creator Spiritus canon

Come Creator Spirit.

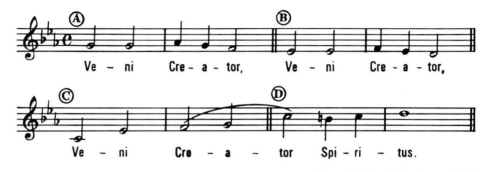

(from *Joy on Earth*, Collins Liturgical Publications 1986)

Resources

Books

There seems to be a dearth of material about Pentecost for both teachers and pupils. These two books intended for use within the Christian community may be noted first.

M Eastman, *The Pentecost Book*, Geoffrey Chapman 1983 (written for a Roman Catholic community, a colourful children's book with stories on the theme of the Spirit, songs, and activities)

M Freeman and B Miller, *Steps & Stones 4*, Church House Publishing 1986 (includes a series of six lessons leading up to Pentecost from which teachers may take ideas; intended for 7–11s)

F Sampson, *Ascensiontide and Pentecost*, RMEP 1986 (the publishers suggest this is for 9–15s; it looks at the festivals, but contains a long section on regional customs, eg Well Dressing, which are not integral to the festivals)

AVA

Christian Festivals, E745, Pictorial Charts Educational Trust (set of 4 posters with notes; one is related to Pentecost/Whitsun)

TAIZÉ Vitrail de Pentecôte, Editions Les Presses de Taizé (glowing red stained-glass window of the Dove, available from St Paul's Bookshop, 199 Kensington High Street, London W8 6BA)

Cassette recordings of music from the Taizé community are often available from Christian booksellers; A R Mowbray produce a cassette *Songs from Taizé*.

SECTION 3: FOR 9–11 YEAR OLDS

5 Jesus

Aims

The purpose of this unit is for children to recognise that the life and teaching of Jesus provoked responses of worship and discipleship, and to offer an opportunity to reflect on some of these.

Information

By focusing on *responses*, this unit is indicating that in trying to understand the place of Jesus in Christian faith, it is important to take note of the *effect* he has had, and the effect he still has on the lives of many.

Responses in the Christian tradition itself have never been uniform. There have always been many ways of speaking about Jesus and many ways of responding to him and his message.

The information below simply points in some possible directions and teachers will certainly be able to supplement these from other sources. It will probably be helpful to have studied the story of Jesus at a basic level first (see section 2, page 60).

Words for worship

From earliest times Christians have met together for worship. Some of their earliest hymns are from the New Testament. This one about Jesus is well known.

> His state was divine,
> yet he did not cling
> to his equality with God
> but emptied himself
> to assume the condition of a slave,
> and became as men are;
> and became as all men are,
> he was humbler yet,
> even to accepting death,
> death on a cross.
> But God raised him high
> and gave him the name
> which is above all other names
> so that all beings
> in the heavens, on earth and in the underworld,
> should bend the knee at the name of Jesus
> and that every tongue should acclaim
> Jesus Christ as Lord,
> to the glory of God the Father.
>
> (Philippians 2:6–11, from the Jerusalem Bible: New Testament, Hodder & Stoughton 1973)

This hymn shows how early in the history of Christianity (about 63 CE) belief in Jesus was being expressed in a very specific way: Christians believe he was divine yet came to earth as a servant and suffered humiliation and death and God raised him from the dead.

Philippians 2 is probably too difficult for children to study, but they could be introduced to other Christian hymns about Jesus which contain feelings about:

what Jesus is like;
his story;
how the writer responds.

Two well known hymns which could be used are 'At the name of Jesus . . .' and 'Jesu, good above all other'.

Pictures of Jesus

Pictures of Jesus are of course a 'response' because no one knows for certain what he looked like.

Comparing and contrasting different pictures of Jesus can raise some very interesting points for discussion (see *Jesus* by Trevor Shannan, Lutterworth Press 1982).

Here are some questions to think about when looking at pictures:

What is the main thing the picture is trying to say about the character of Jesus?

Does the picture pick up some of the symbols Christians use for Jesus (eg King, Lord, Shepherd)?

Is it mainly concerned with his humanity or does it point to the Christian belief in him as God?

Does the artist 'place' Jesus in first-century Palestine or in his own country and times?

However, pictures don't fit neatly into categories and these questions are only guidelines. Almost every picture has some interesting element of its own.

Responses in the gospels

The gospels provide many examples of individual encounters with Jesus. Here are some examples to consider.

Jesus' disciples: Mark 1:16–21

Each of the gospels recognises that Jesus had disciples: twelve men who were alongside him throughout his 'three years' teaching and preaching. Mark 1:16–21 tells the story of the call of four of them, Simon (Peter), Andrew, James and John. When you read the story you will notice how brief it is, and that as a result it is quite dramatic. It focuses on essentials: Jesus' 'call' to the men, and their willingness to follow, leaving everything. Children sometimes enjoy thinking of all the questions that occur to *them* about this passage. Why did the men just drop everything? Did they go and tell their families? Who looked after their boats and did their jobs? Had they met Jesus before and talked about becoming disciples? These are the kind of questions which children might raise.

Of course they can't be answered; they simply point to information we might like to have. But even if the writer knew it, he didn't include it. Children might suggest why he didn't and whether there are 'advantages' in a short story which focuses on essentials; they might think of what the story would 'teach' Mark's readers about being a disciple, and what the story might mean to Christians today.

The next three stories may be told against the background of Roman rule in Palestine in the first century.

A Roman centurion: Luke 7:1–10

This story is of interest because it shows that it wasn't just his compatriots who turned to Jesus. Notice that Jesus commends the man for his 'faith'. The story offers the chance to discuss what is meant by having 'faith' in a person. This is another aspect of response.

Zacchaeus: Luke 19:1–10

To be a tax collector in the employment of the Romans was to betray your own people. Moreover, many subcontracted their work *and* made a profit through exacting more money than was actually due to the Romans. Against this background the unpopularity of someone like Zacchaeus is not hard to imagine. Notice the 'size' of his response. Consider how the people around might have commented on Zacchaeus' response. What would Zacchaeus' response mean for him? Jesus' own purpose is summed up in the last sentence: he had 'come to seek and save the lost'.

Judas Iscariot—Mark 14:12–21, 42–50

Teachers may prefer not to deal with this response. It does, however, serve as a balance indicating that some responses to Jesus were negative ones in the end. There is a theory that Judas was disappointed that Jesus did not lead an armed revolt against the Romans.

Notice that Mark tells how all the disciples fled when Jesus was betrayed and arrested. Children could explore the 'human' dimensions of this.

Biographies

There are some difficulties in using life stories of Christian men and women. Sometimes the impression is given that only Christians do good things! Sometimes the figures are presented as heroes who seem to have none of the usual human failings. And these stories are very often about white European Christians working 'overseas'; this is a grave imbalance.

Having said all that, the stories of people's lives offer enormous potential in the classroom, not least because such stories are intrinsically interesting. They show in a concrete way what a 'response' can actually mean.

Here are three examples of biographies of people whose lives can be seen to be *modelled in some way on Jesus*. In their actions they parallel Jesus' concerns as portrayed in the gospels. They seriously follow Jesus' commands and their lives *acquire meaning* as they reflect on his story.

All three happen to be located in India.

1 **Mother Teresa's** work with the poor, sick and abandoned is an obvious example and is well documented; her sisters are not all white; nor, with the establishment of 'co-workers' in other places, is the focus only on India: it is for example on Britain too. Her story might be set alongside that of Jesus 'serving' his disciples (John 13:1–17). It can be seen as one response to this story and its concluding command.

2 The work of **Paul Brand** could be similarly approached. Paul Brand, a world-renowned authority on the treatment of leprosy and the rehabilitation of its victims, was born in India in 1914, the son of Baptist missionary parents. He had a troubled childhood. Sent back to Britain to be educated, he was lonely and performed poorly at school. His working life began as a builder's apprentice; but out of his personal faith grew the conviction that he should become a missionary. The Baptist Missionary Society refused his offer of service on the grounds that he needed further training. This prompted him to take a course in tropical medicine. His skills were quickly apparent to his teachers, who advised him to become a medical student. He qualified during the Second World War and only after it was over could he go to India to work. There he began work among those with leprosy.

Paul Brand's personal vision of lepers as the 'sons and daughters of God' prompted his relentless quest for ways to restore and rebuild the lives of those who had long suffered rejection, disablement and disfigurement. Surgery to help lepers owes much to Paul Brand. The New Life Centre which he set up in Vellore, south India, helps leprosy patients to begin to build a new life for themselves; there they can learn to read and write, to become printers, and to handle tools.

Paul Brand's choice of work arose directly from his response to the story of Jesus and offers a modern commentary on passages such as Luke 5:12–16; 17:11–19.

3   The life of **Mary Verghese** offers the opportunity to reflect on another aspect of response: how Christians may find meaning in Jesus' story for their own lives. The story of Mary Verghese was used in a schools broadcast for Easter some years ago, one of its underlying themes being 'death and resurrection'.

Mary Verghese, who was born in 1925 at Kochin, Kerala, south India, grew up in a Syrian Orthodox home. Christianity is said to have arrived in India with the apostle Thomas, and it was certainly established in Kerala earlier than in Britain.

She was educated at the Christian Medical College in Vellore, Madras State. Her ambition to be a gynaecologist was apparently brought to a halt when, shortly after beginning work at the College Hospital, she was terribly injured in a car crash caused by the driver's carelessness. A damaged spinal cord left her paralysed; a long process of recovery from the accident led only to a wheelchair and the daily struggle faced by every paraplegic.

Her faith sustained her. She was able to forgive the young man whose recklessness had seemingly ruined her life. Colleagues and friends supported her in her search for new service to others: Paul Brand persuaded her to join him as a surgeon rebuilding the claw-like hands and feet of those disabled by leprosy. Working from a wheelchair, she became a leading surgeon in this field.

This was not all. Problems of paraplegics needed attention in India; Mary Verghese discovered that her own quiet confidence and her ability to cope with a considerable professional life encouraged paraplegics at Vellore, who were worried that as a result of their injuries life was all but over. After further preparation in Perth, Australia, where her own rehabilitation was taken as far as possible, and in the USA, Mary returned to work at the Rehabilitation Institute at Vellore, built as a result of her tireless energy. The Institute became a centre for new, caring initiatives to enrich the lives of paraplegics.

But of course for every Mother Teresa, Paul Brand, and Mary Verghese there are many, many Christians whose lives are lived unnoticed except by a few. A quick glance at interviews on a popular programme like BBC's *Songs of Praise* illustrates the theme of response very well. So in speaking of 'biography', teachers might also try to draw on local people who can talk about their response to Jesus' life and teaching, and how it affects their daily life. Care must be taken to do this in an objective way, since schools should not be used for evangelistic purposes.

Approaches

1   If you wish to explore 'pictures of Jesus', and think the children will have some impressions of Jesus, begin by exploring their ideas of what he was like. Move on to 'interview' other people and collect their impressions. See if he is represented in stained glass in local churches, for example. Introduce children to a selection of pictures of Jesus, ideally from around the world. Compare them with the impressions collected from the children and other people, and examine them in the light of the questions suggested (see above).

2   Explore the story of the call of the disciples, following the ideas suggested above. Add to this the charge given to the disciples in Mark 6:7–13. Discuss with the children how Peter, Andrew, James and John might have felt. If possible, meet with members of a local church to ask them questions about the meaning of this passage for them.

3   Develop the theme of response through contact with a religious order. Many schools will be within reach of a religious community with whom they might establish some links. The dress of the order, their vows, their disciplined devotional life, and the tasks undertaken by the community will all to some degree express responses to Jesus' story and could be explored by the children.

SECTION 3: FOR 9–11 YEAR OLDS

The many faces of Jesus. In these pictures Jesus is portrayed by a Chinese and an English artist, and in the tradition of the Serbian Orthodox Church.

4   Using the guidelines suggested above, tell the story of Mother Teresa, Paul Brand or Mary Verghese. Mother Teresa's story can be found in *In the Streets of Calcutta* by A Constant (RMEP 1980) and *Mother Teresa* by M Craig (Hamish Hamilton 1983).

Mary Verghese is the subject of J Clifford's *Wheelchair Surgeon* (RMEP 1986), and Paul Brand's story is told in J Young's *Paul Brand* (SCM 1980) and D C Wilson's *Ten Fingers for God* (Hodder & Stoughton 1965).

5   Carry out a project on the hymns people like to sing. This might take the form of a questionnaire to local congregations if they are willing to cooperate, or it might even involve writing to leading local figures. A similar project on favourite Bible passages led to one school writing to many public figures and publishing their replies (see *Best Bible Bits*, Church House Publishing 1984).

6   Look at a selection of hymns to see what they say about Jesus, bearing in mind the guidelines on pages 120–121.

Activities

1   The above approaches lend themselves to a variety of written responses, for example:

Newspaper reports
Scripts for plays or 'radio'
   presentations
Eyewitness/first person accounts
Diaries
Letters to friends

◀ *Christ Pantocrator* (Ruler of all things). Serbian Orthodox Church of St Lazare, Birmingham

▲ *Christ in Majesty* (detail) by Graham Sutherland, Coventry Cathedral

▶ A twentieth-century Chinese painting of Jesus

2 Plan for a class/school exhibition on 'Christian responses to Jesus' which, drawing on all the approaches suggested here, looks at past and present responses and might be open to visitors—or perhaps be mounted in a local church at an appropriate time like Pentecost (see page 118).

3 If you have the opportunity, watch some extracts from films of the life of Jesus, often available on video; eg Zeffirelli's *Jesus of Nazareth*. Let the children read some gospel passages and imagine a scene or incident for themselves, noting down their ideas; look at the appropriate section of the film. Discuss with the children whether it was like or unlike their 'pictures'.

4 Find out more about *icons*, 'special' paintings of Jesus and the saints in the Orthodox churches. Good poster reproductions of icons are available from St Paul's Bookshop, 199 Kensington High Street, London W8 6BA. Read Rumer Godden's *The Kitchen Madonna* (Macmillan 1967), which sensitively recognises the importance of icons in the life of Orthodox Christians as well as telling the story of two children who became involved in 'creating' an icon.

Resources

Books

J Lawson, *A Thousand Tongues*, Paternoster Press 1987 (detailed study of John and Charles Wesley's hymns exploring their relation to biblical teaching; reference work for teacher who really wants to pursue this)

B Lealman, *Christ—Who's That?*, CEM 1983 (booklet for secondary schools; useful background for teachers on exploring pictures; it also includes a section on 'other' religions' views of Jesus)

N Martin, *The Life of Jesus*, Wayland 1986 (for primary schools, one of a new series of religious stories)

T Shannon, *Jesus*, Lutterworth Press 1982 (one of the Chichester Project series for secondary schools; some useful background for primary school)

D Thomas, *The Face of Christ*, Paul Hamlyn 1979 (an attempt to explore the many ways in which Jesus has been portrayed; teacher reference work, but children might look at the pictures)

Two series of books offer biographies: RMEP's *Faith in Action* series and SCM's *People with a Purpose*.

AVA

B Lealman, *Christ in Art*, CEM (24 slides with notes; intended for secondary schools but the pictures are usable with different age ranges)

6 Krishna

This unit seeks to help children to enjoy some of the stories told of Krishna and to begin to discover a little of what these stories, and Krishna himself, mean for **Hindus**.

Information

The names of Rama and Sita have become well known in many classrooms through the celebration of Divali. For many Hindus the name of Krishna may be even more familiar. Stories of Krishna's life are manifold and appeal to all ages. He is the great teacher of the popular Hindu scripture, the *Bhagavad Gita* (section 2, page 68); his image is found in many temples; his birth is celebrated in the festival of *Janamashtami* and he is the focus of devotion for millions of Hindus.

Who is Krishna?

Hindus believe that 'God is one', but affirm also that he can be known, spoken of and represented (see 'Images and pictures of Krishna' below) in many ways. Hinduism thinks of Krishna as an *avatar*, a descent or 'downcoming' of Vishnu. Vishnu is one of the principal Hindu deities and is identified with Brahman, the Supreme Being. To put right all the wrong in the world, Vishnu is said to come down to earth from time to time. He has done so as Rama and as Krishna, as well as appearing in other forms. This idea of restoring order in the world, and of bringing good where there is evil is an underlying theme in many stories of Krishna.

For many Hindus, Krishna is also the focus of *bhakti*—loving devotion; this is one of the traditional Hindu ways to God, combining worship and 'right' living. In the stories of Krishna and Radha, Radha often serves as a symbol of *bhakti*.

Stories about Krishna

It is helpful to separate stories about Krishna into three groups. The first two may be most useful for this age group: they provide some of the popular stories which Hindu children will know.

First, there are stories about **Krishna's birth and mischievous childhood in Vrindaban**. The birth stories are about his miraculous escape from the evil designs of his wicked uncle Kansa. The childhood stories present the boy as a beautiful, immeasurably strong, personally engaging but infuriatingly self-willed child and youth. He steals milk and butter; teaches himself the flute and uses its sounds to charm both the cows and the *gopis* (cowherd girls); he dances on the head of Kaliya, a monstrous serpent which, by poisoning a lake, has killed his friends and cows, and by his dancing subdues it.

A further dimension to the time Krishna spent in Vrindaban focuses on the love which Radha (one of the *gopis*) had for him.

Here is the story of Krishna's escape from Kansa to safety.

The Birth of Lord Krishna

Long ago, there was a wicked king called Kansa, who was told by his sages that one day he would be killed by the eighth child born to his sister, Devaki.

Kansa was terrified and enraged. He decided to kill every child that Devaki had. He plotted to keep a guard on Devaki and her husband, Vasudeva. He had them watched night and day so that the minute a baby was born it would be destroyed.

Kansa wanted to keep his evil plan a secret. He made his guards swear not to tell anyone. 'I don't want the gods to hear about it,' he said.

But the gods did hear about it. Lord Vishnu, the Preserver, God of Goodness and Mercy, heard about it. Vishnu has the power to be born again many times and in many different ways. He decided to be reborn as Devaki's eighth child. 'I will be the one to destroy King Kansa,' he said.

When Devaki's eighth child was due to be born, Kansa had her and Vasudeva imprisoned. They were chained to the walls, and guards sat night and day at the door. Vasudeva clenched his fist with anguish. How could he save their baby?

It was the very middle of the night and a strange calm hung over the world. A full moon floated majestically over a trembling earth. There was not even a breath of a wind to stir the dusty ground.

Suddenly, the moment arrived. Devaki's eighth child was born. As the dark, moist body of a boy wriggled into the world, a shiver of excitement vibrated round the universe. Up in heaven the drums thudded wildly. Lord Indra sent a shower of flowers and raindrops tumbling down out of the sky. All the devas and apsaras, the nymphs and the rishis burst into song. 'Lord Vishnu is reborn as a man, and his name is Krishna!'

Vasudeva held his son fearfully. Everyone was asleep. The women who should have helped with the birth were snoring in a corner. Outside the prison door, the guards were slumped on the floor.

Suddenly the baby opened his eyes. It was like the windows of heaven opening. Devaki and Vasudeva found the chains had fallen from their bodies, and the locks on the door flew open.

'Quick! Escape! Save our baby!' cried Devaki.

Vasudeva gathered up baby Krishna. 'I'll take him somewhere safe,' he whispered.

With tears streaming down her face, Devaki kissed her child, then Vasudeva crept out into the night.

Crossing the river Yamuna or Jumna

On the other side of the River Yamuna lived a cowherd and his wife called Nanda and Yasoda. They were good, honest people, and Vasudeva knew he could trust them. He hurried down to the river banks, and holding his baby close began to wade across.

Suddenly, a storm blew up. The waters swirled and began to rise higher and higher. Desperately, Vasudeva held the baby above his head. Just when he thought they must both drown, the baby Krishna stretched out his little foot and dipped it in the angry waters. Immediately the river became calm. The waters fell and Vasudeva could get across.

In the dark of night, Vasudeva handed his precious son to Nanda and Yasoda. They looked on the beautiful boy and loved him as their own child.

(from 'The Birth of Lord Krishna' in *Stories from the Hindu World* by J Gavin, Macdonald 1986)

Secondly, there are **stories about the hero Krishna** who fought evil wherever he found it and was acclaimed the saviour of his people who were oppressed by evil rulers and their supporters; demons in both human and animal guise attacked him but were overwhelmed. These stories point beyond the hero Krishna to the god Vishnu and in story after story Krishna is recognised for who he 'really' is. His final triumph is over Kansa, the evil uncle who sought to destroy Krishna.

Thirdly, Krishna appears in the **Bhagavad Gita** where he is the divine guru; the *Gita* is a poem, itself part of an even longer epic poem, the *Mahabharata*. In the *Gita*, Arjuna is the hero facing a troubled conscience over whether or not to fight the enemy who are his own kin. Arjuna's charioteer on the battlefield turns out to be none other than Krishna; the *Gita* comprises his advice and teaching to Arjuna, and Arjuna's realisation that in Krishna he has encountered God.

'The Hatred that Led to War' in *Stories from the Hindu World* (see above) tells the story of Arjuna and Krishna in a simple way for children.

Celebrating Krishna's birthday

Krishna's birth is remembered at the festival known as *Janamashtami* or *Krishna Jayanti*, celebrated around August/September. Here is a brief description of how the festival may be celebrated in India:

Krishna is said to have been born at midnight, so many Hindus fast and stay up until that time in order to greet the baby Krishna with singing and dancing, and with offerings of butter and curds. The festival is celebrated with great enthusiasm at such Krishnaite centres as Mathura, Krishna's birthplace, and Vrindaban where Krishna is said to have spent his childhood. Pilgrims from all over India are attracted to these places for the festival where night-long prayers are recited and devotional songs are sung in the temples, which are decorated for the occasion with flowers and fruit. The festival is also celebrated in the home, where an image of the baby Krishna may be placed on a small swing or in a cradle, and pictures showing important incidents from Krishna's life may be displayed.

(*Festivals in World Religions* by Alan Brown (Ed), Longman 1986, p 129)

The story of Krishna's birth is a suitable one to tell at this time.

Images and pictures of Krishna

For most Hindus worship focuses on images. Since some religions (eg Judaism, Islam and Christianity in its Protestant form) have rejected the use of images and representational art, it is important that Hindus' use of images is seen on its own terms. First, it is better not to use the word 'idol'; 'image' is better, but the Hindu *murti* tells us more. The word refers to the 'face' of God. Whilst there are many deities and many images, for the devotee who worships a particular deity the image focuses God's presence.

Approaches

Stories of Krishna could find a place in a number of RE topics: worship; sacred buildings; birth and childhood stories; and festivals would all provide scope. The following ideas are for those wanting to focus simply on Krishna.

1   *Dharma*, 'order' or 'things as they should be' is an important idea in Hinduism: it relates to the natural world, to society and to individuals. Ideas of 'order' and 'disorder' might be explored with children; their ideas about the world as they think it should be, or of what spoils it, might be discussed.

Against this kind of background, introduce the stories of Krishna which explore this theme.

2   The stories of Krishna might be told over a week around the time of Jana-mashtami. Discuss with the children *why* they think the stories are remembered and told and retold. Who do they think will enjoy them most?

With the older children you might discuss carefully whether the stories are 'true', not in the sense of 'Did they happen?' but attempting to discover what they 'say' about God, and about human fears and hopes.

3   An artefact approach may prove helpful. Small, colourful plastic images of Radha and Krishna can be bought quite cheaply or borrowed from a resource

Radha and Krishna luxuriously dressed in royal robes are the focus for worship in this shrine. The sight (*darshana*) of the image can be understood as a favour granted by the deity to the worshipper.

SECTION 3: FOR 9–11 YEAR OLDS

centre. Children can be invited to comment on what they see: a dancing, crowned, flute-playing, handsome, blue male figure with a beautiful companion (often carrying a pot on her head). Children can be helped to 'read' such images by reading or listening to stories that Hindus tell about Radha and Krishna. *The Shap Handbook on World Religions in Education* (CRE 1987) has a useful section (pp 118–120) on religious artefacts and their use.

An opportunity to visit a Hindu temple or to look at worship in a Hindu home and see images *in situ* would complement this work very well.

Activities

1 Telling stories through puppet plays is popular in India. Make stick puppets to tell some of the stories of Krishna. Prepare simple scripts for individual voices and a narrator. Perform for parents, another class or an assembly.

2 Miniature paintings of Krishna and the *gopis* (cowherd girls), especially Radha, always show them in idyllic surroundings in the great forest of Vrindaban (see Resources). It is still a tradition to paint such scenes.

Create and colour some 'forest miniatures' in a similar style and very beautifully.

You might go on to discuss why Krishna is shown in such lovely surroundings. Is it just because Vrindaban was forested, or is there a hidden message about who Krishna is and his purpose and influence in the world?

Radha and Krishna in a beautiful grove of the forest of Vrindaban. The love which Radha showed for Krishna is symbolic of the devotee's love for God.

3 If you have told some of the stories of Krishna early in the autumn term, mark Hindus' celebration of Krishna's birth. Set up a small shrine (see under 'Celebrating Krishna's birthday' above); surround it with pictures (commercial or prepared by the children). Make it as colourful as possible.

Discuss the offerings Hindus might make at this festival: milk, butter and sweets. Why these?

Make some Indian sweets—a recipe for *burfi* is given here—and share them on the day of the festival, ideally inviting in some guests to learn about Krishna from the children.

Burfi

Ingredients

2 packets of desiccated coconut
1 cup of sugar
$\frac{1}{4}$ cup of melted butter
1 large tin of evaporated milk
3 cups of water

What to do

1 Mix the coconut with the evaporated milk.
2 Melt the butter.
3 Boil the sugar and water until it thickens (be careful).
4 Lower the heat and add the coconut mix.
5 Gradually add the butter, stirring all the time.
6 Allow mixture to thicken. You can add nuts or fruit or flavouring here if you want.
7 Spread the mixture in a shallow tin.
8 Wait a few moments and then mark into squares. Leave to cool.

(from *Divali and other aspects of Hinduism*, Resources Centre for Multi-Racial Education Peterborough 1981, p 74)

Resources

Books
M Aggarwal, *I am a Hindu*, Franklin Watts 1984 (focuses on a child in a Hindu family who are devotees of Krishna)
P Bahree, *The Hindu World*, Macdonald 1982 (information book for this age range; it has a section on Hindu gods and Brahman)
J Green, *Childhood Pastimes of Krishna: Krishna, master of all mystics*, Bala Books 1981
J Green, *Childhood Pastimes of Krishna: Kaliya King of serpents*, Bala Books 1979
(Bala Books publish classics from India. The first of the two mentioned here has illustrations in the style of Indian miniatures (see Activities 2). Bala Books are available in England from Bhaktivedanta Book Trust, Croome Court, Severn Stoke, nr. Worcester WR8 9DW.)
H Kanitkar, *Hindu Stories*, Wayland 1986 (five stories including 'Krishna's escape' and 'Krishna tames Kaliya')

Sister Nivedita, *Cradle Tales of Hinduism*, available from Ramakrishna Vedanta Centre, Bourne End, Bucks SL8 5LG (a classic telling of Hindu stories; gives the Krishna ones in some detail; useful for the teacher)

AVA
The Hindu Gods, E731, Pictorial Charts Educational Trust (small posters of miniature paintings of a number of Hindu gods including Krishna)
The Krishna Legend, Ann & Bury Peerless, 22 Kings Avenue, Minnis Bay, Birchington, Kent (a set of 24 slides, again based on miniatures; brief notes included)
Artefacts can be obtained from C M Winstanley, Articles of Faith, 123 Neville Road, Salford M7 OPP.

SECTION 3: FOR 9–11 YEAR OLDS

7 Muhammad

The aims of this unit are that children should become familiar with some stories about Muhammad and encounter him in the context of a believing community who remember and speak of him today.

Information

The First Revelation

Muhammad grew up in Makkah [Mecca], where he married Khadija, a wealthy widow.

At the time, the people of Makkah worshipped idols, but Muhammad was different. He believed in only one God.

He often used to leave the bustling city streets to go away to a cave where he could pray in peace.

The cave was in Mount Hira, just outside the city. It was the Prophet's custom to spend the month of Ramadan there, praying and fasting.

It was during this month, when the Prophet was forty years old, that the Archangel Gabriel appeared to him in the cave, and commanded: 'Read!'

'I cannot read!' stammered the Prophet, for like many people at that time, he could neither read nor write.

Then the Angel embraced the Prophet, holding him so tightly that he thought he would faint. Just when he thought he could bear it no longer, the Angel released him, and commanded him again: 'Read!'

'I cannot read,' the Prophet repeated.

A second time, the Angel embraced the Prophet and commanded him to read—but the reply was the same. Then after a third embrace, the Angel said:

'Read! In the name of thy Lord, who createth,
Createth man from a drop of blood.
Read: and thy Lord is Most Generous:
Who teacheth man the use of the pen,
And teacheth him that which he knew not before.'

Muhammad repeated these words, and knew that he would never forget them. But he was very much afraid, and as soon as he thought he was alone again, he ran from the cave and rushed towards the city.

As he ran, he heard the voice once more:

'Oh, Muhammad, you are the Messenger of Allah, and I am Gabriel.'

He stood still, and looked up. The Archangel stood on the horizon before him, so huge that his figure filled the sky. And whichever way Muhammad turned, the Angel towered before him.

By the time Muhammad had reached his home and his wife, he was shaking with fear. She wrapped him in a blanket, and he told her what had happened.

Khadija knew the story was important—but she did not know what it meant. So she sought out her cousin Waraqa, who was a wise and learned Christian.

'It is the same message that Allah sent to Moses,' Waraqa told her. 'It means that Muhammad is the Prophet of our people. Tell him to be of good cheer.'

But later, he met the Prophet at the Ka'aba, the holy place in Makkah, and he gave him this warning:

'No man has ever brought the message you bring without being opposed. They will call you a liar, and they will cast you out and fight against you. Truly, if I live to see that day, I will help you all I can.'

(from *Stories from the Muslim World* by H Khattab, Macdonald 1987, pp 16–17)

Reading this story takes you immediately to the heart of Muslim belief about Muhammad and the Qur'an. For Muslims the Qur'an is the word of God; it was set down in writing exactly as it was told to Muhammad by the Angel Gabriel. Notice too that Muhammad is unable to read or write: he has to repeat or 'recite' the words he is given by Gabriel. Although Muhammad was unlettered, the words he recited were in the most beautiful Arabic. The language itself points to the divine origin of the message. The revelation of the Qur'an continued throughout Muhammad's life and is believed by Muslims to be God's final message to mankind. Because the Qur'an is literally God's word it is treated with great respect (see section 2, pages 66–67). Translations of it are not adequate and it is important to be able to read it in Arabic. Many Muslims commit all of it to memory, and gain the title of *Hafiz*.

Muhammad's place in Muslim belief

Arabic, the language of the Qur'an, has inspired beautiful calligraphy. The *Shahadah*, the Muslim profession of faith, although shown in two distinct styles here, is recognisable by the bold upright strokes of the pen.

SECTION 3: FOR 9–11 YEAR OLDS

'There is no god but God and Muhammad is his messenger.'

These words are the *Shahadah* (the first of the Five Pillars and declaration of faith); to speak them with serious intention is to become a Muslim and to follow the path of Islam. The words recognise the importance of Muhammad and his role as God's prophet and messenger. Just as the Qur'an is God's final revelation to mankind, so is Muhammad the last prophet. Muslims recognise that there have been many prophets and the Qur'an tells of many of those whose names are familiar to Jews and Christians too. But Muhammad is the 'Seal of the Prophets' and with the message he is given, all earlier revelations are superseded.

Telling Muhammad's story

From an early stage in Muslim history there was an interest in the life of Muhammad. People noted and remembered what he said and did; eventually his words and actions were collected and written down. These collections became known as the *Hadith* ('Tradition'). Writing biography was also of interest to Muslims; three key biographies of Muhammad appear to have been in circulation by the eighth and ninth centuries CE. Stories drawn from sources such as these are now becoming available (see Resources). For those who want to place the stories in a historical context, the following time chart and overview of his life will be useful, though a 'life of Muhammad' is not the main concern here.

Muhammad's life: some important dates

c. 570 CE — Born in Mecca. His father died before his birth.

576 — Muhammad's mother dies; he is then brought up by his grandfather and later by his uncle, Abu Talib.

595 — Marries Khadijah, a wealthy widow.

610 — The date of the first revelation.

613 — Muhammad begins to preach in Mecca.

620 — The year of the night journey to Jerusalem.

622 — Emigration to Medina—known as the *Hijrah*. This is regarded as the beginning of the Muslim Era. The Muslim lunar calendar starts from this year.

630 — Muhammad returns to Mecca; the city is won over to Islam and the idols in the Ka'aba are destroyed.

632 — Muhammad dies in Medina and is buried there.

The message Muhammad received in Mecca declared the existence of one God (Allah); it challenged the wealthy to be generous and take care of the needy and it warned them that one day God would be their judge. Like many prophets before him Muhammad was at first rejected by his own people. In 622 CE he decided to emigrate to Medina, accepting the invitation of some Medinans who had pledged loyalty to him and his message and wanted his help in Medina.

But first he had to leave Mecca, avoiding those who wished him ill. Here is the well-known story of the *Hijrah* as told for Muslim children.

Allah is with us

The night was dark. It was already past midnight. In a few hours the first rays of sunlight would appear. Then the Quraysh would realise that Muhammad, the Prophet (Peace and Blessings be upon him)*, had slipped through their fingers and then the chase would be on. They would leave no part of the city unsearched.

---

* Muslims are required to invoke Allah's blessings and peace upon the Prophet whenever his name is mentioned.

The Blessed Prophet had already left his house and Ali lay asleep in the Blessed Prophet's bed. The house was being surrounded by 12 young men of the Quraysh who, jointly, had plotted to kill the Blessed Prophet that night. He knew the time to emigrate had arrived. The preparations had already been made. From his own house the Blessed Prophet came to Abu Bakr's house in Misfala, the part of Makka [Mecca] which lay just to the south of Ka'ba. Although they wanted to reach Madina [Medina] in the north, they took the route to the south. They knew that the first place the enemy would look after realising that Muhammad had escaped, would be the way to Madina and the house of Abu Bakr. So to confuse their pursuers and gain time they went south.

Soon the Prophet and Abu Bakr came to the mountains and hills which lie south of Makka. They began looking for a place where they could take refuge while the enemy was searching for them. After trudging up and down mountain paths, they found a cave on Mount Thaur. It was desolate, isolated and very deep. It seemed never to have been visited by human beings before.

The night was still dark, except for the light from the stars. Abu Bakr entered the cave first, cleared it of pebbles and stones, and began looking for snakes which might harm the Blessed Prophet. He took off a garment he was wearing, tore it into strips and filled up every hole he could find. After making the cave safe and secure, he came out and invited the Blessed Prophet to step inside.

Abu Bakr loved no one more than the Blessed Prophet. He had faith in him when few were prepared to believe. He spent all his money for the cause of Islam. And now he was given the honour of accompanying the Blessed Prophet on that memorable journey to Madina which would change the course of human history.

Earlier, as they walked from Abu Bakr's house in Misfala to the cave of Thaur, Abu Bakr sometimes fell behind and sometimes moved briskly on ahead. The Blessed Prophet asked him why he didn't stay by his side. Abu Bakr replied 'I am on the lookout for any threat or danger. Sometimes I go back and see if anyone is following us, and sometimes I go ahead to see if there is any danger.'

'You mean', said the Blessed Prophet, 'you love me so much you would face danger rather than let any harm come to me?'

'Yes, O Prophet', Abu Bakr replied.

By the time the Blessed Prophet and Abu Bakr had settled in the cave it was dawn and back at Makka the young men found out that the man who had been sleeping in the Blessed Prophet's bed was not the Blessed Prophet but Ali. They became very angry and frustrated. Immediately they launched a search for the Blessed Prophet. Saddling their horses they galloped along the road to Madina, but found no tracks, so they gave up and came back. Then they spread out around the city searching to the east, west and south. Finally they hired expert trackers to discover by which route the Blessed Prophet had left the city. Soon, saddling up again, they headed for the mountains south of Makka. Now they were on the right trail.

The Blessed Prophet and Abu Bakr were huddled in the cave. Even though they had travelled in the opposite direction to confuse the Quraysh and were in a cave which they believed would not be easily discovered by their enemies, they still did not feel secure.

Abu Bakr looked around again and again and, fearfully, strained his ears for any sounds.

Eventually they heard footsteps. Quite a few people had arrived in the area. Accompanied by the trackers, they covered the hills on foot and by horseback, trying to find where the Blessed Prophet and Abu Bakr were hiding. Finally they reached the mouth of the cave. But they found that a spider had woven a web over the entrance. Obviously, they concluded, no one could be inside. One of the trackers, Kurz bin Alqama, remarked: 'The footsteps come to this point, then vanish. Where did they go from here?'

'Let us go inside', said another, 'maybe they are here.'

Ummayya bin Khalaf, a prominent Quraysh chief, was with them. He shook his head. 'There's no point in going inside the cave. What will you find there? No one has entered recently. The spider's web was woven long before Muhammad was born, I wager. Let's not waste any more time here.'

Another of the pursuers was standing so close to the mouth of the cave that the Blessed Prophet and Abu Bakr could see his feet. Abu Bakr was extremely worried and fearful, not for his own life, but in case any harm should come to the Blessed Prophet. He kept a close watch on the mouth of the cave, while the Blessed Prophet prayed. When the blessed Prophet had finished his Prayer, Abu Bakr, with tears in his eyes, whispered: 'They are directly above us now. They will see us and come inside.'

The Blessed Prophet smiled and looked with kindness at Abu Bakr. 'Why are you fearful, Abu Bakr?' he chided softly. 'There are not just two of us, Allah Himself is the third.'

Abu Bakr said 'I am not fearful for myself but for the harm they might do you before my eyes'.

The Prophet replied, 'Grieve not, for God is with us'.

There was not the slightest sign of worry on the Blessed Prophet's face, so real and intense was his faith in Allah, in His presence, in His succour. He saw with certainty that Allah was there with him, even though no material or physical help was in sight.

(from *Love Your God* by K Murad, The Islamic Foundation 1982)

This story, which marks the beginning of the Muslim calendar, also helps to build a picture of the kind of person Muhammad was. Clearly he was someone who inspired great loyalty and friendship; he is shown to be fearless and to possess courage. Above all he was aware of God's presence and placed his trust in God.

Notice that this story not only helps to build up a picture of the kind of person Muhammad was, but also relates to the life of the first Muslims *and* to Muslims now—through the *Hijrah* (migration to Medina) and the calendar. It is also a story which Muslims tell. These are useful criteria for selecting stories.

The story of Bilal would also meet these kinds of criteria. Bilal was a Muslim, the son of an African and a slave. His story shows Muslim attitudes to slavery (Bilal was freed by Abu Bakr, a companion of the prophet) and to people of different races. Bilal became the first *muezzin*, the first person to call the faithful to prayer, a practice which is still integral to daily prayer in Islam. Bilal's story can be found in *Stories from the Muslim World* (Macdonald 1987). This collection also tells of Muhammad's birth and of his childhood encounter with Bahira the monk; both stories point to Muhammad as a great prophet.

Remembering Muhammad's example

We noted earlier that Muhammad's words and actions were remembered by his followers. As well as stories which relate to key events in his life—such as those we have noted above—there are many which are based on these kinds of recollections. Muslims believe that Muhammad in all his words and actions was at one with the message he preached. His life can therefore be an example to them: it expresses what it is to be a Muslim.

The following story is taken from a collection about Muhammad and children, based on Hadith and written primarily for Muslim children.

Kindness towards children of an enemy

The love which the Prophet had for children was not love for Muslim children only, but love for all little ones, no matter who they were. This was why the Prophet became very deeply distressed on the day when some of his people told him that in a battle, some children had been killed by accident.

The Prophet's friends were puzzled to see him so terribly upset. 'Why are you so sad, O Messenger of Allah?' they said. 'The children who were killed were not Muslim children. They were children of our enemy.'

The Prophet's friends said this to lessen his sadness, but their efforts did not succeed. The Prophet remained sad and depressed by the news that little children had been killed in war. As far as he was concerned, children had nothing to do with war or fighting or death in battle, and that went for non-Muslim as well as Muslim children.

'Remember,' he told his friends 'these children were innocent.' They had committed no crime, nor had they committed an act of war against the Muslims. Children were not capable of doing such things.

'Wars are not of children's making', the Prophet said. Wars were made by adults and children should be kept out of wars.

Certainly, they should not be killed in war. It was because the Prophet believed this very deeply that he strictly forbad the killing of children, no matter who they were.

(from *A Great Friend of Children* by M S Kayani, Islamic Foundation 1981, pp 33–5)

Approaches

1   Familiarity with some of the stories about Muhammad is the main aim of this unit, and simply telling a range of stories to let the children build up a picture of Muhammad and the kind of person he was provides an immediate approach.

2   It may be possible to show children a Qur'an, and to use pictures and slides to show how it is sometimes illuminated. How can the children tell this is a special book? The ways in which it is handled also indicate that it is special. This discussion may lead to the question of what makes it so special, and so to the story of the first revelation.

(Note that some Muslims may not like a non-Muslim to handle an Arabic Qur'an.)

Activities

1   The *Shahadah* is frequently found as a decoration in the mosque, and so are 'Allah' and 'Muhammad' (see illustration on page 139). Calligraphy like this may

SECTION 3: FOR 9–11 YEAR OLDS

be found on cards, wallhangings, plaques, plates, car stickers, badges and pendants. Children might try to design one of these items, incorporating these symbols and perhaps using geometric designs (see page 100).

2 Prepare a play based on the story of the *Hijrah*. Since Muslims do not portray Muhammad in any way, Muhammad should not appear in the play.

3 Here are some sayings of Muhammad.

The believer is not he who eats his fill while his neighbour at his side is hungry.

Food for two is sufficient for three and food for three is sufficient for four.

Beware of envy, for envy devours good [deeds] like fire devours firewood.

The strong man is not the one who is strong in wrestling, but the one who controls himself in anger.

When you are three together, two [of you] must not converse privately without the third until you are in company of other people, because it makes him sad.

(from *A Day with the Prophet* by A von Denffer, The Islamic Foundation 1979)

Think about the meaning of the sayings with the children. They can then try to write their own stories which lead up to and end with one of the sayings.

'Allah' and 'Muhammad' written in Arabic
are central to this simple wall hanging which
might be found in a Muslim home or a
mosque.

Resources

Books
L Azzam and A Gouveurneur, *The Life of the Prophet Muhammad*,
 Islamic Texts Society 1985 (based on early Muslim sources, and
 written for 10–15 year olds; useful for teacher reference too)
M Davies, *The Life of Muhammad*, Wayland 1987 (written and
 illustrated by Muslims; intended for primary school)
The Islamic Foundation, 223 London Road, Leicester LE2 1ZE,
publishes a range of story books for 8–11 year olds. They are
primarily for Muslim children but can be adapted for school use. In
addition to those referred to in the text the following also relate to
Muhammad.
M S Kayani, *Love all Creatures*, 1981
K Murad, *Love at Home*, 1983
M A Tarantino, *Marvellous Stories from the Life of Muhammad*, 1982
Most of these stories are also available on audio-cassette.

AVA
Postcards of some of the beautifully illuminated Qur'ans in their
possession are available from the British Museum; a set of 18 slides
is also available from them under the title *Islamic Calligraphy and
Illumination*.
Quranic Alphabet, Islamic Circle Organisation 1983 (a book of
 pictures, calligraphy and quotations from the Qur'an; pleasing to
 handle and look at)
Islamic Worship and Devotion, REAP Poster Pack, CEM (a pack of
 three posters with notes; one poster shows a Qur'an open for
 reading)
Cassettes of the Qur'an being read in Arabic are available from shops
specialising in Middle Eastern publications.

SECTION 3: FOR 9–11 YEAR OLDS

8 Dying and Living

This unit helps children to explore stories which are concerned with death and life and to begin to understand how some stories express some of the deepest human questions and hopes.

Information

This unit continues the study which was proposed in section 2, page 72.

Stories are one of the most important ways in which religious meaning is expressed.

Sometimes the word 'myth' is used for the special kind of story which is at the heart of every religion. Special definitions need not detain us here, but it is important to understand that the common use of the word 'myth' to mean an 'untruth' is exactly the opposite of its meaning in religious expression. Myths hold the *deepest* truths of religions and grapple with the big questions such as:

Where did life come from?
Why is there suffering and evil?
How did death come into the world?

Sometimes they also contain a whole community's beliefs about humankind, or about God and the gods.

The stories studied in this unit are not all 'myths' in this strict sense but they all show how the dynamic of a narrative can hold ideas which cannot be satisfactorily expressed in propositions.

Approaches

Questions about death and life are fundamental to religions, and stories and myths on these themes occur again and again in every country and culture. In studying the examples provided and others which the teacher can find, the opportunity should be used to elicit children's own thoughts and feelings about these great issues without in any way trying to settle the matter.

Myths and stories of death and life: some examples

In section 1, page 22, the story of the Buddha's encounter with poverty, suffering, disease and death is told. The story of Kisagotami, a distressed mother, tells of how the Buddha himself urged his followers to perceive death as part of everyone's experience; it reflects also Buddhist belief in the impermanence of life.

The Story of Kisagotami

Kisagotami was born into a very poor family and had the reputation of being frail and tiring easily. When she was old enough to be married she went to live with her husband's family. Because she had come from a poor home they treated her without much respect until she gave birth to a son. Then their attitude was quite different and she was treated with both kindness and honour. Her situation was now a happy one, but this did not last for long. When her son was old enough to run about and play he become ill and died. Kisagotami was desolate. She had not only lost the child she loved, but also her respected position in her home. In her grief she picked up the body of her child and wandered from one house to another, asking for medicine for her son.

The people who met her laughed and sneered. 'Whoever heard of medicine for the dead?' they said.

By now Kisagotami was almost driven out of her mind by her sorrow. A wise man saw her wandering about and realised how much she needed help. He had heard some of the teaching of Gautama Buddha, and thought that he might be able to help her come to terms with her grief. He approached Kisagotami gently and told her that the Buddha was staying nearby and that he might have medicine for her son. 'Go and ask him' he said.

Kisagotami went to find the Buddha and stood on the edge of the crowd, listening to him. When she had the chance, she called out to him.

'O, Exalted One, give me medicine for my son.'

Part of the Buddha's greatness was his skill in knowing how to help other people. He told her kindly to go to the city nearby and visit every house. 'Bring me some grains of mustard seed from every household in which no one has ever died.'

Kisagotami was delighted. Here was someone who took her seriously. She went to the city, knocked on the first house and asked for some grains of mustard seed from the householder, if no one had ever died there. The householder told her with great sadness that he had recently lost his wife. Kisagotami listened to his story with growing sympathy, understanding his grief from her own. She eventually moved on, but found that in every house there was a story of sickness, old age and death. Her own grief seemed different now that she shared that of others, and she realised that the Buddha had known when he sent her out that she would find that her predicament was the common experience of human beings. Death is the law common to all that lives.

She now took the body of her dear little son to the cremation ground and let it be cremated, fully realising that all is impermanent.

Kisagotami then returned to Gautama Buddha. He asked her whether she had brought him the grains of mustard seed. She told him what had happened, and what she had realised. She then asked him to accept her as his follower and to teach her more about the nature of reality and the path to understanding.

(from *Buddhist Stories* presented by Peggy Morgan, Westminster College, Oxford)

Death is a fundamental part of human experience, and the question of how death came into the world, as well as suffering and other evils, is the theme of many myths. The story used here is no longer part of a living religious tradition, but the phrase 'Pandora's box' has entered idiomatically into the language of those influenced by Greek culture.

Prometheus had given fire—the possession of the Gods—to humankind: the only gift he could think of after Epimetheus has distributed *all* the other gifts the Gods had provided for men. In the version of the story from which this extract is taken, the Gods have bound Prometheus and seek to curb men's power. They create Pandora, and then . . .

SECTION 3: FOR 9–11 YEAR OLDS

Pandora's Box

Then Zeus prepared a box and filled it with all kinds of evil things—pain, fear, envy, pride, deceit, hate, sickness and death. Turning to Mercury, Zeus said, 'Take Pandora down to the earth and give her to Epimetheus. As you leave her to return to Olympus, give her this box and tell her it is a good gift only if she never opens it. The day she looks inside the box, evil will come to her and to all men.'

Long weeks and months went by and Epimetheus and Pandora were happy together. They visited the homes of men, they walked through the fields and knew many joys. But again and again, Pandora became very curious about the box. 'The gods and goddesses gave me many beautiful things. The things in the box may be lovelier still.'

Finally one day when Epimetheus was not at home, Pandora could no longer control her curiosity. 'I simply must see what is in the box,' she thought. 'I will just lift the lid a little bit and see inside.' But the moment the cover was loosened, all the evil creatures imprisoned inside came forth. Pandora ran away screaming, not knowing which way to turn.

Epimetheus was not far away and came running home. When he saw what had happened, he fastened the lid down again. But it was too late. Pain and hate, jealousy and fear, deceit and envy, sickness and death—all had come forth. Now that they were free, they rushed into every corner of the world.

Late that night, Epimetheus and Pandora heard a faint noise coming from the closed box. A voice seemed to cry, 'I am Hope. Let me out.' For a long time they would not go near the box. But Epimetheus finally said, 'It cannot be worse than the things that were freed. Perhaps it really is Hope as it claims to be.'

So they opened the box again, and Hope came out. She went forth into the world . . .

(from *Beginnings: Earth, Sky, Life, Death* by S L Fahs and D T Spoerl, Beacon Press 1958, pp 129–30)

The story of Adam and Eve, shared by Jews, Christians and Muslims, deals with this same problem: how suffering and death came into the world.

Myths worldwide speak also of a great flood in which humankind is destroyed because of its wickedness. The biblical story of Noah is one such story. In the Hindu tradition the story of Manu is well known. The fish is actually an *avatar* (see page 126) of the great god Vishnu, who once more 'comes down' to save humankind.

Manu and the Fish

Manu was a wise and holy man who devoted his life to the worship of the gods. One day he was praying by the banks of a river, when he heard a tiny voice calling.

'O great and holy Manu,' the voice said, 'I appeal to you for help. You're a holy man; it's your duty to help and protect the weak.'

Manu looked round to see who was speaking. But there was no one there. Then the voice came again. 'In here,' it said. Astonished,

Manu saw that it was coming from a tiny fish in the river in front of him.

Carefully, he filled his cupped hands with water, bent and brought out the fish.

'Tell me what I can do for you, little one,' he said. 'Help me,' said the fish. 'You see how small I am. In the river I'm the smallest living thing: my life is in danger from enemies of every size. 'What must I do to help?' asked Manu. 'Put me in a jar, safe on land,' said the fish. 'In return, I'll save your life as well. A great flood is coming, all mankind will be swept away. If you help me, you alone will escape.'

Manu did not take this promise very seriously: even if there was a flood, how could a tiny fish save him? Nevertheless, he fetched a large clay jar, filled it with water and placed the little fish in it.

Now this was no ordinary fish. In no time it had grown too big for the jar, and Manu had to dig a pond for it outside. Before long, even the pond was too small, and Manu carried the fish, which was now huge, to the river Ganges.

Before it flopped into the river and made off to the ocean, the fish spoke again to Manu. It told him when the flood would come, and gave him instructions. He was to build a large boat, in good time, so that he would be safe when all the land was flooded. In it he was to put seeds of every kind of plant, and a length of strong rope. The fish promised that he himself would reappear, and save Manu when the floods came. Manu would recognize him by a large horn on his head.

As the fish swam away, Manu realized that it was not really a fish at all, but the god Vishnu, preserver of life himself. No mortal could look at a god and live; so Vishnu had appeared to him as a fish, in a form he could recognize and understand.

Respectfully, Manu bowed his head; when he looked up, the fish had gone. Manu hurried home and began to build a boat, as he had been instructed. He gathered seeds of every kind of plant, and plaited a length of rope. When all was done, he waited for the flood.

When the storms began and the waters rose, Manu set out in his boat across the sea. Before long, the great fish reappeared, and Manu made a noose in his rope and fastened it to the horn on the fish's head. Towed by the fish, Manu's boat was safe from all danger.

At last the waters began to subside. The boat grounded on a mountain-peak high in the Himalayas, and the fish ordered Manu to moor it to the rock. Manu was the only survivor of the flood that destroyed mankind. He was the first of a new race, the father of all.

(from *Gods and Men* by J Bailey, K McLeish and D Spearman, OUP 1981)

And so life continues, but humankind's nature does not seem to change and death is still part of everyone's experience, as the Kisagotami story showed.

So what is the way through? Religions usually offer a 'vision' of the resolution of the problems of suffering and death, and they speak of ways and paths through life until the vision becomes a reality. The theme of the journey and quest is another popular one in mythology.

SECTION 3: FOR 9–11 YEAR OLDS

But the pictures they give to describe the final goal of humankind provide the other side of those about suffering and death with which this topic started. The pictures are many; they point to symbolic or mythical places.

For the Buddhist the concept of *nirvana* expresses the ultimate goal for which he or she strives. The word suggests the blowing out of a flame: perhaps the extinguishing of all those things—greed, hate, desire—which for the Buddhist tie humankind to rebirth after rebirth after rebirth. *Nirvana* itself is beyond the description of words and images, and may take many rebirths to reach.

As the Buddha's teaching spread to China and Japan, many sects emerged. One of these is known as the Pure Land sect (belonging to the Mahayana branch of Buddhism). It teaches that it is possible to be reborn in a 'pure land'. From there it is possible to go on to reach the supreme enlightenment of *nirvana*.

This description is written as if it were the words of the Buddha to a disciple, Ananda, about the Pure Land. Amitabha is Lord of the Pure Land, one of innumerable *buddhas* (enlightened beings) who live beyond the world that humans know.

The Pure Land

This Pure Land, Ananda, which is the Land of the Lord Amitabha, is rich and prosperous, comfortable, fertile, delightful and crowded with gods and men. There are no jewels in our world to compare with the splendour of those which exist in the Pure Land. And nowhere in the Pure Land does one hear of anything bad. Nowhere does one hear of problems or punishments. Nowhere does one hear of sadness or bad luck or suffering. Indeed one does not hear about bad *or* good things at all.

And the beings in the Pure Land don't eat food as we do, like soup or raw sugar. Whatever food they want to eat, it is as if they had eaten it. They feel satisfied in body and mind, without having to push food into the body! And if they would like to smell certain perfumes, then the whole place becomes scented with just that kind of heavenly perfume. But if someone doesn't want to smell that perfume, then the scent doesn't reach him!

And all the beings who have been born, who are being born and will be born into this land, all of them are on the way to Nirvana. Why is this so? Because there is no place here for those who are set in wrong ways or for those who are completely aimless. For this reason the Pure Land is called sometimes 'The Happy Land'.

And if any people in earth, Ananda, reverently direct their minds to Amitabha, if they will really try to do right, if they long for Enlightenment and if they vow to be reborn in the Pure Land then Amitabha, the fully Enlightened One, will stand before them surrounded by hosts of monks. Then, having seen that Lord, and having died with hearts serene, they will be reborn in that Pure Land. And if there are sons and daughters of good family, who desire to have a vision of Amitabha in their earthly life, they should turn their thoughts with resoluteness and perseverance to that Pure Land and dedicate their store of merit from their good deeds to being reborn therein.

(from *Looking at Myth* by J Rankin, Lutterworth 1979; adapted from the Sukhativyuha in *Buddhist Scriptures* translated by Edward Conze 1959, reprinted by permission of Penguin Books)

Amida (Amitabha) Buddha, Japan

This then is a picture of people 'on their way' to their ultimate goal: note that many Buddhists will not take this description literally. It is a picture which offers insight about the goal towards which they are moving.

Muslims too have their picture of where they are going; they speak of judgment and then of heaven or hell. Heaven, or paradise, is pictured as a beautiful garden (see for example *surahs* 55 and 76 in the Qur'an). It is a garden full of trees; there are palms and pomegranates. The climate is just right too—there is neither sun nor bitter cold—and within the garden there are fountains and streams. Here those who have striven faithfully in the way of Allah find their needs satisfied and their striving rewarded. The idea of paradise as a beautiful garden is mirrored in some of the beautiful carpets from Muslim countries—a helpful 'aid' for exploring a Muslim vision of heaven with children.

SECTION 3: FOR 9–11 YEAR OLDS

The Qur'an speaks of paradise as a 'garden traversed by rivers'. Carpets produced in the Muslim world have often made use of this motif — and even depict rivers and water channels. Notice the trees and flowers in this design.

Using the stories

The stories are included under Approaches in this unit because the most obvious approach is simply to tell these stories, and others you may collect. They could perhaps be grouped under the broad themes used above.

> The experience of death
>
> Why death and suffering and evil?
>
> The destruction of evil and a 'fresh start'
>
> Beyond physical death: visions of 'heaven'

If other starting points are wanted, the following could be helpful.

1 In the context of a theme of 'Mystery', encourage children to think about their 'Top Ten' questions—questions they would most like answered. Draw up the

lists. Then 'sort' them with the children: extract questions to which there *are* answers, identify those which they think people will always ask, and those which seem most 'mysterious'. Use this questioning to introduce the topic of death and life.

2   Use the seasons to point to patterns of growth, change and death and rebirth. Explore feelings and moods about spring and autumn/winter.

Link with human experience—does this parallel the seasons, or is it different? What do the children think? With older children this may give rise to discussion of rebirth.

3   Open up the issue of stories and their meaning by using children's stories which share the themes of some of the myths. Two books for younger children (but with an appeal to all ages!) could be used here. Both are by Michael Foreman: *The Two Giants* (Hodder & Stoughton 1967) and *Panda's Puzzle* (Pocket Puffin 1987).

Activities

Myths appeal to the 'inner self', to emotions and the senses. The stories used will naturally lend themselves to creative activities in music, art, drama, dance and movement. In addition children might:

1   Discuss and create a visual display on the 'light' and 'dark' sides of life. This could draw on newspapers and news items, on the local environment, and children's own experiences.

2   Imagine Pandora's box had been full of good things. What would they have put into it?

3   Think about, and write or paint, their ideas of 'heaven' or 'paradise'. What would they like to be there and what things would they exclude?

4   Write their own stories about how greed, envy, suffering, for example, came into the world.

5   Read and listen to other myths on the themes of this unit.

Resources

All the extracts used in this section are from books of myths and stories which are useful collections. In addition teachers may find the series *Library of the World's Myths and Legends*, published by Paul Hamlyn, helpful. This offers up to about 18 titles, each well illustrated, on major mythologies of the world, eg Indian, Scandinavian, Greek, Chinese. These books are useful for putting stories/myths in context.

SECTION 3: FOR 9–11 YEAR OLDS

9 The Holy Land

Aims

The aims of this unit are that children shall begin to discover why Israel is a special place for **Jews, Christians** and **Muslims**; that they identify particular places which are special for these faiths and are introduced to some of the stories these faiths tell of the land.

Information

Children are likely to be aware of the 'Holy Land' under its present name of Israel—though possibly less likely to have heard it called Palestine—and may know of it as a place of conflict. This unit is not primarily concerned with that conflict, but with the country's significance for three religions: Judaism, Christianity and Islam.

Judaism

Although most Jews today live outside of Israel, and many would not wish to live in Israel, the land and the city of Jerusalem in particular evoke a response. In Jewish life the country is remembered in many small but significant ways: Orthodox Jews use no musical instruments in their worship as a sign of mourning for the destruction of the Temple; a wine glass is broken at a wedding—in the middle of celebration and rejoicing—for the same reason; prayers are said facing in the direction of Jerusalem. Similarly the major festivals remind Jews of the land, since they relate to the seasonal cycle in Israel: Passover, Shavuot and Pentecost were when harvest offerings were made to God, and pilgrims once travelled to Jerusalem for them. At the Passover *seder* (see section 2, page 76) the closing greeting 'Next year in Jerusalem' again shows attachment to the land of Israel and for some expresses a real hope. This seasonal cycle is also overlaid with historical events, but the rhythm of life to which it points is that of the land of Israel.

The Promised Land

The Torah (see section 2, page 76) tells how the land was promised first to Abraham and then to Isaac and Jacob and their descendants. Not only was the land promised, it was also given, by God. But possessing the land carried responsibilities too. Just as the land was set apart for the people, so the people were to be 'holy', living righteous lives. This was to be their response and the Torah indicated the way. The Writings and the Prophets (see section 2, page 67) tell of the ancestors of the Jews living in the land, but also of their exile from it. In fact a pattern can be seen in their history: possessing the land, being in exile, returning to the land. The prophets often saw exile from the land as God's judgment on the people for their failure to live by the commandments they had been given. Some prophets spoke of a future age and of God's anointed ruler (Messiah), of a time when righteousness would flourish. They painted a picture of a perfect future when God's people would live as a holy people in the land, an example to other nations who would be drawn to Jerusalem. The city became an important symbol in such visions of the future.

Against this background, stories and other passages from Jewish scripture may be used with children. Some biblical passages are suggested here, and story books are included under Resources.

The story of Abraham and God's promise to him   Genesis 12:1–9

The story of Joshua entering the land   Joshua 1:1–9; 6:1–17, 20

A psalm about Jerusalem	Psalm 122
Another psalm telling how the people felt when they were in exile, far from Jerusalem	Psalm 137:1–6
Visions of the future	Isaiah 2:2–4; 11:1–10

Important places

Outside the period covered by biblical sources, three places associated with later events in Israel's history deserve to be mentioned.

In Jerusalem today the most important place is probably the *Western Wall*, all that remains of the precincts of the Temple. It is a place where Jews pray, often leaving written prayers on small pieces of paper which are pushed into crevices in the wall. It is a popular place for the celebration of a *bar mitzvah* (literally, son of the commandment—the ceremony that takes place when a boy is 13 years old and takes on adult responsibilities in religious practice). The wall is also a reminder of the destruction of the Temple and violation of the city by the Romans in 70 CE. Why did this wall remain? Different stories are told. One, that the angels wept as they saw the destruction of the city and their tears quenched the flames which would have destroyed this wall. Another, that when the Temple was built the rich paid for various sections to be constructed; the poor wanted to help too but all that was left was the building of the outer wall. This they did with meagre funds and their own hands. When the Temple was destroyed their contribution alone remained. A further story tells that it was the Romans' decision not to destroy it; had they done so, their great victory would have had no witness.

The Western Wall in Jerusalem: a place of Jewish prayer and pilgrimage

A symbol of Jewish resistance against the Romans is found at *Masada*, a huge outcrop of rock overlooking the Dead Sea, a natural fortress where Eleazar ben Yair and his followers resisted the Romans for three years after the fall of Jerusalem. The story of the resistance and the ultimate fall of Masada is dramatically and imaginatively told in David Kossof's *The Voices of Masada* (Fontana/Collins 1975).

Many pilgrims to Jerusalem visit *Yad Vashem* ('Eternal Memorial') which is a memorial to those Jews who died in the Holocaust, as well as to non-Jews who

SECTION 3: FOR 9–11 YEAR OLDS

bravely helped some Jews to survive. Engraved in the floor of a bare room, lit only by one flame, are the names of the concentration camps where six million Jews were put to death.

Islam   Muslims speak of Abraham as the first *monotheist* (a person who affirms there is one God and who worships only one God), and the story of Abraham, Hagar and Ishmael plays a significant part in Islam, especially in the *hajj* (see page 159). The tombs of the Patriarchs—Abraham, Isaac and Jacob—in Hebron are thus a place of Muslim prayer and piety. But it is the Dome of the Rock, in Jerusalem, which is one of the three holy places of Islam. This is the place to which Muhammad was brought in his night journey and from which his miraculous ascent to heaven took place. This experience occurred at a time of crisis for Muhammad: his preaching in Mecca was meeting with hostility, and both his wife Khadijah and his uncle Abu Talib, who had been his protector, had recently died. Here is the story of Muhammad's ascent as it is told for Muslim children.

This Arabic seal in the texts of this section is the traditional salutation 'May the Peace and Blessing of Allah be upon him' used by Muslims after mentioning Muhammad.

The Night Journey and the Ascent to Heaven
One night as the Prophet ﷺ lay sleeping in the same spot where 'Abd al-Muttalib used to sleep, next to the Ka'bah, he was woken by the Archangel Gabriel. Later the Prophet ﷺ described what happened: 'I sat up and he took hold of my arm. I stood beside him and he brought me to the door of the mosque where there was a white animal for me to ride.'

The Prophet ﷺ told of how he mounted the animal and, with the Archangel Gabriel at his side, was transported from Mecca to the mosque called al-Aqsa, in far away Jerusalem. There the Prophet ﷺ found Abraham, Moses, and Jesus among a group of Prophets. The Prophet Muhammad ﷺ acted as their leader, or imam, in prayer. Then he was brought two jugs, one containing wine and the other milk. He chose the milk and refused the wine. At this, the Archangel Gabriel said, 'You have been rightly guided to the *fitrah*, the true nature of man, and so will your people be, Muhammad Wine is forbidden to you.'

The Prophet ﷺ also related how they passed through Heaven's gates and saw countless angels. Among them was Malik, the Keeper of Hell, who never smiles. Malik stepped forward and showed the Prophet ﷺ a view of Hell and the terrible plight of those who suffer in that place.

Then the Prophet ﷺ was taken up by the angels, through the seven Heavens, one by one. Along the way he again saw Jesus, Moses, and Abraham, and the Prophet ﷺ said that he had never seen a man more like himself than Abraham. He also saw John, called Yahya in Arabic, Joseph or Yusef, Enoch, that is Idris, and Aaron.

At last he reached the Lote Tree of the Uttermost, the *sidrat al-muntaha*, where no Prophet had been before. Here the Prophet ﷺ received a Revelation of what Muslims believe.

In the Name of Allah, the Beneficent, the Merciful.
The Messenger believeth in that which hath been revealed unto him from his Lord and (so do) the believers. Each one believes

in Allah and His Angels and His Books and His Messengers—
We make no distinction between any of His messengers—and
they say: We hear, and we obey. Grant us Thy forgiveness, our
Lord. Unto Thee is the homecoming.

(Qur'an ii.285)

Then he was taken into the Light of the Divine Presence of Allah,
and was instructed that Muslims should pray fifty times a day. The
Prophet ﷺ recalled:

> On my way back I passed by Moses and what a good friend
> to you he was! He asked me how many prayers had I been
> ordained to perform. When I told him fifty, he said, 'Prayer
> is a serious matter and your people are weak, so go back to
> your Lord and ask Him to reduce the number for you and your
> community.' I did so and He took away ten. Again I passed
> by Moses and he said the same again; and so it went on until
> only five prayers for the whole day and night were left. Moses
> again gave me the same advice. I replied that I had been back
> to my Lord and asked Him to reduce the number until I was
> ashamed, and I would not do it again. He of you who performs
> the five prayers faithfully, will have the reward of fifty prayers.

On the morning following these events and the Prophet's return to
Mecca, he told the Quraysh what had happened. Most of them said,
'By God! This is ridiculous! A caravan takes a month to go to Syria
and a month to return! Can you do that long journey in a single
night?'

Even many Muslims were amazed by this and wanted the Prophet
ﷺ to explain. Some ran with the news to Abu Bakr who said, 'By
Allah, if Muhammad ﷺ himself has said so, then it is true.
Remember, the Prophet ﷺ tells us that the word of Allah comes
to him directly from heaven to earth at any hour by day or night, and
we believe him. Isn't that a greater miracle than what you are now
doubting?'

(from *The Life of the Prophet Muhammad* by L Azzam and A Gouveurneur,
Islamic Texts Society 1985, pp 54–6)

The Dome of the Rock is the third holy
place of Islam.

The place of Muhammad's ascent was later to be marked by the building of the Dome of the Rock. Inside, the shrine does literally house the rock. As well as its association with Muhammad, this site is associated also with Abraham's sacrifice of Isaac and, variously, with the altar of sacrifice of Solomon's Temple or with the Holy of Holies, the innermost sanctuary of the Temple. So this place is sacred too for Jews.

Architecturally the Dome of the Rock is unique in Islam. Its decoration inside is ancient, whilst the mosaics outside are recent. The decoration displays distinctive features of Muslim art: geometrical design, calligraphy, and *arabesque* (stylised plant forms).

Arabesque, stylised and intertwining plants, interlaced geometric designs and calligraphy richly decorate this mosque.

Christianity

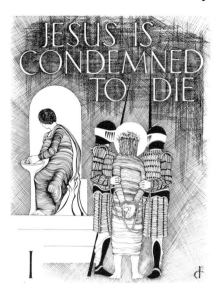

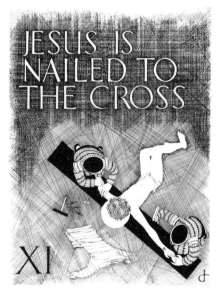

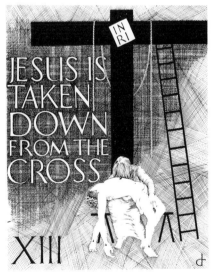

Three of the fourteen Stations of the Cross recalling the last events in Jesus' life.

For the Christian, as for the Muslim, the land of Israel is important; but it is not 'a promised land' for the Christian in the way that it is for the Jew. Since Christians are heirs to Jewish scripture, places of interest to Jews are of interest to them also, but the Christian's main interest in Israel is as the place where Jesus was born, lived and taught, died and was raised from the dead. In the earliest centuries of the Common Era, Christians lived in Israel, but the development of churches elsewhere in the Mediterranean world was equally significant. Any interest the early Christians had in places associated with the events of Jesus' life had come to a sharp halt when in 135 CE the Emperor Hadrian brought destruction to Jerusalem, and especially its Jewish or Jewish-Christian sites. It was under Constantine, when Christianity became the official religion of the Roman Empire, that many sites associated with the life of Jesus were sought out by the Emperor's mother, Helena, and marked by building projects sponsored by her son.

The following are some of the places which are now the focus of Christian pilgrimage and are associated with particular moments in Jesus' life.

The Church of the Nativity, Bethlehem

This church was dedicated by Helena on 31 May 339 CE. Narrow steps lead down from the church into the Grotto of the Nativity. A place below the altar is marked with a many-pointed silver star, declaring that it is here that Jesus was born. A small chapel, the Chapel of the Manger, richly decorated, lies to one side.

Galilee

Galilee, in the north, was where much of Jesus' ministry took place. Pilgrims surveying the hills and the lake (known by various names: Sea of Galilee, Lake Genessaret, Lake Tiberias) may sometimes feel closer to gospel events here than in the crowded places of Jerusalem. Capernaum, often featuring in the gospel story, is on the northern shore of the lake, and has been excavated. Overlooking the lake to the north-west is the Mount of the Beatitudes (Matthew 5:1–12), now marked by a church. Nazareth, which lies some distance west of the lake, is seen as the home of Mary and Joseph, and childhood home of Jesus (Luke 2:40). It is now a popular place of Christian pilgrimage, second only to Jerusalem and Bethlehem, but it remained insignificant until the time of Constantine, who in 326 CE had a church built to mark the place of the Annunciation (Luke 1:26–31). Luke also tells how Jesus preached in the synagogue here (Luke 4:16–22).

Jerusalem

The Christian sites in Jerusalem mark especially the events of the last week in Jesus' life.

The *Via Dolorosa*, or the 'way of the cross', leads through the narrow streets of the old walled city of Jerusalem. Fourteen places mark significant events of Jesus' progress to the cross. The custom of following the way of the cross appears to go back at least to the fourth century CE and by the fifteenth century pilgrims had started to reproduce it in their own countries, using pictures, carvings or sculptures of the incidents recalled, hence the Stations of the Cross found in many churches today. The *Via Dolorosa* ends in the Church of the Holy Sepulchre, a very complex building, again associated with Constantine but built on a still more ancient site which marks the place of Jesus' death and burial.

Approaches

General approaches to the topic are suggested here, whilst some activities specific to each faith are given in Activities, below.

1 Slides of Israel borrowed from an RE centre (or from someone who has been in Israel) are ideal to begin to build a picture of Israel. Try to illustrate, for example:

the new and the old, to convey a sense of a land with a long history;

three faiths in Jerusalem: show pictures of the Western Wall, the Dome of the Rock, the Church of the Holy Sepulchre;

the different kinds of land found in such a small country: fertile and cultivated, plains and mountains, deserts, coastlines.

2 Collect suitable travel posters and brochures. Consider with the children how you might travel to Israel from where you live. What clues are there in the posters/brochures to suggest *why* people might want to go there? Which times of year would be popular? Distinguish general answers—holidays, sun—from any 'religious' answers which may emerge (eg seasons corresponding with Passover, Christmas, Holy Week or Easter).

3 Talk with children about guidebooks. What would you need to include in a guidebook for your town/village? Plan to make a simple class guidebook to Israel which will include something about the importance of the land for Jews, Christians and Muslims.

4 If you have access to a resource centre, borrow audio material which will help you to build up a 'sound picture' of Jerusalem. Listen to the sounds whilst looking at a good picture which 'looks over' Jerusalem. You will need the sound of bells, of the *adhan* (the Muslim call to prayer), and of Hebrew being read. Imagine early morning in Jerusalem, waking up with these sounds in the distance; begin to introduce these three living faiths in the city today.

5 Tell the story of the Holy Land imaginatively through the eyes of three people—perhaps children visiting Israel—a Jew, a Muslim and a Christian. Provide a name and brief biography for each and follow and mark their paths through Israel.

Activities

The approaches suggested above lead into activities. They might be supplemented or extended in the following ways.

1 If possible invite to the school visitors who belong to these three faiths and who have been in Israel. Prepare the children to ask questions. Ask the visitors to bring pictures to show; they may also have things they have bought in Israel to show to the children and which the children might carefully handle.

2 Design badges for the places which people of these three faiths might visit; devise symbols which indicate what is special about each place.

3 Make travel brochures to attract people from each of these faiths to Israel: include itineraries and information about the places each might visit.

4 Use some of the biblical material suggested above to explore Jewish feeling for the land.

 a Tell the story of Abraham leaving Ur for an unknown destination. Focus on how Abraham might have felt; on the life he was leaving behind and on the unknown future.

 b Explore with the children the idea of a perfect place, a town or city, perhaps one they know which they could make even better. How would they change it? Introduce some of the poetry about Jerusalem suggested above (Psalm 122; Isaiah 2:2–4 and 11:1–10). Explore the way the person writing felt about the city. What kind of things make a place special?

5   Tell the story of Masada. David Kossof's book (see page 149) gives plenty of ideas for characters involved in the stand against the Romans. Prepare short plays about Masada, or write a series of news bulletins.

6   Use the idea of Christians visiting Israel to build up an overview of the life of Jesus (cf section 2, pages 60–61) and to make a class wall display: 'A Map of Israel for Pilgrims'. The map should include key places associated with Jesus. Some of these might be marked with small pictures; all could carry a caption and a biblical reference. (Such maps do exist and could provide a useful reference for the teacher.) Travel brochures would be useful for pictures here; children will need to have Bibles and help in using them (note that individual gospels can be bought cheaply).

7   Look carefully at a picture or slide of Jerusalem which gives a view of the city showing the Dome of the Rock. Discuss how you can tell it is a special building (dome, gold, raised high up, spacious setting in otherwise twisting streets). Look at close-up pictures. What do children think the blue and gold might symbolise? Notice the kind of patterns. Do some mosaic work which is based on patterns of this kind (see Resources).

Resources

Books

J Bourgoin, *Islamic Patterns: an infinite design colouring book*, Dover 1977 (45 designs, limited photocopying permissible)

A T Dale, *Winding Quest*, OUP 1972 (the heart of the Old Testament in plain English)

M Davies, *The Three Holy Places of Islam*, The Muslim Institute 1984 (an inexpensive pamphlet guide designed for Muslim children)

R Gonen, *Biblical Holy Places, an illustrated guide*, A & C Black 1987 (useful reference for the teacher on Israel, as well as other countries; includes biblical references)

M Kretzmer, *Adventure in the Holy Land*, 1983 (guidebook for children today; available from the Jewish Educational Bureau (address on page 115), but highlights places of Muslim and Christian as well as Jewish interest)

Photo-Guide to the Old Testament, Lion 1973
Photo-Guide to the New Testament, Lion 1972
(picture books picking out significant places)

J G Priestley, *Bible Stories for Today: The Old Testament*, REP 1981 (retelling of stories for young audience)

M A Tarantino, *Marvellous Stories from the Life of Muhammad*, The Islamic Foundation 1982 (written primarily for Muslim children, but intended to interest a wider audience)

AVA

Israel, Ann & Bury Peerless, 22 King's Avenue, Minnis Bay, Birchington, Kent (54 slides with notes)

Bethlehem, IL 13; *Masada*, IL 20; *Jerusalem: Dome of the Rock*, IL 09/1; Woodmansterne Ltd (slides and brief notes)

Holy Places, E724, Pictorial Charts Educational Trust (set of 4 wall charts and notes; includes Christian and Muslim places)

'The Dome of the Rock', Muslim Information Service (45 piece jigsaw puzzle)

'Religions of the Middle East', Argo ZFB 54 (record)

SECTION 3: FOR 9–11 YEAR OLDS

10 Pilgrimage to Mecca

Aims

This unit will help children to discover the importance of Mecca in **Muslim** belief and practice, and through looking at the pilgrimage to Mecca to reflect on what it means to be a Muslim.

Information

To make the pilgrimage to Mecca just once in a lifetime is the duty of every Muslim who can afford the journey. It is estimated that some two million Muslims now travel to Mecca each year to fulfil this duty. They come from every quarter—from Africa and the Middle East; from Pakistan, Bangladesh, and India; from Iran, Central Asia, and the Chinese border lands; from Malaysia and Indonesia, Turkey and Yugoslavia; from Mauritius, Trinidad and Surinam; and from the United States and the British Isles. To begin to list the countries immediately points to the worldwide appeal of Islam, as well as its capacity to bring together people of many nationalities, and to bring them together with a single purpose—worship of one God.

The spirit of *hajj*

In discovering *hajj* with children, it is crucial to catch the excitement—setting out after years of saving, putting on the pilgrim dress, touching down in Jedda, acquiring your pilgrim's visa and waiting for your guide to take you to Mecca . . . and then glimpsing the Ka'ba encircled by thousands of pilgrims, for the first time.

Alongside the excitement, something of the spirit of *hajj* needs to emerge too: a spirit of sacrifice is the essence of *hajj*. In past centuries the journey to Mecca was full of dangers and could take many months; some travellers would never return. Today travel is easier and speedier, but this spirit still prevails in the giving up of personal comfort, pride in dress; and frequently also in doing without the companionship of family and friends and without the distinctions that can arise through wealth and education. The simple dress adopted by those on *hajj* points to equality and brotherhood, a visible reminder that all are equal before God, whatever their race or colour or personal status in life.

To go to Mecca is also to follow in the footsteps of Muhammad who restored the Ka'ba for the worship of one God and made the pilgrimage to Mecca himself.

Mecca

Each day when Muslims pray they will find the direction of Mecca and face that way. When a mosque is built it must be aligned in that direction and when a Muslim is buried the face must be turned towards Mecca.

A Muslim home may have pictures of Mecca and the Ka'ba, and in some countries those who have made the journey to Mecca may paint a picture of the Ka'ba over the door or on the wall of their home.

For Muslims, Mecca has a long history: in Muslim belief it is the place where Abraham and Ishmael built the first house for the worship of one God. This house is known as the *Ka'ba*, a word which means 'a cube-shaped structure'. The Ka'ba today is covered with a black cloth (*kiswah*) richly embroidered in gold with Arabic calligraphy. This is renewed each year at the time of the *hajj*.

Many of the places visited on the pilgrimage are associated with the story of Abraham. Abraham is important for Jews, Christians and Muslims. He believed in one God, and the story of Abraham and the destruction of his father's idols is told by Jews and Muslims. It would make a useful introduction to Abraham's thinking about God. It is told from a Muslim perspective in the book from which the following extract is taken. We take up Abraham's story as he leaves his father's home.

Abraham and Mecca

Imagine how terrible it must have been for Abraham to leave his home, his family and all that he knew, and set out across the wilderness into the unknown. But at the same time, how could he have remained among people who did not believe in Allah and who worshipped statues? Abraham always had a sense that Allah cared for him and he felt Allah near him as he travelled.

At last, after a long hard journey, he arrived at a place by the Mediterranean Sea, not far from Egypt. There he married a noble woman by the name of Sarah and settled in the land of Palestine.

Many years passed but Abraham and his wife were not blessed with any children. In the hope that there would be a child, and in keeping with tradition, Sarah suggested that Abraham should marry Hagar, her Egyptian handmaid. Soon after this took place, Hagar had a little boy named Ishmael.

Some time later Allah promised Abraham another son, but this time the mother of the child would be his first wife, Sarah. This second son would be called Isaac. Allah also told Abraham that from his two sons—Ishmael and Isaac—two nations and three religions would be founded and because of this he must take Hagar and Ishmael away from Palestine to a new land. These events were an important part of Allah's plan, for the descendants of Ishmael would form a nation from which would come a great Prophet, who would guide the people in the way of Allah. This was to be Muhammad, the Messenger of Allah, ﷺ . From the descendants of Sarah's child, Isaac, would come Moses and Jesus.

So it was that Abraham, Hagar, and Ishmael left Palestine. They travelled for many days until finally they reached the arid valley of Bacca (later to be called Mecca), which was on one of the great caravan routes. There was no water in the valley and although Hagar and Ishmael only had a small supply of water left, Abraham left them there knowing Allah would take care of them.

Soon all the water was gone. The child began to grow weak from thirst. There were two hills nearby, one called Safā and the other Marwah. Hagar went up one hill and looked into the distance to see if she could find any water, but found none. So she went to the other hill and did the same. She did this seven times. Then sadly she returned to her son, and to her great surprise and joy she found a spring of water bubbling out of the earth near him. This spring, near which the mother and child settled, was later called Zamzam. The area around it became a place of rest for the caravans travelling across the desert and in time grew into the famous trading city of Mecca.

From time to time Abraham travelled from Palestine to visit his family and he saw Ishmael grow into a strong young man. It was during one of these visits that Allah commanded them to rebuild the Ka'bah—the very first place where people had worshipped Allah.

They were told exactly where and how to build it. It was to be erected by the well of Zamzam and built in the shape of a cube.

In its eastern corner was to be placed a black stone that had fallen to earth from heaven. An angel brought the stone to them from the nearby hill of Abū Qubays.

Abraham and Ishmael worked hard to rebuild the Ka'bah and as they did so they prayed to Allah to send a Prophet from among their descendants.

When the Ka'bah was completed, Allah commanded Abraham to call mankind to pilgrimage to His Holy House. Abraham wondered how anyone could hear his call. Allah said, 'You call and I will bring them.' This was how the pilgrimage to the Ka'bah in Mecca was established and when Muslims make the pilgrimage today they continue to answer the age-old call of Abraham.

(from *The Life of the Prophet Muhammad* by L Azzam and A Gouveurneur, Islamic Texts Society 1985, pp 5–8)

Mecca is also the place of Muhammad's birth. For Muslims he is the prophet whom God sent in answer to Abraham's and Ishmael's prayer. It was in the hills outside the city that Muhammad was called to be God's messenger and prophet. Here he received his first revelation and message from God, and experienced rejection by the Meccans. The migration of Muhammad and some seventy followers to Medina in 622 CE marked a turning point for the Muslims. In Medina they grew in strength and faith, and in 630 CE Muhammad was able to return to Mecca. He restored the Ka'ba to the worship of one God and removed the idols which the people had placed there.

The pilgrimage (*hajj*)

The *hajj* takes place in Dhul Hijjah—the twelfth month of the Muslim calendar. Setting out on the pilgrimage—*hajj* means to set out with a definite purpose—is an emotional occasion and pilgrims take leave of families and friends with prayers at the mosque. Their preparations will have started long before this. Those who wish to travel to Mecca must be in good health, free of debt, and able to support families at home whilst they are away. They will already have purchased their pilgrim dress; for men this is two pieces of white seamless cloth and simple backless sandals to indicate simplicity of life. Men's heads are left uncovered as a sign of humility. Women have no prescribed dress; they will dress discreetly and often in white—but their faces should remain uncovered.

The pilgrim dress must be put on before reaching Mecca, for being a pilgrim demands personal consecration. This is shown in other ways too, for example no perfume will be used, suggesting that the enjoyment of ordinary life is left behind. No forms of life—plant or animal or insect—must be harmed within the sacred territory of Mecca, thus recognising that all belongs to God and fostering respect for the created world. Peace and harmony must be the hallmarks in relations with others. All that distracts and detracts from the worship of God must be set aside.

Pilgrims normally approach Mecca with a guide, who will make sure they know exactly how to carry out the rites of *hajj*. When they arrive in Mecca they will go first to the Ka'ba and walk round it seven times in an anti-clockwise direction, and try to touch the sacred stone. The great prayer of the pilgrim:

'Here am I. O God, at Thy Command, here am I'

will be on everyone's lips.

A covered passageway goes from the Great Mosque to the running water of Zamzam and the hills of as-Safa and al-Mawa. The pilgrims will recall the story of Hagar and Ishmael as they climb these hills and drink the water of Zamzam.

Together these actions comprise the lesser pilgrimage or *umra* which can take place at any time of year, but they have become part of the *hajj* too.

The most important ceremony of the *hajj* takes place on 9th Dhul Hijjah at Arafat—a huge barren plain capable of holding thousands of pilgrims. Here the pilgrims gather at noon for the ceremony of standing before God. A small hill called the 'Mount of Mercy' rises from the plain. The thousands of pilgrims stand on the plain until sunset recalling their wrongdoings and declaring their repentance. At sunset they must move to Muzdalifah, ready to go next day to Mina.

At Mina stand three stone pillars marking places where Ishmael resisted Satan. The pilgrims collect small stones to throw at the pillars, thus affirming their rejection of evil too. This 10th day of Dhul Hijjah is also *Eid ul Adha*, the Festival of Sacrifice. Here at Mina pilgrims sacrifice an animal; its meat will be shared with the poor. The festival recalls the great sacrifice Abraham was prepared to make for God. In Islam the story is told of Abraham dreaming that he was to sacrifice his most precious thing. He knew this to be Ishmael, his son. As he was about to make the sacrifice, God intervened and provided a ram for sacrifice. For Muslims the sacrifice at Mina points to the spirit of sacrifice which should characterise a Muslim's life.

Festivities will continue until the 13th day of Dhul Hijjah. Throughout the Muslim world those who are not on pilgrimage will also celebrate this festival. Where families are waiting for the return of pilgrims, the celebrations may be extended, and friends and relatives will gather to welcome the return of the pilgrims—who may now add the title *Hajji* to their names.

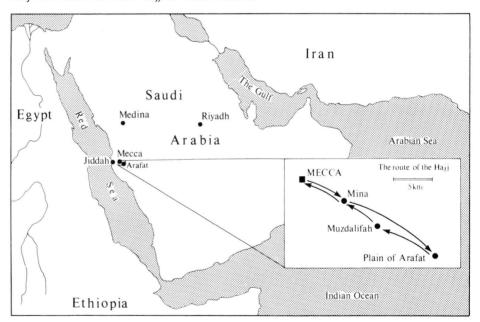

Only Muslims may visit the holy city of Mecca. Mecca and the surrounding area is *haram*, that is set apart and dedicated to God. The sacred places around Mecca visited during the *hajj* are shown on the small inset.

Approaches

1 Encourage children to talk about 'the place which is special for me'. Discuss feelings when planning to go there; feelings when there, when leaving. How do they remember the place afterwards? (What about scrapbooks/ photographs/souvenirs?) Note too that children may have quite local places which are 'special'—this allows for those who simply don't go anywhere. Think about places they hope to visit one day.

2 If you can obtain good pictures of Mecca and other places visited on the pilgrimage (see Resources) use them as stimulus for introducing *hajj*. A picture of the Ka'ba and pilgrims might prompt the following questions:

What do the children notice about the people?
(Dress in common; shared movement)

What shape is the building they can see?
(Cube—introduce its name)

What clues are there about its importance?
(People walk round it; *kiswah*; set inside great courtyard)

Notice the crowds. What does it feel like to be among such crowds?

Begin to introduce a pilgrim's experience of Mecca.

3 Use the following story to explore 'the spirit of *hajj*'.

The Cobbler's Pilgrimage

Dreams are not usually true. But some dreams, especially those of prophets and some godly people are true.

Once Abdullah bin Mubarak went to Hajj. After performing the Hajj, he felt sleepy and lay down on the floor. While sleeping he saw two angels come down from the sky. They were talking to each other about the Hajj. One said, 'How many people came for Hajj this year?'

The other said 'Six hundred thousand.'

'And how many of them were lucky?'

'None. Nobody's Hajj was accepted,' the second angel answered.

'What a state of affairs' said Abdullah bin Mubarak to himself. He felt sorry for all those people who had taken a lot of trouble and travelled from far-off places to perform Hajj. The angels were still talking. He heard the second angel saying 'In Damascus there is a cobbler by the name of Ali bin al Muwaffiq. He did not come for Hajj. But his Hajj has been accepted by Allah and because of his Hajj all those people who performed Hajj this year have been blessed.'

When Abdullah woke up he remembered the conversation between the two angels. He also remembered the name Ali bin al Muwaffiq of Damascus. He decided to go and meet him.

So, Abdullah went to Damascus and asked people about a cobbler by the name of Ali bin al Muwaffiq. When he found the house, he knocked at the door, and a man came out. Abdullah asked, 'Brother, what is your name?'

'Ali bin al Muwaffiq,' said the man.

'What do you do for a living?' asked Abdullah.

'I mend shoes. I am a cobbler' said the man.

Abdullah then proceeded to tell Ali all about his dream concerning the Hajj, and the conversation between the angels. 'Now,' said Abdullah, 'tell me all about yourself.'

Ali was hesitant at first, but, encouraged by Abdullah, he made himself comfortable and began to tell this story: 'For thirty years I have been saving money for Hajj. I had saved up three thousand dirhams and I was planning to go this year. Now it so happened that my wife was pregnant. One day she asked me to go to the next door neighbour's and ask for some meat curry that they were cooking. So, I went to my neighbour and asked for some curry. He said "For the past seven days my children have had nothing to eat. I could not watch them die from starvation. As it happened, I found this dead donkey lying in the back street so I cut a piece of meat from it and cooked that. I just can't offer you this curry. It is not halal, it is not permissible for your wife, for you." After that I felt pretty ashamed of myself. Here I was with three thousand dirhams but my own neighbour hadn't eaten for seven days. So I went home, took those three thousand dirhams and gave them to my neighbour. "Here, take this," I said, "feed your children with this money as long as it lasts. This will be my Hajj."'

Abdullah went home satisfied. 'Those angels in my dream were right,' he said to himself.

(from *Love Your Brother, Love Your Neighbour* by K Murad, The Islamic Foundation 1982)

Activities

This frontispiece from an Arabic atlas of 1551 CE draws the eye to its centre, the Ka'ba in Mecca. Similarly the Muslims of those countries named in Arabic in the 'niches' on the circumference of the circle turn to face Mecca in prayer and set out in that direction on *hajj*.

1 Write diaries for a week of Dhul Hijjah, including 8th–10th of the month. Design an appropriate cover, eg include the Ka'ba, perhaps showing it in the centre of the world. (Mercator's projection places Mecca very centrally.)

2 If you have contact with a local Muslim community, ask if there is someone who has been to Mecca for *hajj* who is willing to talk to the children. Let the children plan the questions.

3 Tell the story of Abraham and the idols. Encourage the children to talk about ideas they may have of God. Show them some Muslim prayer beads which they use to remember God. Learn about the names Muslims have for God. Allah means simply 'God': but Muslims may use the beads to think of the Ninety-nine Beautiful Names of God. Look at some of the names as they are written in Arabic.

4 This is the cover of an Arabic atlas from the sixteenth century CE. Mecca is at the centre and around the edge are the names of countries from which Muslims might travel to Mecca. A similar design on a large scale for the classroom might identify the names of countries where there are many Muslims today—perhaps by a band indicating names and another one showing their flags. The design is also reminiscent of a compass. Children might learn about how Muslims must determine the direction of Mecca for their daily prayers. (Note too that Muslims were interested in astronomy and geography from an early time—inspired by the requirements of prayer and pilgrimage. As long as this fact is not forgotten, the topic could extend into learning a little of Muslim scientific achievement.)

Resources

Books

M M Ahsan, *Muslim Festivals*, Wayland 1985 (for this age range; has sections on *hajj* and *Eid ul Adha*)
M Davies, *The Life of Muhammad*, Wayland 1987
H Khattab, *Stories from the Muslim World*, Macdonald 1987
(two recent story books, the first useful on Muhammad in Mecca, the second tells the story of Ishmael and Zamzam)
R Tames, *The Muslim World*, Macdonald 1982 (useful map of Muslim countries; section on *hajj* and one on 'Scientific Wonders')

AVA

Islamic Festivals, E747, Pictorial Charts Educational Trust
(4 posters including *hajj* and *Eid ul Adha*)
The Islamic Tradition, Argus Communications 1978 (2 filmstrips, 2 tapes plus scripts and notes; one filmstrip is on *hajj*, and individual frames could be used with this age group)

SECTION 3: FOR 9–11 YEAR OLDS

11 Amrit

The aim of this unit is that children should become familiar with a well known story from the **Sikh** religion, and begin to think about some of the ways in which belonging to a religion may be expressed.

Information

Amrit Pahul is the Sikh ceremony of initiation. Not every Sikh goes through the initiation ceremony: some decide to, others don't. Those who do will wear symbols distinctive of the Sikh and take on certain duties. Those who 'take *amrit*' (see below) today are the heirs of those who chose to follow the Sikh way of life at the call of the tenth guru—Guru Gobind Singh—and like them they become members of the *Khalsa* ('the pure ones', the community of initiated Sikhs). A favourite but not the only time for the ceremony to take place is the festival of Baisakhi (13 April). This is the beginning of the Sikh new year, but also the commemoration of the 'birthday' of the Khalsa, the story of which is told below.

This topic also offers the possibility of exploring themes within children's experience: belonging, identity, sharing, choosing, responsibility, 'brotherhood' and equality.

Beginnings

Sikhism began in the fifteenth century CE with the experience and teaching of Guru Nanak in northern India (see section 2, pages 88–91). A further nine gurus followed Nanak, the line of human gurus ending in 1708 CE with the death of the tenth guru. In these early times Sikhs often found themselves under persecution from other groups, and in particular from the Mogul rulers: the temptation for Sikhs to give up their faith must often have been great. It was in this kind of climate that Guru Gobind Singh took action and summoned all Sikhs to Anandpur in 1699 CE, at the time of the spring harvest celebrations of the month of Baisakhi. In that year Baisakhi was to take on new significance for Sikhs. At this point the story of Guru Gobind Singh's 'call' to the Sikhs may be taken up.

The Creation of the Khalsa

This story is about Guru Gobind Singh who was the tenth Guru of the Sikhs. He was also the last Guru. He created the Khalsa which means 'good and pure human beings'. He decided that Sikhs should consider the holy book, the *Guru Granth Sahib*, as the Guru.

On *Baisakhi* day in 1699, Guru Gobind Singh asked all the Sikhs to come to Anandpur Sahib. He was worried that the Moguls were going to destroy the Sikhs. His father, Guru Tegh Bahadur, had been killed by the Moguls. Guru Gobind Singh wanted to make the Sikhs strong and brave. He did not want them to be afraid of death. So on *Baisakhi* day Guru Gobind Singh stood in uniform and fully armed before his people, he said to the Sikhs, 'You need to be strong. You need to fight together. You need to organize yourselves as a group.'

He then took his sword out of its sheath and said, 'My sword needs a head. Is there anyone in this *sangat* (congregation) who is willing to offer his head for his Guru? Is there anyone who is willing to offer his head for religion?'

A popular calendar picture showing Guru Gobind Singh and the Panj Pyare. The *amrit* is being stirred by Mata Jito Ji — the Guru's wife. Tradition tells that she was responsible for sweetening the *amrit* with *patashas*, symbolising sweetness of character and a peace-loving nature.

Everyone was silent. No-one moved. They were all scared. After a few minutes, the Guru repeated his demand, 'Is there anyone in this *sangat* who is not afraid to die? Is there anyone who is willing to offer his head for his Guru?'

Still no-one moved. Once again the Guru repeated his demand. Then one man came forward. He said, 'You can take my head. I will give up my life for you.'

Guru Gobind Singh took him into a tent nearby. There was a loud thud. After a few minutes Guru Gobind Singh came out of the tent. His sword was dripping with blood. He repeated once again, 'My sword needs another head.' Another man came forward. He said, 'You can take my head. I will die for you.'

Once again the Guru went into the tent. Once again he came out with a sword dripping with blood. People began to get worried. Some left the *sangat*. Some said, 'The Guru has gone mad.'

Guru Gobind Singh repeated his demand three more times. Each time the Guru came out of the tent with a sword dripping blood.

After the fifth man had entered the tent the Guru came out with the five men. They were all dressed in saffron-coloured uniforms, like the uniform worn by the Guru. They were all carrying swords. The Guru called these men 'the immortal five' and *Panj Pyares* (five beloved ones). He said to the five men, 'My brothers, I have made you the same as I am. There is no difference between us. You have passed my toughest test. You are not afraid to die. You are my five beloved ones. You are chosen by God.'

The people in the *sangat* were very surprised. They were happy that the Guru had not killed these men. The Guru then told the *sangat*, 'These five men are the first five members of the new brotherhood, the *Khalsa*. They are the pure ones. To become a member of the *Khalsa* you have to be brave. You have to be ready to give up your life for the Sikh faith.'

He also told them, 'These five men are of different castes. But they are all brave men. Members of the *Khalsa* must drink *amrit* together from the same bowl. They should all have a common surname. This name should be *Singh* for men and *Kaur* for women.

Guru Gobind Singh made it clear that women can also be members of the *Khalsa*. They can also partake of *amrit* and be the *Panj Pyares* (five beloved ones).

Guru Gobind Singh then prepared *Khande Ka Amrit*. He put some water and sugar in a steel bowl and stirred it with a double-edged sword. He recited five hymns from the *Guru Granth Sahib*. He then initiated the *Panj Pyares* into the holy order. He asked them to drink *amrit* from the same bowl. This was to make it clear that everyone was equal.

After this the Guru himself took *amrit* from the five beloved ones. This was followed by a ceremony at which large numbers of people were baptized into the Sikh faith.

Ever since that day the *Amrit* ceremony takes place on the *Baisakhi* day. But it can also take place on any other day. Any five people who are members of the *Khalsa* can organize such a ceremony at any time or any place.

Guru Gobind Singh made the Sikhs strong. He removed the fear of death from their hearts. But he was also humble. He himself was the authority and power of the *Panj Pyares* (five beloved ones). To this day Sikhs remember Guru Gobind Singh with respect and admiration. They sing his praises as a great man who was a Guru himself but also a disciple of the *Panj Pyares*.

(from *Guru Nanak and the Sikh Gurus* by R Arora, Wayland 1987)

(Note that it has become usual to write 'Panj Pyare*s*' in transliteration, although 'Panj Pyar*e*' already denotes the plural.)

Understanding the story

Caste
A person's name in India indicated their occupation, or *jati*; in turn their occupation indicated their social standing or *caste*. The Panj Pyare, except for one, were from low caste groups. Caste divided people in India; for example there were strict rules about who you might eat with, or about which castes might intermarry.

Names
When Guru Gobind Singh introduced 'Singh' (Lion) and 'Kaur' (Princess) to replace 'occupational' names, he was making a statement about equality and indicating that the Sikh way did not find caste important. The names also conferred dignity on every Sikh.

Amrit
The Panj Pyare, and the other Sikhs, *shared amrit*—again this radically challenged caste rules and affirmed brotherhood and equality.

The five Ks
You will find some versions of the story tell how Guru Gobind Singh and the Panj Pyare adopted the same distinctive style of dress, this marked them out from those around them and came to have a religious and symbolic significance. Each distinctive feature begins with a 'k' in Punjabi:

kesh	uncut hair
kangha	comb
kara	bracelet
kach	shorts
kirpan	sword

A sixth feature of Sikh dress, which may be the one which is most familiar to children, is the turban.

Amrit Pahul today

The Guru Granth Sahib
Guru Gobind Singh was the last human guru. After him, leadership was invested in the Adi Granth (or Guru Granth Sahib, or sacred scriptures). These are now at the heart of Sikh worship and practice. Amrit Pahul like other Sikh ceremonies requires the presence of the Guru Granth Sahib and of a *granthi*—one who can read the scriptures in their original script, Gurmukhi. (See also section 2, pages 67–68.)

The ceremony
The table below highlights key features of the ceremony which might be explored with children.

1	Making a decision	2	Preparing and receiving *amrit*
3	Instruction Prayer	4	*Karah parshad* *Langar*

1   When a Sikh joins the Khalsa he or she must take on responsibilities. These must be agreed to before initiation takes place. Here are some examples of them:

> Recognise the Guru Granth Sahib is Guru.
>
> Obey its teachings.
>
> Worship one true Lord.
>
> Meditate daily and recite the set hymns.
>
> Treat members of the Khalsa as brothers and sisters.
>
> Serve Sikhs and the community where you live.
>
> Give a tenth of your savings to charity.
>
> Be ready to fight in the service of the Sikh community and for any who suffer injustice.

When such duties are accepted, initiation can take place.

2   In front of the Guru Granth Sahib, water and *patashas* (sugar crystals) are stirred with a short two-edged sword by the Panj Pyare, whilst words from the scriptures are recited. Then those to be initiated come forward and kneel on one knee, alert like warriors. They drink *amrit*; it is sprinkled on their eyes and forehead five times and the words 'The Khalsa is of God and the victory is to God' are recited. Then all drink *amrit* from the one bowl.

3   The most senior of the Panj Pyare will speak of the Sikh faith and way of life and teach the '*Mool Mantra*', the most well known Sikh prayer, which speaks of God. All will share in '*Ardas*', another well known prayer.

> **The Mool Mantra**
> There is one God,
> Eternal Truth is His Name;
> Maker of all things,
> Fearing nothing and hating
>   nothing,
> Immortal, unborn, self existent:
> By the grace of the Guru made
>   known to men.

The Guru Granth Sahib is opened at random and a verse is read out. This is called *Hukam*, which means 'command'. It is a word of advice, God's word, on which to reflect and act.

4   Sikh services always end with everyone present—even non-Sikhs—receiving the sweet food *karah parshad* together. It is symbolic of God's grace and blessings and the human family sharing as one.

> Karah parshad
> Take equal quantities of flour or semolina, sugar, water and melted, clarified butter.
>
> Mix the flour or semolina with the butter, and stir for a short time over a low heat.
>
> Dissolve the sugar in the water, and then add it slowly to the butter mixture, stirring all the time.
>
> When the mixture leaves the sides of the pan it is ready. Let it cool.

SECTION 3: FOR 9–11 YEAR OLDS

5   Service (*sewa*) is at the heart of Sikhism, and the hospitality given to anyone, Sikh or non-Sikh, who visits a Sikh place of worship is well known. Everyone will share *langar*, a meal together, before going home. While sharing *langar* everyone sits together on the same level, indicating that all are equal.

Approaches

1   Exploring Amrit Pahul offers many starting points within children's experience; for example:

Talk about 'belonging' with the children. To which groups do they belong? How can/do people show belonging? (eg names; visible symbols—dress, badges; things they do together).

Discuss uniforms and special dress with the children. Why is uniform important? What does it 'say' to people who see it? What is it like for people who wear it—how do they feel?

What is in a name? Explore names, beginning with the children's—what do they know about their names? Do names have meanings? Where do names come from? Discover cultural variations. Introduce Singh and Kaur. Link to belonging, to equality and to character.

2   Bring together a collection of Sikh artefacts to use as a stimulus in the lesson (see Resources), or use a picture of a Sikh wearing the 5 Ks and turban, to lead into the story of Guru Gobind Singh and the Panj Pyare.

3   Use a picture of the Panj Pyare (the five loved ones) of the story and a picture of a Sikh Amrit Pahul today. Identify any similarities between the pictures.

4   Talk with the children about stories they know well. (In a multifaith classroom this may lead to the realisation that different cultures, countries or religions have 'their own' stories—but stories which can be shared.) Tell the story of Guru Gobind Singh and the birthday of the Khalsa as a story Sikh children hear.

5   It can be difficult to look at a 'service' with children, but children who have become familiar with the stories of the birthday of the Khalsa might begin to think how they would *create* a similar ceremony today. So, for example:

What about the Guru? (Here one would introduce the presence of the Guru Granth Sahib.)

How would you represent the Panj Pyare? (By having present five Sikhs who are already members of the Khalsa.)

How would *they* dress? And what about those to be initiated—how should they be dressed?

What else would be necessary for the ceremony? (Clearly water and *patashas* and a bowl in which to prepare *amrit*, as well as a *khandra* to stir the mixture.)

In these ways children might deduce the physical requirements of Amrit Pahul, and suggest what might happen. This active involvement of the children is more important than working through an 'order of service' at this stage. The information about the initiation ceremony given above will help to 'fill out' the suggestions children make.

Activities

1   Prepare a play—perhaps for assembly—about the formation of the Khalsa by Guru Gobind Singh. (But note that some Sikhs do not like the Guru to appear as a character in a play.)

2   Many stories from Sikh history are available in cartoon form. Children might tell the story of Guru Gobind Singh and the Khalsa in this form individually, or together construct a wall cartoon.

Initiation today. Entry to the Khalsa must take place in the presence of five Khalsa members who represent the Panj Pyare (shown here). *Amrit* will be prepared and used during the ceremony.

3 Prepare radio news reports about the formation of the Khalsa. Include interviews of some key people.

4 Design some Baisakhi cards. Make sure that you use pictures and symbols appropriate to the season.

5 If possible invite a Sikh who is a member of the Khalsa into school to talk about his/her initiation or about the 5 Ks and the turban.

6 Explore further the importance of names and uniform/symbolic dress. The story of the Donkey in the Lion Skin, told by W O Cole and P S Sambhi in *Baisakhi* (RMEP 1986) and in some books of Sikh stories, would be useful here.

Resources

Books
M Aggarwal, *I am a Sikh*, Franklin Watts 1984
W Owen Cole, *A Sikh Family in Britain*, RMEP 2nd edition 1985
D Singh and A Smith, *The Sikh World*, Macdonald 1985
(three general books suitable for this age range, the first and third containing a wide range of colour photographs)

AVA
Comics
Amar Chitra Katha (an extensive pictorial classics series from India, covering Indian history and mythology; titles include *Guru Nanak* and *Guru Gobind Singh*; details from Books from India, 45 Museum Street, London WC1A 1LR)

Posters
Initiation Rites, E721, Pictorial Charts Educational Trust (4 posters on Christianity, Judaism, Sikhism and Buddhism)

Slides
Living a Faith: Sikhism—beliefs and worship, Sacred Trinity Centre, Chapel Street, Salford, Manchester M3 7AJ (73 slides, teacher's notes and cassette; includes the formation of the Khalsa and the 5 Ks)

Artefacts
A list of artefacts available for purchase can be obtained from Articles of Faith (see page 131, Resources).

SECTION 3: FOR 9–11 YEAR OLDS

12 The Synagogue

Aims

This unit helps children to discover the synagogue as the meeting place of the **Jewish** community and to recognise the importance of the synagogue as a place where the Torah is kept, read, heard and studied by the community.

Information

The design and style of synagogues varies from country to country and from one generation to another, but synagogues possess one common characteristic: they provide a place to keep the Torah scroll(s) (see section 2, page 66). The Torah's presence and its use in worship influence the layout and furniture of synagogues; its commandments influence the decoration of the building. The Torah scroll with its ornaments points to the respect people have for its teaching and to the authority it holds.

A meeting place

The Temple in Jerusalem was once the most important centre of Jewish worship. King David had planned to build the first Temple (2 Samuel 7:1–7) but it was his son Solomon who carried out the task (1 Kings 5). This first Temple was destroyed by the Babylonians as long ago as 586 BCE, and most of the people were carried into exile in Babylon.

It is thought that when they were there they began to organise their life in ways which ensured the survival of their faith. The Torah, meeting together to observe the Sabbath, and festivals offered focuses for community life. So these things were already important before the Common Era and were to remain so in later centuries, especially after the events of 70 CE (see page 149). The Jewish way of life became 'portable', and the synagogue—literally a 'meeting together'—evolved into a *place* of meeting where Torah was heard and discussed.

Finding your way round a synagogue

Outside

Traditionally the synagogue was intended to be taller than other buildings in a locality. Both practical reasons and restrictive measures imposed by the countries in which they have settled have often prevented Jewish communities from complying with this requirement.

Other distinguishing features may not be immediately apparent from the outside; clues might be found, for example, on a foundation stone or in the use of Hebrew script, or perhaps in a motif such as the six-pointed Star of David worked in wood or stone.

Inside

Usually a synagogue is entered through a vestibule, so that the main room for worship is not entered directly from the street.

Traditionally an Orthodox synagogue should have windows, a requirement sometimes linked with the story of Daniel, who prayed by the window facing Jerusalem (Daniel 6:10). Another tradition is that there should be twelve windows, symbolic of the twelve tribes of Israel.

The orientation of the synagogue is also important. The ark (see below) is set in the wall facing towards Jerusalem; the main prayers, the *Amidah* (the 'Nineteen Blessings'), are spoken facing in this direction. In Orthodox synagogues (see diagram) there is usually a gallery for the women, who sit separately from the men; this recalls the *mehizah*, a partition screen in older synagogues, which separated the space for men from that for women.

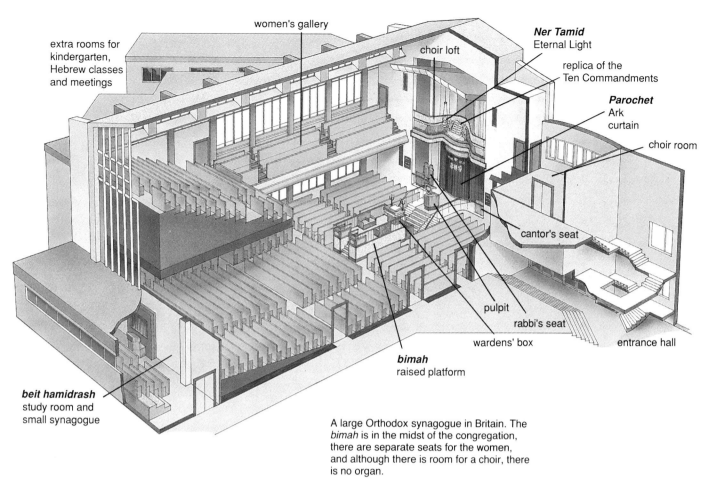

extra rooms for kindergarten, Hebrew classes and meetings

women's gallery

choir loft

Ner Tamid
Eternal Light

replica of the Ten Commandments

Parochet
Ark curtain

choir room

cantor's seat

pulpit

rabbi's seat

wardens' box

entrance hall

bimah
raised platform

beit hamidrash
study room and small synagogue

A large Orthodox synagogue in Britain. The *bimah* is in the midst of the congregation, there are separate seats for the women, and although there is room for a choir, there is no organ.

The ark is basically a cupboard to contain the Sefer Torah—Torah scroll. The doors may be plain, or ornate and decorated. The cupboard is named after the Ark of the Covenant kept in the first Temple, which was a cedar wood box covered with beaten gold and containing, according to Jewish tradition, the two stone tablets with the Ten Commandments.

The parochet is a curtain which hangs in front of the ark. It is usually made of a rich material, and its colour may be changed at festival times. White is usual for Rosh Hashanah (New Year) and Yom Kippur (Day of Atonement). The curtain may be decorated with traditional symbols (see below) and with biblical texts.

The ner tamid is a perpetual light, traditionally an oil lamp symbolic of the *menorah*, the seven-branched candlestick of the Temple. The placing of the lamp above the ark serves to focus the congregation's attention in that direction. A seven-branched candelabrum may also be found in many synagogues—and also the eight-branched (cf pages 111, 113).

The bimah is a raised platform from which the Torah scroll is read. In an Orthodox synagogue it is placed in a central position (see diagram), in the midst of the congregation. The scroll is placed and read facing the ark. Seats in an Orthodox synagogue usually surround the *bimah*. When the appointed portion of the Torah is read on the Sabbath, it is thus read in the midst of the congregation. There is an inbuilt symbolism here too. The Torah is raised above the people: the *bimah* thus recalls Mount Sinai and the giving of the Torah.

The diagram on page 170 shows a different positioning of the *bimah* in a Reform or Progressive synagogue. Here the Torah is read facing the congregation.

SECTION 3: FOR 9–11 YEAR OLDS

169

A plan of the synagogue of a Reform Jewish congregation. Notice how it differs from the Orthodox synagogue, but identify what it has in common too.

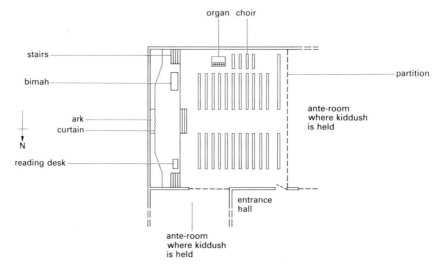

Decoration and symbolism

In the synagogue, as in the mosque (section 2, page 93), there will be an absence of any representational art. Popular symbols are the Shield of David, its interlaced upright and inverted triangles sometimes seen as representative of the covenant between God and man; the rampant lion, ancient symbol of the kingdom of Judah; and the two tablets of the Law, indicating the opening words of the Ten Commandments in Hebrew. There is also the *menorah* or seven-branched candlestick. And Hebrew inscriptions may be found: above the ark, 'Know before whom you stand' is a typical example.

Some synagogues have stained-glass windows, perhaps incorporating symbols we have already noted and sometimes depicting scenes from Torah or other biblical writings. In accordance with Exodus 20:4, human and animal forms are not depicted, but the days of creation, or the story of the Flood, for example, may occasionally provide subject matter.

The Torah scroll

The Torah, housed in the ark, is treated with great respect when it is taken out for reading. Since the scroll itself is the 'carrier' of God's revealed will for humankind, it is itself the focus of attention. Torah scrolls are handwritten in Hebrew by a trained scribe on carefully prepared parchment; the wooden rollers are symbolic of the Tree of Life; the scroll is covered and protected by a mantle which may be decorated with appropriate symbols (see above). Silver decorations—*rimmonim*—may adorn the end of the rollers when the scroll is 'dressed', or a Torah crown may take their place (indicating the Torah 'ruling' over human activity). A silver breastplate hung over the mantle recalls the dress of the high priest in Temple days. A binder may hold the scroll at the point where reading has ended and must recommence, whilst a pointer or *yad* will be available to guide the reader along the line of Hebrew as he reads to the congregation. (The reading of the Torah in the synagogue is described in section 2.)

The Torah is held in such esteem that when a Torah scroll is worn out it is never destroyed, but buried.

Approaches

1 Talk about special belongings—about books which are special—and how to handle them and treat them (see section 2, page 66).

If possible use a scroll from a set of Jewish artefacts, or use slides, to indicate some special features: Torah mantle; Torah crown; bells or *rimmonim*; breastplate; *yad*. Why is the scroll 'dressed' in this way? What do we learn from this about how people feel about the scroll? How would you store it, or keep it? Build up the idea of a special possession and of a special place to keep it.

2   Make a map of the area in which your school is situated. Mark on it any buildings where people meet together for particular events and purposes. Identify the kinds of occasion when people choose to meet together. Do certain events or activities require special kinds of buildings? Which buildings in your locality belong to religious groups? Begin to introduce the synagogue as a meeting place. What kinds of events take place there? Introduce the importance of the Torah in worship and in study—think about the synagogue as a place for the Torah as well as for meeting.

3   Use a set of posters of buildings belonging to religions; for example, *Places of Worship* (E728—Pictorial Charts Educational Trust). Match the name of the building with the name of the religion. Introduce the idea of each religion having its own kind of meeting place/building. Perhaps make a chart to record some distinguishing features of each (see section 1, page 34, section 2, page 92, section 3, page 178). Focus especially on the synagogue and its features and perhaps plan to work on the others later.

Activities

'For out of Zion shall go forth the Law, and the word of the Lord from Jerusalem. Blessed be he who in his holiness gave the Law to her people Israel.' With these words the ark is opened during the Sabbath morning service. The scroll is then taken 'in procession' to the *bimah*.

The Torah is a guide through life and is to be read and heard; respect and honour for Torah is shown in the richly 'dressed' scrolls, adorned here with mantles, breastplates and *rimmonim*. The *yadot* (plural of *yad*) will mark the way when the Torah is read.

1   If at all possible visit a synagogue with the children. Organise your visit around a theme, Discovering the Torah in the synagogue, for example. Make sure you will be met by someone who is able to open the ark and show you the Torah scroll(s).

and/or

Try to see the video *Judaism through the eyes of Jewish children* (CEM/PEP), which includes a short sequence from a children's service. They are shown:

opening the ark and taking out the Torah scroll; taking the scroll in procession to the *bimah*; removing the mantle and ornaments from the scroll; calling up a person to read the Torah; reading the Torah; lifting the scroll for all to see.

The accompanying prayers and blessings are in Hebrew, but the notes supplied provide a translation.

2   If a visit has been possible, prepare class guidebook(s) to the synagogue, picking out important features. Prepare it/them very carefully so that it/they can be sent for the community to see.

3   Design arks and *parochets*. Discover by using Bibles some texts which could be appropriate to place above them. Here are some suggestions.

> Joshua 24:24
> Deuteronomy 7:12; 8:11
> Psalm 119:1, 2, 105, 174

4   Convert your classroom (or another room) into a synagogue for a day. Involve the children in the planning; for example:

> Which direction is Jerusalem?
> How will you arrange the seats?
> Where will you place the ark?
> How will you indicate its importance?

Invite visitors in; let children be guides.

5   Encourage reflection on different parts of the synagogue and their importance; try for example short pieces of writing beginning:

> I am the ark . . .
> I am the *bimah* . . .
> We are the seats . . .

and so on.

Resources

Books

Douglas Charing, *The Jewish World*, Macdonald 1983 (for ages 9–11; contains a good cross-section diagram of a synagogue)
Douglas Charing, *Visiting a Synagogue*, Lutterworth 1984 (written for secondary schools, a detailed look at a Reform synagogue in Manchester)

AVA

C Lawton, *A Synagogue Tour*, Central Jewish Lecture and Information Committee, Woburn House, London WC1H 0EP (filmstrip—44 frames—notes and glossary)

The Jewish Museum, Woodmansterne Publications Ltd (slide sets 010J and 010K, each of 9 slides, include a Torah scroll and its ornaments, as well as pictures of other artefacts, eg Passover plate, Hanukah lamp and *mezuzah*.
Holy Books 1, E726, Pictorial Charts Educational Trust (a set of 4 posters; that on Judaism shows the Torah and its ornaments, and the Torah being read from the *bimah*)
A list of artefacts available for purchase is obtainable from the Jewish Education Bureau (address on page 115).

SECTION 3: FOR 9–11 YEAR OLDS

13 Serving in Religion

Aims

This unit explores the ways of life of people who have a special role within a religion, and encounters the idea of 'being called' and/or charged with particular tasks.

Information

This topic could be set within a wider context of people who serve the local community; or it could be complementary to exploring local places of worship of different faiths. The *local* community is stressed since arranging for children to meet individual people seems the most appropriate approach to this topic (see Approaches).

Most religions invest certain individuals within their community with importance or significance which may distinguish them from the rest of the community, place them in a position of leadership, and give them particular responsibilities and duties.

Judaism, Christianity and Islam each offer distinctive examples.

Judaism: the rabbi

The following extract gives a picture of the work of a rabbi of a Reform synagogue in Jackson's Row in Manchester.

The rabbi and his work

A rabbi in some ways is like a clergyman of the Christian religion. This is because he conducts services, officiates at various ceremonies, and visits the sick. However, a rabbi is firstly a teacher of the Jewish religion (*rabbi* in Hebrew means *teacher*), and it is his task to bring to his people God's message and laws. By his teaching and preaching, he will help them to understand and love their Jewish heritage. He is the spiritual leader of the synagogue and is there to give guidance, encouragement and comfort whenever the need arises. The rabbi is a friend to young and old alike. Progressive Judaism allows women to train as rabbis but this is forbidden within Orthodox Judaism. At present, the Progressive movement in Britain has ordained four women. They serve as rabbis of London synagogues. One of them in fact was brought up at Jackson's Row. Some synagogue ministers are not rabbis but have the title *Reverend*. This means that they lack a deeper knowledge in rabbinic studies. However, they usually carry out all the duties of a rabbi.

Jackson's Row synagogue is fortunate to have a young and energetic rabbi. He trained at a Jewish theological college in London for five years before being *ordained* and given the title of rabbi.

It is usual for a rabbi to be married. The rabbi of Jackson's Row is supported in his work by his wife and children. His wife is a member of the synagogue choir and she also works full time.

A busy life

Since Jackson's Row is a large and thriving synagogue, its rabbi leads a very busy life. Most weekdays he can be found in his study at the synagogue. Many of his congregants will come to see him to arrange a wedding or a funeral, or perhaps to discuss a personal problem. Others may find a telephone call the most useful way of making contact.

There will be days when the rabbi is out and about. He may be at a meeting of rabbis in London or in another northern city, or have a number of house and hospital visits to make. He may be a guest speaker at a luncheon or conducting a happy ceremony such as a wedding or a sad ceremony such as a funeral.

The rabbi's day does not finish around five in the afternoon. Most evenings will be taken up with meetings with groups such as the synagogue council, the wardens or the synagogue education committee or perhaps he will visit the youth club. Weekends too are busy periods. In addition to regular Sabbath services, Sunday is a popular day for Jewish weddings. Sometimes two or three can take place in one afternoon! Rabbis usually take off one day in the week. At Jackson's Row the rabbi makes Wednesday his free day.

Holding office

The rabbi at Jackson's Row also finds time to work with many organisations in Manchester and elsewhere. These include the *Assembly of Rabbis of the Reform Synagogues*, which is a national organisation. Other organisations are Manchester-based such as the *Council of Christians and Jews*, the *Council of Faiths*, and the *Anglo-Israel Friendship League*.

Special clothes

When he is conducting a service the rabbi wears special clothes. These consist of a black gown and hat. On the Day of Atonement and at New Year, the gown and hat are white. In some synagogues, the rabbi simply wears his ordinary clothes and, like any other male Jew, has a tallit over his shoulders and a yamulkah on his head.

(from *Visiting a Synagogue* by Douglas Charing, Lutterworth 1984, pp 21–3)

Christianity: priests and ministers

The Roman Catholic, Orthodox and Anglican churches have a threefold ministry of bishops, priests and deacons. They are *episcopal* churches; that is they have bishops, 'episcopal' coming from the Greek word for bishop. A local church will normally be served by a priest, who may be assisted by a deacon. Some of the Free churches (eg the Methodist church, the United Reformed church, the Church of Scotland) also ordain ministers, but they do not follow the threefold pattern. But the following is likely to be common to all.

The man (or woman in some churches) will feel called to serve God in the church; he or she has a vocation.

The person will usually undergo a period of study and spiritual and pastoral training.

He or she will be ordained with the laying on of hands and prayer, usually by others who already hold office in their church (for example, a priest will be ordained by a bishop).

The laying on of hands, with prayer, is a very ancient custom, not confined to ordination but also used in other ceremonies (eg confirmation, the anointing of the sick) and symbolises the receiving of *grace* (God's power and strengthening). During the ordination service those to be ordained may be reminded of the tasks which will be theirs. Here is an extract from the words spoken to someone about to be ordained a priest in the Anglican church:

A priest is called by God to work with the bishop and with his fellow priests, as servant and shepherd among the people to whom he is sent. He is to proclaim the word of the Lord, to call his hearers to repentance and in Christ's name to absolve and declare the forgiveness of sins. He is to baptise and to prepare the baptized for Confirmation. He is to preside at the celebration of Holy Communion. He is to lead his people in prayer and worship, to intercede for them, to bless them in the name of the Lord, and to teach and encourage by word and example. He is to minister to the sick and prepare the dying for their death. He must set the Good Shepherd always before him as the pattern of his calling, caring for the people committed to his charge, and joining with them in a common witness to the world.

(*Alternative Service Book*, Hodder & Stoughton 1980, pp 371–2)

Few clergy appreciate such comments as 'It's your busy day' (Sunday!) or 'Busy time of year for you' (Christmas!), but children may come to see the priest or minister has a special role in the worship of the Christian community. At the same time it should be clear he or she has other varied tasks. Many are listed in the extract above, but you might consider prayer and study; teaching and preaching; visiting the sick; meeting people on joyful and sorrowful occasions; involvement with the local community; availability to people with problems; care of the place of worship and perhaps of a school.

Islam: the imam

'He who is the most excellent reader of the book of Allah from a people shall be their Imam.'

In this saying you have the basic qualification for being imam: an ability to read the Qur'an, in Arabic (see section 2, page 67). In Islam there is no 'ordained' ministry. Any man who has studied the Qur'an and the Hadith may be chosen to lead the prayer in the mosque. The imam is primarily the leader of the prayers, and in doing this he follows in the footsteps of Muhammad who guided the Muslims in prayer. Although any man with the required knowledge may lead the prayers, many mosques have a full-time salaried imam. The following tasks give a glimpse of the duties such an imam might have.

Leading the prayer five times each day

Giving an address at Friday prayers

Giving a lecture on the Qur'an on Sundays

Leading the prayer and preaching at the celebration of festivals and organising such events at the mosque

Producing the monthly prayer-time-table

Studying the Qur'an and its commentaries

Performing ceremonies for initiation, marriage and death

Teaching the children

Interpreting Islamic law for the community

Giving advice and help to families, eg when sick

(based on *The Bengali Muslims of Bradford* by S W Barton, University of Leeds 1986, Ch 5)

Approaches

1 With the help of the children, make a large wall map which has sufficient space to mark in the places of worship in the locality of your school.

Draw on children's knowledge to supply the names of streets and key buildings; some may be able to think of places of worship. Alternatively arrange a walkabout of the locality to identify buildings and to collect any basic data available from noticeboards (eg religion, name of church/denomination, name of building, distinctive symbols). Mark the information on the map in an interesting way. Plan to meet people associated with some of the places. Where a number of religions are present you may decide to select two or three; where there is only a Christian presence, select two contrasting groups (for instance, you might try to meet a Roman Catholic priest and a Salvation Army officer). Involve children in writing invitations and preparing questions to ask a visitor.

2   Since the focus here is on people serving in religion, approaches which can involve direct contact with local people are best. Certain 'ground rules' are important here. The teacher needs to meet and talk beforehand with the person children are to meet, and be clear about the purposes of the meeting. Consider whether school or the place of worship is the best location for the meeting. Go for interaction between the visitor and the children: don't ask for 'a talk'.

Do think of any expenses a visitor may have incurred in coming to school, and do involve the children in expressing their thanks in some way.

3   Some teachers may prefer to come to this topic rather more obliquely by identifying a range of people who have particular roles in serving the community. Or such a topic might begin by considering school. *Who* is the school?—the children of course; but also the teachers, and other staff, and the head. Identify their responsibilities. From this you may move on to do a similar study of a faith community approached through different people who belong as well as its leaders.

Activities

1   After interviewing visitors, and with the help of books, make diaries for the people you have met: 'A day in the life of . . .' or 'A week in the life of . . .'.

2   Discuss the similarities and differences in the ways of life of the people you have met. Try to identify clearly what *they* felt was most important in their work.

3   Follow up in more detail particular aspects of the people's life and work, for example:

rabbi reading the Torah;

imam leading prayers;

priest celebrating Eucharist.

What does each need to know? What do they wear? What do they do?

4   Consider what kind of person you would need to be to do the tasks the visitors have spoken of: try to draw up a list of 'qualities' a person would need.

5   If you have used Approach 3 (above) prepare a 'Who's Who' for the community you have studied. This might involve brief biographies, details of individuals' association with the community, 'job descriptions' relating to their roles in their faith community.

Resources

Books

O Bennett, *Exploring Religion People*, Bell & Hyman (designed for 9+ age group; focuses on a priest, a rabbi and an imam)

S Tompkins (Ed), *Meeting Religious Groups*, Lutterworth (a series of books which includes an Anglican church, Roman Catholic church, Methodist church, Salvation Army citadel, Synagogue and Mosque. Each book looks at people as well as the building and what happens there; useful information for the teacher)

P Watkins and E Hughes, *Here are the People*, Julia MacRae Books 1984 (reference book on people in church context; gives historical perspective)

14 Churches

The aim of this unit is to discover **Christian** belief and practice through exploring church buildings and the communities who meet in them.

Information

Towns and villages in Britain usually have more than one place of Christian worship. So for most schools it is possible to visit different places of worship, and discover some of the things which Christians share and some of the ways in which they differ. Localities will vary in the opportunities they offer, but the following are some which might be considered: Baptist church, Methodist church or chapel, Friends' meeting house, Roman Catholic church, Salvation Army citadel. Each of these places of worship would have its own story to tell about Christian belief and practice.

Identifying important features

Within each of these Christian traditions the buildings may vary according to the period when they were built. Recent buildings will not always reflect fully the emphases of the earliest buildings of a particular group. For instance Methodist chapels built in the last century were dominated by the pulpit (and frequently the organ): the importance of preaching and hearing the Word of God was clear. Buildings today may have a more modest pulpit and lectern, and the table for communion may be given more prominence.

The following attempt to provide a guide to some key features of different buildings must not therefore be seen too rigidly.

CHRISTIAN GROUP	WHAT TO LOOK FOR IN THEIR PLACE OF WORSHIP	NOTES
ANGLICAN	Most churches will have an **altar** or table as the main focus point, traditionally at the east end of the church. A **pulpit** and **lectern** are also usual features. At the west end of many churches is the **font** used for baptism. Older churches often have stained glass, many will have cross and candles placed on or near the altar. Often the church itself is built in a cruciform shape, some will have chapels in the transepts.	*The balance of altar and pulpit and lectern, points to Anglicans' emphasis on word and sacrament. The font and the altar point to recognition of two essential sacraments: baptism and the Eucharist. The baptism of infants is the norm in this tradition, but this does not of course exclude the baptism of adults.*
BAPTIST	**Baptistry**: a pool for total immersion—often covered. The **pulpit** and **table** may be given equal importance in designs today. In the past pulpits dominated and the people faced the preacher.	*The baptistry points to a distinctive belief in baptism by total immersion, symbolising death and resurrection. Baptists practise Believers' Baptism: those baptised must make the decision to be baptised and follow Jesus for themselves.*

CHRISTIAN GROUP	WHAT TO LOOK FOR IN THEIR PLACE OF WORSHIP	NOTES
METHODIST	In old buildings the **pulpit** may dominate. An **organ** may be placed behind this (or elsewhere). Below the pulpit a **table** with an 'empty' cross is common, perhaps surrounded by a rail where people may kneel for communion.	*This older style of chapel reflects John Wesley's emphasis on Methodism as a 'preaching order', and the importance of hearing the Word of God. Both pulpit and table may provide a focus today. Notice 'table': this recalls the Last Supper—Jesus shared a meal with his followers.*
ROMAN CATHOLIC	**Altar**: the focal point of the building, placed on the eastern facing wall or sometimes centrally placed today. **Tabernacle**, near the altar: a safe place where the Host (wafers) consecrated at Mass are kept. A lamp will burn nearby. **Font**: for baptism—by 'sprinkling', not immersion. There may be places set aside for confession; in many churches these are **confessionals**, places where confession may be made to a priest and absolution given. There may also be: a pulpit, a lectern, a holy water stoup by the door, statues of saints, Stations of the Cross, stained glass, crucifix and candles.	*The features (in **bold**) point to the importance of sacraments in the life of the Roman Catholic Church—to the Mass, to baptism and to the sacrament of penance. The altar recalls Jesus' sacrificial death for mankind; the tabernacle his continuing presence with his people. The Stations of the Cross point to Jesus' death, and to a rich devotional life. Belief in 'the communion of saints', and praying to them is reflected in the statues.*
SALVATION ARMY	The building is called a citadel—linking nicely with the idea of an army. Inside is a **raised platform with a lectern** for the officer who leads the service and space for the songsters and maybe the band too. On the wall behind them will be the symbol of the Army. The most distinctive feature is the **Mercy Seat** (or Penitents' Form) just below the platform; here people may come to pray for forgiveness and to have someone pray with them, and also to receive help.	*William Booth, the Salvation Army's founder wanted to bring the message of Jesus to those who were the least in society—often as the result of social evils. Christians had to fight like an army against evil, and to bring the salvation Jesus offered to poor people. The Mercy Seat points to the possibility of repentance and a fresh start, and to God's mercy.* *(Note that Salvationists do not practise baptism and have no 'communion' service.)*
SOCIETY OF FRIENDS (QUAKERS)	Place of worship known as 'meeting house'. This is basically a room providing space for people to gather together for worship. Seats will be arranged 'in the round'. A table may be in the centre, with a Bible on it, and perhaps flowers. No visual symbols are used. It should be a quiet and peaceful room.	*This reflects the Friends' understanding that the Spirit is within each person. All are equal, so there are no special seats for anyone. Worship is silent—though anyone may speak if moved by the Spirit. This is referred to as 'ministry'. Since all life is believed to be sacramental, Friends do not have any sacraments (such as Baptism, Eucharist).*

SECTION 3: FOR 9–11 YEAR OLDS

What can be learnt from church buildings?

Churches, especially 'the parish church' often find a place in environmental studies topics: they can reveal a lot for example about local people and events; or about the use of local building materials; or about styles of architecture. Here the question above is asked from an RE perspective; four ways of thinking about the buildings are suggested.

1 Discovering 'the Christian story'

Buildings point to Jesus' story in different ways. For example, they may have special places from which the story is read and explained (lecterns, pulpits): Bibles are always placed in churches and sometimes prominently displayed. Reading 'the story' will be important in worship (section 2, pages 66–68). But the content of the story may influence the building too. Texts may be found on memorials; scenes may be depicted in stained glass or carved in wood and stone. Passages of scripture may have prompted symbols (see pages 184–189). The altar or table points to the story of the Last Supper which many Christians recall in the Eucharist, whilst the Stations of the Cross point to the story Christians tell of the last week of Jesus' life.

2 Discovering Christian belief

Some of the features which point to 'the Christian story' may also point to belief. The symbol of the empty cross affirms Christians' belief in the risen Jesus; the tabernacle in a Roman Catholic church speaks of a belief in God's continuing presence with his people, whilst the bareness of a Friends' meeting house points to that presence within the individual person and Friends' belief that God is not found in outward things. Confessionals and the Mercy Seat are evidence of belief in a God who forgives and of the possibility of reconciliation. The font and the baptistry—especially in a Baptist church—point to death and resurrection and to 'new life in Christ'.

3 Discovering the Christian community

By focusing on those who use a church now, for worship and perhaps for other events, and on whoever has care and responsibility for the building, it is possible to build up a picture of a living community. This is especially effective where people are available to meet children (see section 1, page 34).

Church buildings often witness too to the community in the past. Memorials and gravestones may list the qualities for which people were known, and can be the starting point for discussion on the characteristics of a Christian community. Biblical texts might reveal attitudes to death and Christian hope in a future life, which could prompt discussion or comparison with the community's ideas in the present.

A church may be served by a priest or minister, whose work in and for the community might be explored. How does his or her work 'in the building', in leading worship for example, link with other tasks?

4 Discovering Christian worship

Church buildings may be used for many purposes, but their *raison d'être* is of course worship. Some will be *consecrated*, blessed and set apart, for this purpose alone. Since school visits usually have to be made to empty buildings, experiencing a community's worship isn't often possible. However, children can themselves be invited to experience being together in the building. Sitting very still and quiet in a Friends' meeting house for a short time would not be intended as worship, but might contribute to children's understanding of it. Finding a seat alone in a church and sitting for a few moments might introduce the idea of church buildings as places to be alone for quiet thought and prayer.

Special moments in the life of a Christian community are another way of discovering worship: what happens for example at a baptism in a Roman Catholic church, and by contrast in a Baptist church? Meeting people recently involved with such ceremonies, or 'reconstructing' the event with the priest or minister would obviously add to understanding here.

Similarly children might encounter churches on the occasion of a festival to discover ways in which buildings are 'decorated', and to talk to people about their church's celebration. Looking at a Roman Catholic church during Holy Week, and then on Easter Day, could offer insight into the community's 'experiencing' of the events of Holy Week and their rejoicing on Easter Day. For this purpose a careful use of slides is a possible alternative to visits. Other churches may have fewer visible reminders of the season but they will share in its 'mood' through appropriate readings and hymns.

Approaches

The four ways above of discovering a church building already begin to suggest approaches. They also show that one visit to a church does not have to use up all the possibilities. Churches can be used in different ways at different times (see number 1 below).

1   Use one church, or two contrasting ones, to explore just *one* theme; for example:

What to look for in a church (key features)

Symbols

Colour

Discovering the story Christians tell

Becoming a member of . . .

Holy Week and Easter at . . .

People past and present at . . .

2   Where it is possible to create a link with individual members of local churches, you can explore a theme of 'Belonging to . . .'. Invite them (they don't have to be a minister!) to show the children round the church building and explain what it means to them. Explore why they belong to *this* church. Discover how they became a member. How often do they go to the church and what happens at a service? Why is the church important to them? Have any important events in their life been celebrated in the church (eg wedding, dedication or baptism of a child)? Clearly this calls for careful planning with the church member and the children.

Activities

It is worth thinking about the 'activities' which can be carried out *in* a church. These might include sketching; making rough plans; listening (perhaps to an organ); making rubbings; 'collecting' symbols; sitting and standing where the congregation normally are; standing at a lectern or in the pulpit (with permission); experiencing silence, alone and together; using Bibles to look up stories connected with the building; learning a song or hymn Christians sing.

Back in school:

1   Allow for some reflective activities in which children explore their own feelings about the church(es) they have visited: creative writing, poetry, pictures/collages to present the mood of the building or a feature they particularly liked.

2   Make plans or models of the church(es) you have visited. Make sure the main features are included. Label them and provide a key which describes each feature and explains its importance.

SECTION 3: FOR 9–11 YEAR OLDS

3   Let the children design their own church building—working individually or in groups. They will obviously be influenced by the work you have done, but discussion before the activity might consider:

> Atmosphere: influence of light/darkness, sound, colour
>
> Main features it might have
>
> Plain or 'decorated' building—which and why?
>
> How people will be seated (eg in rows, semi-circle) and why?

The children's designs could be a mixture of plans, drawings and writing.

4   This is a follow-up to the 'portrait gallery' idea in section 1, page 39. If you have met people from the church who hold special positions, write simple 'job descriptions' for them.

This style of Methodist church belongs to the end of the last century and the beginning of this century.

Resources

Books

O Bennett, *Exploring Religion: Buildings*, Bell & Hyman (for
 primary/middle age range; includes church, synagogue and Hindu
 temple)

P Curtis, *Christianity*, Lutterworth Press 1986 (written for middle
 years; could support a 'Churches' topic in a variety of ways)

H Hay, *The Quakers*, Ward Lock Educational 1981 (introduction
 which gives overview of Quaker worship, as well as origins,
 organisation and social commitment, useful reference for teachers)

M and J Killingray, *I am an Anglican*, Franklin Watts 1986

B Pettenuzzo, *I am a Roman Catholic*, Franklin Watts 1985
(these two books are for primary school; both pick up the theme of
belonging to a particular church, seen through the eyes of a child)

S Tompkins (Ed), *Meeting Religious Groups*, Lutterworth
 Educational (series designed for secondary schools; useful
 background information; includes visiting an *Anglican Church*, a
 Methodist Church, a *Roman Catholic Church, Salvation Army
 Citadel*)

AVA

The Slide Centre (RE list available from Reckitt Educational Media,
 Ilton, Illminster, Somerset TA19 2BR) produces a variety of slide
 packs, with notes, on churches and their worship (eg *Christian
 Initiation; Holy Week; Christian Symbols; Christian Worship;
 Christian Churches*)

Christians Photopack, The Westhill Project 5–16, Mary Glasgow
 1986 (a pack of 20 colour photographs in A3 format, picking up
 many aspects of Christianity; some would support this topic)

SECTION 3: FOR 9–11 YEAR OLDS

15 Symbols: Christianity

| Aims | The purpose of this unit is to help children to discover symbols as a fundamental way of human expression, and to begin to meet some of the ways in which they are used in religion with particular reference to the **Christian** tradition. |

Information

Everyone uses symbols! They are part of everyday life. Children become familiar with many signs and symbols at an early age: road and traffic signs, shop signs, manufacturers' labels, school badges, flags and football team colours, for example, are all part of a *visual language* which is all round us and created by us.

Language too makes use of symbols: simile and metaphor are part of everyday speech. Some we create ourselves, some we simply learn because they are so much a part of colloquial language. We speak for example of being 'in the same boat', 'exploring every avenue', having 'a chip on the shoulder' and 'sitting on the fence'. Metaphors like these never tempt us to start looking for wood shavings, street maps, boats or fences! We know they are not to be taken literally. They simply point succinctly and vividly to a situation or experience we know. Using language in this kind of way is common to religions. Jesus' teaching in the gospels illustrates this well. Similarly, when Christians speak of their experience of God they use words symbolically; for instance, the Lord's Prayer begins 'Our Father . . .'.

As well as thinking of the words and pictures we use as 'symbols', it is not unusual to talk about 'body language'. A frown, a smile, a shrug of the shoulders, a glance, a handshake, for example, can indicate a mood, or a particular attitude,

or a response. When this kind of 'language' is intentionally used we can begin to speak of 'symbolic actions'.

Signs and symbols

These two words are often used together and distinguishing signs from symbols isn't always easy. It is perhaps helpful to use an example. On an ordnance survey map a + indicates a church: it is simply a sign to indicate a building. Now imagine a Christian looking at a cross in a church; it reminds him of the story of Jesus and especially of his death and resurrection; he reverently bows before the cross and goes away thinking of Jesus' words about Christian discipleship. On the map the cross has *one meaning*, it's just a sign. In the second context *it has many associations and also invites a response*; here it can be called a symbol.

Where do symbols come from?

Some symbols are universal. They are a kind of data bank on which all religions may draw. Often they derive from the natural world: fire, light, darkness, wind, water, earth are just a few examples. Human relationships and roles may also provide a fund of symbols: husband, wife, lover, child, sister, brother, mother, father and judge, king and shepherd, for example, are all used in Judaism and Christianity. These symbols (and others) seem to be intrinsic to human experience in and of the world. Drawn on by a religion, they are able to express some of its deepest beliefs and evoke a response.

Other symbols seem to derive more especially from the stories which religions tell of themselves: the symbolic dress of the Sikh (page 164) and the foods on the *seder* plate at Passover (section 2, page 77) and the cross or crucifix of the Christian tradition, for example.

Visual signs and symbols

From earliest times Christianity seems to have used visual signs and symbols. Particular signs came to indicate key people: crossed keys for St Peter (after Matthew 16:18–19); a scallop shell for St James—calling to mind his burial place in northern Spain and the shells which pilgrims to his tomb collected on the beach at Santiago de Compostela. The X representing St Andrew (and incorporated into the Union Jack) recalls the manner of his death. The first Christians used fish and bread to represent both the Last Supper and the Eucharist and perhaps to point to the Feeding of the Five Thousand too. Later, wheat and the vine came to symbolise the Eucharist, as well as Jesus, the 'living bread' and 'true vine' (see John 6:35 and 15:1). The fish itself—in Greek IXθUS (ichthus)—has a hidden meaning:

I	—	Jesus
X	—	Christ
θ	—	of God
U	—	Son
S	—	Saviour

The monogram ☧ came to stand simply for XPIΣTOS (*Chr*ist), as its letters denote, whilst A and Ω or α and ω (the first and last letters of the Greek alphabet) recalled the words of Revelation 21:6. The anchor was another popular symbol, indicating Christian hope, after Hebrews 6:19. In all these examples we have a kind of visual shorthand. All served as pointers to the Christian story and perhaps evoked memories and responses. The cross itself was to become the most potent symbol. An empty cross signified Jesus' resurrection, whilst the crucifix bearing his body became a reminder of his sacrificial death. But the cross was not among the earliest symbols used by Christians.

Symbolic actions

It is in the context of worship that this kind of action may most often be found in the Christian tradition.

Firstly, people may adopt certain physical postures in worship: standing, simply sitting, kneeling, being very still and quiet, closing eyes, raising the arms (in prayer), dancing. Different Christian traditions relate these kinds of actions to different parts of worship. At this stage children's awareness of some of them and *their* reflections on what they might mean are probably sufficient. The act of using a rosary, lighting a candle or making the sign of the cross could also be explored here.

Whilst these kinds of actions have a personal dimension, although 'done' in community, others may be much more 'community acts'. For example, Christians may greet each other with 'a sign of peace'. This greeting operates in two ways: it is the 'peace of the Lord', but of course it also has a practical dimension for the community. Children thinking about this might put forward their ideas for a 'peaceful' community, or even a peaceful world.

A further kind of symbolic action is much more closely linked with recalling and re-enacting the Christian story; for example, the foot washing (see John 13:2–20) on Maundy Thursday in some churches. Symbolic actions also permeate the Eucharist when bread is taken and broken, and shared and eaten, and wine is offered and shared, often from one cup.

This drawing of a sixth-century mosaic shows Jesus and his disciples at the Last Supper. Curiously, bread and fish are on the table. The five loaves and two fishes recall the story of the feeding of the 5,000 (John 6), which John associated with the Eucharist; they became symbols of the Last Supper in early Christian art.

Symbolic words

Children at the upper end of the age range may begin to explore some of the words which Christians use in a symbolic sense, and in particular the words used to help them speak of God.

Children like to be confronted with mystery. The story of Moses and the Burning Bush is full of such mystery—and it is helpful to keep it that way ('explanations' of the bush add nothing to *understanding*). Let the mystery remain!

Moses and the Burning Bush
Moses spent his time looking after his father-in-law's sheep. One day he found himself in the western part of the desert.

He looked—a bush was on fire, but the fire went on burning brightly.

'I must have a look at this remarkable sight,' thought Moses. 'I wonder why the bush doesn't burn out.'

GOD saw that he went out of his way to have a look at it.

'Stay where you are,' he said. 'Take your sandals off. You are standing on holy ground. I am your ancestors' God.'

Moses hid his face; he was frightened at meeting GOD like this.

'I have seen the brutal treatment of my people in Egypt,' GOD went on. 'I have heard their cry for help under their savage foremen. I know what they are going through and I have come down to rescue them. I'm going to send you back to rescue them from the Egyptians.'

'But—I'm not the man to rescue them,' said Moses.

'I'll stand by you,' said God. 'And this will prove to you that I myself have given you your orders: when you've escaped from Egypt, you shall worship me here on this mountain.'

'But if I go back to Egypt,' said Moses, 'and tell the Hebrew labourers that their ancestral God has sent me to them, they'll only say "Well, you tell us what his name is, then". What shall I say?'

'I AM—that is my name,' said God. 'Tell them that I AM has sent you to them. Go and get the heads of the great families together. Tell them that the God of their fathers has appeared to you, and that he told you to tell them this: "I have been watching. I have seen what you are going through in Egypt. I promise to rescue you from this savage suffering".'

(from *Winding Quest* by Alan T Dale, OUP 1972)

As you can see there is more than one mystery in the story. Much to his surprise, Moses is clearly being given a task—and he wants to know just who is giving it! So what is God's name? Whichever version of the Bible you take, the name that is given is mysterious and may be translated in a number of ways: 'I am who I am', or 'I am what I am', or 'I will be what I will be'. Children might try to say what they think this means. Does it for example simply say 'God *is*', he exists? In Jewish and Christian scriptures God is always a God who *acts*, and humankind may recognise his activity. But how can they describe him? They resort to symbolic words like Father, King, Judge, Shepherd. But let children encounter the *mystery* first through a story such as that of Moses.

'I am the Good Shepherd'

Sheep and the shepherd have often found a place in primary school RE! They provide at first sight a problematic symbol: on the one hand children don't have a lot of contact with shepherds; on the other a lengthy study of the life of a sheep farmer can miss the point altogether. Read John 10:1–16 and then this extract about the Palestinian shepherd.

The shepherd (or in the case of large flocks, the head-shepherd) had to find adequate pasture and water for the flock, and this often involved seasonal migrations. He also needed to know the location of caves, where he could shelter from storms, cold nights and wild animals, and of wadis and rocks where he could find shade on hot days. He carried a sling and a wooden club to fend off lions, bears, wolves, jackals and hyenas which would attack the flock; and a staff to prod the sheep as they moved on or rescue them from crevasses.

When the flock was far from home the shepherd set up a camp near a water source. A fire provided warmth and discouraged wild animals. A simple pen or 'sheepfold' built from stones lying around would have kept the animals together at night. People who owned only a couple of sheep would send their animals out each morning under the care of a village shepherd, who led them to pasture beyond the cultivated fields and returned them at night to their owners' houses.

The shepherd developed a close relationship with his sheep, and had a distinctive call which the sheep could recognize. At a watering place several flocks might mingle together, but each shepherd could extract his own sheep from the rest simply by calling them. Unlike most modern shepherds, he would lead the sheep from in front rather than drive them from behind.

(from *Handbook of Life in Bible Times* by J A Thompson, IVP 1986, pp 138 & 140)

You are now in a position to explore some of the key ideas underlying this symbol. Notice some of the features which emerge.

The shepherd:

knows the sheep by name;

will be concerned for each;

will protect them;

will go to extraordinary lengths for them—even death;

leads the sheep;

will stay with them, even in trouble.

This symbol thus has a deep underlying theme of a relationship.

At the children's level you might explore the question 'What do you think makes for a good shepherd?' Think about the qualities together. You could reinforce this work by looking at visual representations of this symbol and talking with the children about which of the qualities of the Good Shepherd are portrayed in the pictures.

Water: a complex symbol

So far we have looked at visual symbols and symbolic actions and words. Water is included here because it cuts right across these categories and because it is an important symbol in many religious traditions. As we saw earlier, it is part of a data bank of natural symbols. It is 'given'—we can see it, feel it, and even taste it; it is part of everyone's experience. In stories it can symbolise both life and death; and used in religious ceremonies it may similarly point to dying, new life and purification.

In the Bible, water is a recurrent symbol. In the psalms, for example, it is seen as a gift from God, since it ensures harvest and life; its restorative nature is expressed in Psalm 23. In the great hymn of creation in Genesis 1, water lies over the face of the earth, waiting for life to emerge.

Water is also a symbol of darkness and chaos, threatening and to be feared. In the story of Noah it represents God's judgment, in Jonah the sailors believe it is Jonah's wrongdoing which causes the sea to rage. Then of course there is the stilling of the storm (Mark 4:35–41); perhaps the sea is a symbol here too! And in the vision of heaven in the last book of the New Testament, there is the promise of no more sea.

So water has both a beneficent and a threatening side to it.

The life-giving aspect of water can perhaps be most readily explored with children—and in practical ways and experiments. Pictures of arid land and the contrast when irrigation is possible are further evidence of its life-giving nature. But you might also think of the heat and the dust of a hot country and of hospitality shown in offering water for washing as well as drinking. This introduces the cleansing and purifying properties of water, which wash away the dust of the day.

The three aspects of water we have noted: a symbol of life, of 'washing away' and of chaos and trouble, are all contained in the symbolic action of baptism (section 2, page 96). In baptism an *old way* of life is left behind—hence the idea of cleansing, or 'washing away'—and a *new life* is entered on. Here water acquires a new layer of meaning as a symbol for Christians. Going into and under the water, where the community practises total immersion, is symbolic of dying with Christ, whilst emerging from it signifies not only rising to new life now, but participation in Christ's risen life.

Other symbols of course come into play in baptism: the sign of the cross, a lighted candle, a new garment, anointing with oil (chrism), a handshake of welcome into the community. Different branches of the Christian church have their own traditions, but water is fundamental to the ceremony.

Approaches

1   Discovering and collecting visual signs and symbols is a practical way into this topic. Where possible, explore a local church to do this. Let the children collect signs and symbols, making drawings or rubbings of them and noting where they found particular ones. For example, symbols of wheat or the vine found near the altar or table in a church provide an opportunity to link them with what happens when the Christian community gathers there.

As well as the visual symbols, you may be able to collect significant texts used in a church, or perhaps outside on graves, which use symbolic language. Note too that stained glass and other art forms such as carving or sculpture may depict a verbal symbol (eg 'I am the Good Shepherd').

2   Provide opportunities for children to explore 'symbolic action', beginning with their own experiences of 'body language'. For example, let them try drawing a series of faces to express as many moods as they can. Or perhaps they might try out different facial expressions themselves to convey feelings and attitudes. Here is a suggested list: sad, excited, angry, calm or peaceful, pleased, suspicious, puzzled, tired, bored.

Children might also consider a range of other actions which they and others may engage in: for example, clapping, shaking hands, waving, patting a person on the back, saluting, bowing. What do these actions 'say'?

Communications of this kind might also be explored through the collection of pictures, and through the use of good poster material. Whichever approach is taken, the basic intention is that children should become aware of this kind of non-verbal communication and then begin to understand that actions of this kind may be more consciously used within religious traditions.

3   Tell the story of Moses and the Burning Bush with the emphases suggested above. Depending on your knowledge of the children you may want to go on and talk about ideas of God: Have they heard the word 'God' used? What do they think it means? These are the kind of 'open' questions to ask.

4   Take the theme of water and let children explore it at their own level. An approach to this topic might begin by giving children time to enjoy a display of pictures or posters showing water in many different forms and moods. (You may want to display other images too, not least a parched earth and a fertile earth, to extend the theme of water.) Let the children choose one or two which they like best. They might write down words which come to mind when they look at them, or you might have a time when you and the children share your feelings about the pictures. The underlying concern here is to allow the pictures, and more particularly 'water', to 'speak' and the children to respond. This is fundamental to the way in which symbols work.

SECTION 3: FOR 9–11 YEAR OLDS

Activities

1 If you have collected signs and symbols in a church (or perhaps discovered them through slides) they can be used in a variety of ways. For example:

Use reference books and Bibles to check out their meaning(s).

Use the information you have collected to begin to answer a question such as 'What do we learn about Christians' beliefs from these symbols?'

Discuss *why* symbols are used. Are they just decorative or do they 'work' in other ways: eg, carry a message in a concise way; remind Christians of important events and beliefs; help to provide a suitable 'atmosphere' for worship?

2 Extend work by considering artefacts on which Christian signs and symbols may be used today: eg vestments; altar frontal; pulpit fall; chalice and paten; cards for occasions like baptism or confirmation, dedication, and first communion. Try designing or even making some of these.

3 Listen to poetry and music which explores the theme of water; explore the theme too in some of the psalms. Look for example at Psalms 65:9–13*; 104*; 107:23–28.

*Modern versions of these passages can be found in *Winding Quest* by Alan T Dale (OUP 1972).

Resources

Books

O Bennett, *Exploring Religion: Signs and Symbols*, Bell & Hyman 1984 (for children; looks at Christian, Jewish and Hindu signs and symbols)

J Bradner, *Symbols of Church Seasons and Days*, SPCK 1979 (a reference book to have to hand when exploring symbols in a church)

H Child and D Colles, *Christian Symbols*, Bell & Hyman 1971 (very useful reference book with a wealth of information and examples)

Christian Objects, CEM 1977 (a booklet for children exploring the meaning of some Christian artefacts)

J Mayled, *Religious Symbols*, Wayland 1987 (for primary and middle schools; looks at symbols of six world religions)

AVA

People at Worship: Christian Symbols, S1465, The Slide Centre 1982 (set of 24 slides with notes exploring central Christian symbols)

Index

Acknowledgements

We are grateful to the following for permission to reproduce copyright material:

The Bodley Head Ltd on behalf of the Author, Roger Lancelyn Green for an extract from *Tales of Ancient Egypt*; William Collins Sons & Co Ltd for 'Veni Creator Spiritus' from *Joy on Earth* © Les Presses de Taizé (France); James Clarke & Co Ltd for an adapted extract from *Looking At Myth* by John Rankin and an extract from *Visiting a Synagogue* by D. Charing; The Hamlyn Publishing Group for a slightly adapted extract from *The Life and Times of St. Francis* (1967) by A. Childari, trans S. Attanasio; The Islamic Foundation for extracts from *Love Your God* (1982) by K. Murad, *A Great Friend of Children* (1981) by M. S. Kayani and *Love your Brother, Love your Neighbour* (1982) by K. Murad; The Islamic Texts Society for extracts from *The Life of the Prophet Muhammed* (1985) by L. Azzam & A. Gouverneur; MacDonald & Co Ltd for short stories by J. Gavin from *Stories from the Hindu World*, 'The First Revelation' by H. Khattab from *Stories from the Muslim World* and short story by Leo Pavlat from *Jewish Tales: The Eight Lights of the Hanukiyya*; Macmillan Accounts & Administration Ltd for recipe 'Eid Sweets' by Rosalind Kerven from *Festival: Ramadan and Eid-al-Fiter*; the Author, Peggy Morgan for short story from *Buddhist Stories* (1984), (P. Morgan *Buddhist Stories* available from Westminster College, Oxford); James Nisbet & Co Ltd for short story 'Muhammed and the Cave' from *Stories from the Faiths* by Alison Sinclair & Jill Essame; Octopus Pubg. Group plc for recipe for 'Potato Latkes' from *The Gourmet Guide to Jewish Cooking* (1973) by B. Carr & P. Obermann; Oxford University Press for an extract from *Gods and Men* (1981) by J. Bailey, K. McLeish & D. Spearman and text to carol 'Now the Green Blade Riseth' by J. M. C. Crum from *The Oxford Book of Carols*; Penguin Books Ltd for an adapted extract from *Buddhist Scriptures* trans. Edward Conze (Penguin Classics, 1959), copyright © Edward Conze, 1959; Schicken Books/Patheon Books, a Division of Random House Inc for an excerpt from 'Hanukkah Prayer' from p 30 *The Hannukkah Book* by Mae Shafter Rockland; Scholastic Publications Ltd for extracts 'Festival Garland' and 'Making a Minaret' from *Junior Education* October 1987; Wayland Publishers Ltd Hove, England for short story 'Tricks of the Trade' by J. Snelling from *Buddhist Stories* and extracts from *Guru Nanak and the Sikh Gurus* (1987) by R. Arora.

We are grateful to the following for permission to reproduce photographs:

Andes Press Agency/Carlos Reyes, page 35; Aramco Magazine, page 36; Art Gallery of Western Australia, with permission from the Stanley Spenser Estate, page 18; The Bible Society, page 66; Bibliotheque Nationale, Paris, page 161; British Library, pages 67 and 82; Camera Press/Ferhervary MTI page 13, Yael Braun page 115, Bernard Silberstein page 149; W. Owen Cole, page 167; Michael Day, page 12; Douglas Dickins, pages 15 (above) and 85; EDITA, S. A. Lausanne, page 125 (right); Format Photographers/Raissa Page, page 26 (left); Michael Holford, pages 52, 73, 74 and 130; Jewish Chronicle, pages 16, 64 and 77 (below); Jewish Museum, Warburg Institute, page 70; Junior Education/Leonard E. Goode, page 95; Abdul Lahf al Hoad, *Islam*, Wayland, page 159; Lawson and Fairclough, *I am a Jew*, Franklin Watts, photo Chris Fairclough, page 171; Mansell Collection, page 80; Martin Mulcahy, page 45; Mayhew and McCrimmon, page 153;National Gallery, page 8; Network Photographers/Katalin Arkell page 39, Dennis Doran page 182; Christine Osborne, pages 60, 100, 151 and 152; Editions d'Art Olray, page 63; Ann and Bury Peerless, pages 29, 68 (above), 88 and 127 (by kind permission of Chandigarh Museum); David Richardson, pages 25, 26 (right), 32, 41, 68 (below), 69, 92, 111, 112, 129, 172 and 183; Jonn Topham, page 48; Woodmansterne, page 125 (left); Zefa, page 10.

Cover photograph by Camilla Jessel